Building Business Solutions

Business Analysis with Business Rules

First Edition

by Ronald G. Ross
Co-Founder and Principal, Business Rule Solutions, LLC
Co-Chair, Business Rules Forum Conference

with Gladys S.W. Lam
Co-Founder and Principal, Business Rule Solutions, LLC
Director, Building Business Capability (BBC) Conference

BUSINESS RULE SOLUTIONS, LLC
THE BUSINESS RULE TECHNIQUE COMPANY

(BRCommunity.com

Building Business Solutions

Business Analysis with Business Rules

First Edition

by Ronald G. Ross

with Gladys S.W. Lam

ISBN 978-0-941049-10-8

To Gladys' parents,

Victor Shao Zeng Zhao and Siu Jane Zhao

趙紹曾   袁笑珍

Acknowledgments

Thanks to Kristen Seer *and* Cindy Scullion *for numerous suggestions and ideas.*

Special thanks to Keri Anderson Healy, *editor of* BRCommunity.com, *for her time and diligence in patiently and sometimes painfully editing this and lots of other material too.*

Colleagues who most graciously reviewed the original material presented in Chapters 12 and 13: Don Baisley, Rik Gerrits, John Healy, Keri Anderson Healy, Kristen Seer, Silvie Spreeuwenberg, *and* Jan Vanthienen.

Special thanks for helpful feedback on Chapters 4 and 14 from Kevin Brennan *and* Don Baisley, *respectively.*

Colleagues on two standardization efforts have made this material structurally sound — the Business Rules Group *for the Business Motivation Model and the* OMG SBVR Task Force.

Last but not least, we have worked with so many companies and organizations over the last 15 years, and with so many really great people in them, we wouldn't know where to begin in thanking them. Without all of you this book simply wouldn't have been possible.

Contents

Preface

In the March 1999 issue of the *Business Rules Journal* on www.BRCommunity.com I wrote: "The key role in requirements development for the 21st century business will be that of Business Analyst." I went on to ask, *"Does your company have them? Can you define who they are? What they need to know? What they need to be able to do?"*

Gladys and I have been planning to write this book since early that same year. According to my notes, it was to be titled: *Business Analysis: What It Is and How You Do It.*

A bit of background: Gladys and I founded Business Rule Solutions, LLC in 1996 specifically to focus on business models and business rules — *jointly*. By 1999 we had developed and field-tested key components of our approach, applying them in dozens of consulting assignments. Since then we've applied the techniques successfully in hundreds of companies worldwide.

Memory fails as to why the book didn't happen in 1999. One factor was undoubtedly the Y2K issue — change the legacy code or the company dies. Today, another threat looms large for business — the double-edged sword of business alignment and business agility.

We had successfully addressed the problem of business alignment with our Policy Charter technique by 1999. In truth, though, we hadn't fully addressed business agility. That problem requires business practices to express and manage business rules *at scale*. We had a good start by 1999, but there was much to learn. So perhaps the book would have been premature. (But isn't that what second and third editions are for?!)

In the interim, a whole new community of Business Analysts has emerged worldwide. Many books are now available on the subject. That's hugely important and very exciting.

Is there still a place for this book? We're confident the answer is *yes*. Not all Business Analysts have yet lived up to the "business" part of their title. And the community has not yet successfully solved the twin challenges of business alignment and business agility. What should *business* requirements be about anyway?

So, Gladys and I think Business Analysts (and others) will get real value from this book. Inside are our answers for the key questions: *What do you need to know? What do you need to be able to do?*

About the Annotated Glossary

To keep chapters as short and as focused as possible, we've created an *Annotated Glossary* at the back for easy reference. In it you will find additional explanation and background (if you need it) for key concepts that appear in the text (often repetitively). Such concepts are indicated like this: **business rule**.

About the Tips

When you see this icon it means the text to its right provides a tip about how to apply or better understand the material being presented.

About the Pattern Questions

When you see this icon it means the text in the box provides a **pattern question** for the Business Analyst to apply in harvesting business rules from business models.

About the Book's Scope

This book doesn't try to do everything. It can't. Although it explains all the relevant techniques you need for business analysis with business rules, it doesn't:

- Provide a step-by-step guide for applying them. You'll need that. Our complete methodology is **Proteus®**. Visit www.BRSolutions.com for more information.

- Explain business rules in-depth. The book provides a good overview and shows how business rules fit with business analysis, but there's much more. For that refer to *Business Rule Concepts, 3rd Ed.* (relatively short and easy to read). See www.brsolutions.com/b_concepts.php.

- Discuss tools to manage business rules and business vocabulary as an ongoing business concern. For a look at a best-of-breed platform, see www.RuleArts.com.

You'll also need some specialized skills not explained in the book, including how to:

- Express business rules. The book does provide a great many examples of business rules, but does not explain how to express them in structured English. For that you need **RuleSpeak**®. Refer to www.RuleSpeak.com (free).

- Develop decision tables. Decision tables are an important best practice for business rules, but this book cannot get into examples. Refer to the in-depth white paper *Decision Analysis Using Decision Tables and Business Rules* (free on www.brsolutions.com/b_decision.php).

About "See the Elephant!"

The refrain **See the Elephant!** in this book is based on two intersecting threads of traditional wisdom. You'll see how it fits.

First is the tale "The Blind Men and the Elephant," which has a rich and varied history. In the version most familiar to people in the West by John Godfrey Saxe, six men "to learning much inclined" set out to see an elephant "though all of them were blind." Each touches a different part of the elephant, then all "prate" (*to talk at length and to little purpose*) about what the others mean. The true nature of the beast eludes them.

Second is the tale "The Elephant's Child" by Rudyard Kipling, which explains how elephants got their long trunks. A young elephant "... was full of 'satiable curtiosity [sic], and that means he asked ever so many questions." The poem at the end of the story is frequently mentioned as the literary source of the six interrogatives *what, how, where, who, when,* and *why.*

CHAPTER 1

Introduction

Business Analysis with Business Rules

Continuous change is a central fact of life for business these days. The techniques you use for business analysis must be based on the assumption that business rules *will* change, often quite rapidly. The best business solution is one that caters to such change, always doing so in the manner friendliest to business people and Business Analysts.

What other issues should techniques for business analysis address in this second decade of the 21st century? In addition to continuous change:

- Capturing, managing, and retaining business **know-how**.
- Enabling more effective **business governance**.
- Making compliance *(with business rules — what else?!)* more effortless.

None of these challenges is well served by the kinds of information systems we've built in the past. This book provides the basis to engineer a new kind — **business operation systems**.

Let us warn you, this is not a book about fixing software engineering practices. It's about *changing* them fundamentally. We think it's way past time they were. Current practices probably miss as much as 90% of everything important in running the business(!).

What a Business Rule Is

A **business rule** is a criterion used to guide operational business behavior, shape operational business judgments, or make operational business decisions. Business rules are only indirectly about system design or behavior. *Your business would need its business rules even if it had no software.*

Alignment

Everyone asks: *How do you close the gap between the business and IT?* We think that's the wrong question. You want to do that, sure. But the question as posed more or less implies the solution will be organizational, whether by new styles of interaction, better project management, restructuring, or other means.

Instead, we think the key to an effective solution is architecture. Use the right architectural approach and the organizational issues will take care of themselves (one way or another). So we ask: *How do you align business operations with business strategy?*

To be frank, most Business Analysts lack the standing in their organizations to pull off enterprise-level solutions. We hope that situation changes (and over time, we believe it will). Experience suggests taking smaller steps is wise. (We didn't say *small* steps, just *smaller*). So we right-size the question to the more achievable, smaller-scale equivalent: *How do you align business capabilities with strategies for solving business problems?*

You will find success at that level of alignment fruitful (and challenging) enough. Read more about it in the next Chapter.

What a Business Capability Is

A **business capability** is not an application system, database, set of use cases, enterprise architecture, or any other IT artifact. Its design and implementation might depend on some or all of those things, but that's a different matter.

Instead, a business capability is created as a *business* solution to an operational *business* problem. That solution and the problem it addresses have a scope (definite boundaries) that can be identified in terms of what business items make it up. The business solution is initially developed and expressed as a business strategy (**Policy Charter**).

The **business model** you create in business analysis is the business architecture for the business capability, a blueprint enabling business people and Business Analysts to engage in a business discussion about what needs to be created, managed, operated, changed, and discontinued. Developing a business solution using a business model does not necessarily imply software development, but if software development does ensue (and it usually does), the business model provides a solid grounding.

Our definition of *business capability* comes down to this: What the business must know and be able to do to execute business strategy.

 You'll notice we keep repeating **business** as a modifier (*business* solution, *business* problem, *business* capability, *business* model, *business* strategy, *business* rules, and so on). We do so throughout the book. And we do it in practice too. It's a reminder that our focus is *always* on business things, not system or IT things. When we say *business*, we mean *business*.

Basic Principles for Business Analysis

You can see already we're very careful about how (and when) to ask questions. You'll find that's true throughout the book. You'll see it in developing a strategy for the business solution (**Policy Charter**), **pattern questions** for harvesting business rules from various kinds of business models, **decision analysis**, and other techniques in *Proteus*. *How* you ask questions makes all the difference in the world. *Question the questions!*

> **Basic Principle for Business Analysis:** Always seek to ask the right question in the right way of the right people at the right time.

In creating a business model we also take great care never to use *ITspeak* in talking with business people. IT terminology provides an easy and understandable reason for business people to drop out of business discussions. A business model is always about *real-world things*, represented using terms that business people would naturally use.

> **Basic Principle for Business Analysis:** Use no term in talking with business people about the business they wouldn't use naturally.

Avoiding all *ITspeak* is hard. Many familiar terms *assume* development of software systems. Two examples: *use case* and *data model.* Both terms originated from IT and imply a system. In developing business models you don't need those terms(!).

Here's a related point. 'Users' exist only if you're thinking about building an IT system. We avoid the term. In the business context, business people are not 'users', they are the central actors in the day-to-day drama of business activity. Anyway, everybody is a 'user' of *some* system these days, so 'user' doesn't much discriminate anything.

> **Basic Principle for Business Analysis:** *Never say 'user'.*

Now we confess that last one is hard. It takes practice. We still slip up once in a while ourselves. Watch closely to see if you catch any misuse in this book.

Change Deployment Hell

A business manager at a very large health care organization recently confided to us that making a change to business rules of even moderate complexity took their organization 400 person-days over a 4-month period. That's staggering. How could it be sustainable? Their organization, like many today, is living in *change deployment hell*.

The manager went on to observe that a subtle stagnation had crept into the staff's very way of thinking about the business. He noted that they often don't even consider business innovations they know from experience to be difficult for the existing systems to handle. He wondered out loud whether they could even think through any real business innovation effectively any more. The bottom line: They needed a new approach, *not* more of the same.

By the way, the people at this organization were hard-working and very engaged in their activities — they did want to deliver good quality. That wasn't the problem. Indeed, we find most people in our field to be very professional and to have the best of motivations.

We can do better than that, smarter than that — we can and we should. Ask yourself this fundamental question: Do you really want to continue embedding the business rules you need to run the business in application programs?!

This book assumes you don't. It explains pragmatic, proven approaches for identifying and externalizing business rules from all other artifacts produced in business or system analysis. In short, we treat business rules as a *first-class citizen*. We think everybody should.

Can you really engineer business rules separately from requirements for application software? *Absolutely.* It's a proven fact.

Business Rules vs. Requirements

Let's be very clear that business rules and requirements are not the same thing. When you set out to create a software system, business rules can *imply* requirements — but that's a different matter.

Here's a major difference: Requirements evolve *before* deployment of a system; business rules evolve *after* deployment of a system. That affects *everything*.

To bring the distinction into perspective, consider *data* for a moment. Would you consider actual business data — not the data definitions but the actual data itself — to be part of requirements? *No!*

The life cycle of data and the life cycle of requirements are simply not the same. The life cycle of requirements, no matter what methodology you use, more or less ends with official software release. For data, in contrast, that's just the *beginning* of life. The data persists. More importantly it changes over time. That's the very essence of doing business. It's so obvious we take it for granted.

Real Life Begins at Deployment

The very same is true for business rules. Official software release is just the beginning of their life. They persist. More importantly they change, sometimes rapidly, because a business constantly needs to adjust its business parameters.

> **Basic Principle for Business Analysis:** *Always remember the business rules live on.*

The distinction between the software development life cycle and the life cycle of business rules is sometimes hard for those in IT to grasp. Indeed, if you're looking through the lens of software development methods, you're almost certain to be confused. When you look at business rules from the *business* point of view, however, seeing the distinction is far easier.

Eventually all companies will appreciate the distinction. Then the need for managing rulebooks as a separate resource (just like databases) will be obvious. We call that activity **rulebook management**. Leading companies are already doing it.

Order-of-Magnitude Improvement in Business Agility

Today's information systems aren't agile — even when agile software methods are used to develop them. Companies need **business agility** and in most cases, IT simply isn't delivering it.

We believe you should aim for nothing less than *order-of-magnitude* improvement in business agility. Is that possible? *Absolutely!* Here's a brief case study.

Order-of-Magnitude Improvement: Case Study

A medium-sized financial services company we visited specializes in detection of credit card fraud. Suspicious transactions are kicked out to fraud specialists for manual inspection. These fraud specialists are an expensive and largely non-scalable resource.

Suppose the bad guys pick up and move shop from Idaho to Manhattan. Transactions deemed suspicious only by *zip code* suddenly yield a 10x increase in volume. To keep the volume of kick-outs relatively constant, additional selection criteria (e.g., *location of store, type of store, frequency of use, size of transaction,* etc.) must be introduced.

Before using business rules, the elapsed time to deploy revised selection criteria was 30-60 days. By then *smart* bad guys are already operating somewhere else. Using business rules, the company decreased the elapsed time to 3-6 days. Would you say their business had become more agile? *You bet!* That's an order-of-magnitude improvement.

Summary

Our world is fast-changing, highly-regulated, and knowledge-intensive. Business operations are highly complex and becoming more so by the day. Business Analysts didn't invent the complexity — they are simply the ones who must come to grips with it.

Success requires special thinking tools to structure the analysis of business complexity. Business Analysts must be able to bring those tools to the table. This book shows you what the tools are and how to apply them with business people.

> **Basic Principle for Business Analysis:** *Be the master of thinking tools to address business complexity.*

Is there any other way? We don't see any. One thing for sure — doing more of the same, just faster, is *not* going to work. Existing IT techniques have simply maxed out. As Kathleen Barret, CEO of the IIBA says, *we need to take it to the next level.*

We concede the problem is big one. It's all around us everywhere we look. It's like what an ant crawling up an elephant's leg can't see. The elephant is just too big. We *don't* concede, however, there's no solution. We've proven there is. But first you must **see the elephant!**

CHAPTER 2

Alignment

What's Really Needed to Align Business and IT

A Cautionary Tale

Let me tell you a story. One of our clients is an auto insurance company. Their existing business process went like this: When an insured gets into an accident, the insured calls the claim center by telephone, reports the damage, then takes the vehicle to a claim center. The claim center gives an estimate for repairs and provides a claim form. The claimant takes the claim form to a repair shop to have the car repaired.

The company had conducted an in-depth study of claims. The study indicated that over 80% of claimants were honest and, surprisingly, most

repair shops too. A large majority of claims were fender-benders and glass breakage with no bodily injury (i.e., 'simple').

So someone came up with a bright idea. For simple claims from honest claimants, the claimant could just phone-in the claim, then take the car directly to a selected list of (honest) repair shops. Claimants would like that — one less step (no need to bring the car to a claim center for an estimate). The claim centers would like it too — less volume.

An IT project was initiated to implement the idea. A competent analyst was assigned. First she interviewed telephone operators at the claims centers to find out what they needed. *Easy.* Claimants usually go to a repair shop close to home or to work. So a key feature for the new system would be for an operator to key-in a claimant's home or work address and access all certified repair shops nearby.

The analyst then interviewed managers of the repair shops. *Easy too.* They simply needed access to claimants' policies to determine coverage.

Six months later an impressive new system had been built, complete with a colorful map of the city. Point to any location (or key-in any address) and the system identified all certified repair shops within an x-mile radius. *Slick.* Lots of bells and whistles.

The IT project team proudly demoed the new system to a group of high-level managers. Fifteen minutes into the demo, a senior director asks: "Are there any legal implications for our organization if we suggest repair shops over the phone?" *Blank stares.* The IT analyst didn't know the answer, nor did any other team member.

That afternoon the senior director phoned Gladys and said, "I don't know what went wrong. A system has been built but I have no idea whether we should roll it out. We have no sense of what business issues it might create. Can you help?" Gladys responded, "If you can get the right people in the room, I can facilitate a session to find out." He asked, "Who do you need?" Gladys replied, "Someone with significant experience from legal, the director of the telephone claim centers, a manager representing the repair shops, and a seasoned adjudicator who understands the needs of claimants thoroughly."

When a senior director wants something done, things happen. Monday morning Gladys was in a room with six managers including the four people she had requested. Here's some of what she discovered within just a few hours.

From the director of the telephone claim centers: "Did you know that an average one-minute increase in talk time on every call means adding six additional operators to the staff? Our call volume is so high our operators have no spare time for additional conversation. Suppose an operator suggests ABC repair shop and the claimant responds, 'My sister went there once and they did a terrible job. What other ones do you have?' The operator must spend time going through alternatives."

From the representative from legal: "We absolutely cannot suggest a repair shop over the phone. We could have legal issues from both claimants and repair shops. Claimants might hold us liable if they feel the repair shop doesn't treat them well or fails to repair the damage properly. Repair shops will have issues if they feel we suggest competitors more often."

Gladys spent several days brainstorming a viable business solution with the group. In the end the group decided on a public, self-help internet system rather than the internal system originally developed.

She led the group through a thorough assessment of business risks. The new business solution would require beefed-up security and extra information about repair shops. Since some claimants might not have access to the web or feel comfortable using it, an automated phone service would allow them to search for near-by repair shops by punching phone buttons. People who dislike automated phone dialogs could still call a claim center, but the response would be limited to a request for a list of all repair shops sent automatically by the mailroom.

The bottom line: The best business solution turned out to be *very* different from the system built originally. *That system basically had to be scrapped.*

Gladys held a post mortem with the senior director. What approach did the organization normally use for figuring out business solutions before jumping into designing a system? *None.* What group or role in the organization was responsible for making sure it happened? *Nobody.*

Lessons Learned

The case study presented on the previous pages and innumerable ones like it demonstrate that:

1. Business Analysts should think and talk in terms of creating *business solutions*, not building software systems.

2. Blind alleys and showstoppers *can* be found early on.

3. Creating viable business solutions involves identifying business risks and ways to address those risks — in other words, *business strategy*.

4. Most IT approaches are fundamentally *deficient* in that regard. It's simply not what they're about.

5. If you have the right people in the room, and conduct the conversation in the right way, it *doesn't take that long* to work out a viable strategy for the business solution.

What's the worst case? You might find out there's *no* viable strategy for the business solution at the present time. (We've never seen that happen.) Still, wouldn't it be better to know?! As they say, *hope is not a strategy*. And given the costs of IT, hope can also prove *very* expensive.

Isn't There a Better Way?

So many IT projects ultimately end in failure and are simply written off. Same old story, time and time again. Why is it so hard? Why can't we figure out beforehand whether some solution will actually work once we roll it out? Most project management approaches and many IT methodologies include steps for building business cases and provide guidelines for project planning and estimating. What's missing?

The answer is simply that business leads are not being properly engaged at the onset in sketching out key elements of a winning business solution. *They're not asking the right questions in the right way of the right people at the right time.*

Correcting the omission must take into account the realities of business life. Business managers and business leads are notoriously busy. They are also understandably hesitant about participating in requirements sessions inevitably slanted toward IT. They dislike being asked questions that have implications they can't appreciate or that are phrased in unfamiliar terms (*ITspeak*).

Business managers and business leads need to be engaged in the right kind of conversation, asked the right kinds of question, and hear only real-world vocabulary. The conversation must be fast-paced, pinpoint, and natural. The effort must use the minimum amount of their time possible and produce compact documentation that can easily be reviewed by busy sponsors to spot holes. The approach must absolutely uncover any blind alleys or showstoppers. And the results obviously need to serve as a foundation for developing requirements. What kind of technique could make all that work?

Enter the Policy Charter

One day in the mid-1990s, Gladys and I were called into a senior manager's office for a hastily arranged meeting. The manager needed help deciding whether to proceed on a very large reengineering initiative.

There were piles of documents all over her desk (and on the floor). Gladys knew this manager pretty well — she was capable, highly respected, and normally calm, confident, and collected. That day, though, she was clearly perturbed.

As we talked about the proposed business initiative and the major software development it entailed, the manager grew ever more agitated. Before long she got right to the heart of the matter: "I have great people working for me. They've worked very hard these past several months and produced a ton of documentation. I've gone through it carefully. I've talked in depth with the team. Still, for the life of me I don't know whether or not we should do this. Do we have a winning business solution or not? I know we need to do *something*, but I'm still not seeing the big picture." She paused for a moment and then added, "And if I'm still missing it, I'm pretty sure the team is too."

A ton of documentation. Winning business solution or not? Still not seeing the big picture. We'd heard similar complaints from senior managers confronting large projects many times before. This sponsor's team had produced use cases, data models, technical architectures, migration issues, support requirements, problem areas, 'open' issues, and still more — hundreds of pages. Yet nowhere did it provide what she really needed.

What exactly was missing? The documentation implied a new way of doing business. Yet nowhere in the documentation was there any concise, direct representation of the business thinking behind that new way of doing business. Perhaps the thinking was *somewhere* in all that documentation, but if so it was *everywhere*.

Previously the team had done high-level cost/benefit analysis. Everyone was fairly satisfied on that score, so ROI wasn't the issue.

The effort would clearly pay-off if the business problem were fixed properly.

There's the rub: *fixed properly*. Specifically what the sponsor wanted to see were the key elements of the business strategy that the proposed design embodied. She wanted to see the underlying motivation laid out — the *why* of it all. She simply wanted to know whether the business problem really was being addressed properly.

Why hadn't their requirements approach given her that answer? The answer hadn't come from the business side because there was too much 'systems' in the approach. And it hadn't come from the IT side because there was too much 'business' in the question.

In response, Gladys came up with an innovative technique, the **Policy Charter**, first published in 1998. (See Chapter 4 for details.) The Policy Charter ended up having significant influence, not the least of which was on the **Business Motivation Model**, now the standard for organizing business strategy.

Why It's Called a Policy Charter

A key element in well-developed business strategy is **business policies**. You can think of business policies as *business rules in the making*. Not just any business rules, but *core business rules* that are make-or-break for the business success of the strategy. The name *Policy Charter* emphasizes the special role of these business policies. The content is laid out in a format that highlights that role.

It doesn't really matter too much, though, what you call the artifact or how you format it. What's important is what it holds — a strategy for the business solution.

Just one thing: *Don't* call it a **business process** or lay it out as a flow. A business process model is something altogether different from a **business strategy**.

Gladys convinced the manager to commit the business leads to several days of facilitated sessions to develop a Policy Charter. The effort was a big success. At the end of the sessions the business leads commented that the discussion was *exactly the one they had wanted all along*.

The key elements of the strategy for the business solution were laid out in a few pages. An even shorter summary was created for higher-level executives. The sponsor got great feedback from the executives, not to mention solid buy-in. As events later proved, they had indeed carved out a winning business solution.

I have to confess something here. It fell to me to develop material to conduct a half-day orientation session for the participants. The material needed to cover business goals, business risks, business tactics, and business policies, and to show how to structure them in coherent fashion. I wasn't sure I could get those ideas across.

I needn't have worried. The participants were all highly-experienced business leads. They knew intuitively all about business goals, business risks, business tactics, and business policies. They had no trouble whatsoever applying those ideas free and clear of any IT and project concerns. They just needed some structure. No more than half an hour into the session, they began telling *me* how it fit together (and to please hurry up).

Since that first experience we've helped create Policy Charters to front-end many scores of initiatives of all shapes and sizes in many different industries and countries. Properly organized the technique always works like a charm.

Credit Due

At least two ideas underlying the Policy Charter originated with John Zachman and the **Zachman Architecture Framework**.

1. Zachman cleanly distinguishes architectural issues from project justification and management concerns. He focuses squarely on architecture for the complex thing you want to engineer (e.g., a business capability). So the focus should not be on project goals but on *business* goals, not on project risks but on *business* risks. Unknowingly, many approaches conflate those issues badly. The resulting misdirection creates huge sinkholes for unwary projects.

2. The *why* question of the Framework concerns motivation and strategy. The generic model for *why* thinking is *ends-means-ends*. In other words, business strategy has inherent structure — *barebones, pinpointed* structure. What *ends* will the business capability constantly try to achieve? What *means* can it employ to achieve those ends? Simple, straightforward, and very business-friendly.

Summary

Does your requirements approach allow you to reliably identify blind alleys and showstoppers *before* your company invests large sums in modeling and software development? What's missing? Most organizations do follow some project management approach. Do you find yours really helps in answering big-picture business questions?

To ensure success with an initiative, business leads must be properly engaged at the very start to carve out the key elements of a winning business solution. The focus is on developing a strategy for the business solution (Policy Charter) to ensure full **business alignment**. The Policy Charter lets management **see the elephant**.

CHAPTER **3**

Architectural Scope

The Scope Lists

Your business solution will have an **architectural scope**. This architectural scope will define the boundaries of the business capability you will build.

The key word in understanding architectural scope is *business model.* A business model is a model of *real-world* things and ideas that are named and represented using words natural for business people. Even the words used for structural elements of the business models themselves must be natural for business people — again, *real-world*.

A **business model** serves as a blueprint enabling business people and Business Analysts to engage in business discussion about what needs to be created, managed, operated, changed, and

discontinued. Developing a business solution using a business model does not necessarily imply software development, but if software development does ensue (as it usually does) the business model provides solid grounding.

Business Model vs. Architectural Scope

A business model is *self-defining* with respect to architectural scope. If a business item is in a business model, then by definition the business item is in architectural scope. If a business item is not in a business model, then by definition it's not in architectural scope.

Establishing scope for harvesting **decision rules** for an **operational business decision** requires specialized techniques. Refer to Chapters 12 and 13.

Getting Started

The first step in creating a business model is to take a quick survey of the target **business capability**. Putting some stakes in the ground produces a first-cut or *ballpark view* of architectural scope.

This ballpark view provides a collective sense of which business items are in scope and which ones aren't. Although not definitive, it provides an informed starting point for brainstorming a strategy for the business solution (**Policy Charter**).

A fundamental role for the Policy Charter, not obvious at first glance, is to help refine and solidify architectural scope.

Establishing a well-grounded architectural scope early, purely in business terms and with participation of business leads, is essential in avoiding subsequent 'scope creep' during design and development of systems. Is it really possible? *Yes,* it's a proven fact.

Business lead is the term we use for the operational business managers and subject matter experts who participate directly and actively in working out an effective business solution for a business problem. Direct participation of business leads in creating a business model is essential.

Architectural Scope vs. Project Definition

Managing the creation and deployment of a business solution for a business problem requires a project. Project definitions (or *charters*) should never be confused, however, with business models. They are *fundamentally* different. Many approaches stumble badly in this regard resulting in confusion, waste, and missed opportunities.

Let's suppose your company today has an inadequate business capability in some area, or none at all. The business wants to address the problem. The challenge you face as a Business Analyst is determining what the new business capability should look like. That's the purpose of a business model. A business model details the new or revised business capability *in the form the business capability is to operate in the future.*

 To refer to "the form the business capability is to operate in the future" in this book we say "future-form" rather than "to-be." "To-be" is often associated with system models (knowingly or otherwise). We emphasize business solutions.

Future Form

Engineering *future form* is an architectural issue. It's the same kind of challenge you would personally face if you needed a new home. Let's say your family is growing and you need more space with the right features for children and pets. You also need more storage space and enough room to entertain a widening circle of friends. What should the new or remodeled house look like? How do you go about envisioning that *future form*?

You hire an architect. Together you brainstorm the new family solution and she draws up a blueprint. *Then* you hire a contractor to build to spec.

As a Business Analyst, you too need to be an architect, but for business capabilities instead of homes. You too need to develop a business blueprint *before* the contractors (read 'software developers') are 'hired'.

Let's say today some business capability in your business is operating at point A. In its future form, the business needs it to operate at point B. The business model should describe the business capability in the new, improved form *it is to operate at point B.*

How will you get the company from point A to point B? For that you need a project. This project, however, is about managing change, *not* architecture per se. *Project definition and business model can and should be cleanly separated.*

About the Scope Lists

A ballpark view of architectural scope can be achieved by creating lists of business items. There should be six *scope lists*, each including from three to twelve *scope items* (7 +/- 2 is generally recommended). Let's say the average for each scope list is just over eight items. Your ballpark architectural scope will consist of approximately 50 scope items (6 x 8, rounded up).

 The actual number of scope items in each scope list is less important than that the scope lists outline architectural scope as clearly and as completely as possible. The scope lists should omit nothing needed for a business solution.

The six lists are based on the fundamental questions: *what, how, where, who, when,* and *why.* For each question, a particular kind of scope item is listed.

If forced to pick, we would rank the six scope lists into three tiers of relative importance, as in Table 3-1. In practice, we bounce between the lists freely. You need all six.

Table 3-1. Tiers of Scope Lists

Tier	Area of Concern	Scope List	Scope Item	Description
1	business motivation	why	business mission & business goals	how to assess whether business success is achieved
2	'customers' & quality of service	who	principal business actors	people and organizations that interact with the business
		when	operational business events	real-world triggers for significant business activity
3	operational support	what	core business concepts	fundamental notions in the business **know-how**
		how	central business processes	business processes producing key business results
		where	business locations	sites where business activity takes place

As illustrated by Figure 3-1, the six scope lists allow you to 'box' the business solution space and to roughly determine its size. It's your first opportunity to **walk the walls** with business leads. Job One is not to leave any of the six sides of the box open; otherwise the contents can and will spill out (*read* 'scope creep').

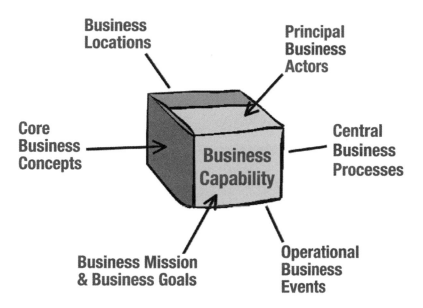

Figure 3-1. Boxing the Business Solution Space

Initial scope lists can be extracted by Business Analysts from many sources: business-case documentation, feasibility studies, problem statement, project description, sponsor(s), etc. These initial scope lists should then be reviewed and approved by the business leads.

The Zachman Connection

The **Zachman Architecture Framework** is the source of several important ideas in our approach to architectural scope. *Ballpark view* and *scope list* arise directly from the Framework. So does our emphasis on the fundamental questions: *what, how, where, who, when,* and *why*. The tiers above, however, are purely our preferences.

About the Scope Items

Let's look closer at each kind of scope item. We'll spend the most time on business mission and business goals since they are central to motivation and the Policy Charter.

Except for business mission, avoid spending a lot of time wordsmithing individual scope items. At this point they lack explicit definitions, descriptions, and motivation anyway. Simply make sure the scope lists are concise and complete.

Why: Business Mission

A business capability has exactly one *business mission*, which identifies what the business capability is responsible for doing in day-to-day operation. The business mission should be crafted carefully, from a purely architectural point of view (not political or promotional). Business goals have meaning only in the context of the business mission.

 By specifying the business mission carefully and accurately, you can often eliminate as much as 90% of the business immediately from scope.

Crafting the Business Mission

A well-crafted business mission is bare-bones — no **fluff**. It has three essential parts, each succinct: *the action, the service differentiation*, and *the beneficiary*. An example of a business mission for a future-form business capability in a large bank:

Business mission: *To offer a retirement savings plan product to customers of all ages.*

- *to offer* — the action part

- *a retirement savings plan product* — the service differentiation part

- *to customers of all ages* — the beneficiary part

 The action part should emphasize ongoing activity, not change in the business.

You should specify both the *enterprise mission* and the *business mission*. The enterprise mission applies to the business as a whole and is normally fixed (not subject to change by the project). The business mission applies specifically to the business capability.

A question to test your business mission: *Does the business mission unnecessarily assume infrastructure or means of delivery?*

> Example: *To publish a fashion magazine covering the latest trends for young professionals.* Questions: *Is "magazine" essential to the business mission? How about delivery via a subscription-based web site?*

Alternative version: *To provide information about the latest fashion trends for young professionals.* This version assumes less about means of delivery and consequently broadens the range of potential business solutions significantly.

 Run the alternative version(s) by the sponsor for a quick-and-dirty first test of architectural scope.

Why: Business Goals

The business mission can be done *directly.* Business goals can be done only *indirectly.*

> Examples: *To keep customers satisfied. To make a profit on operations.*

A *business goal* is an effect a business capability is tasked with achieving on an ongoing basis in day-to-day activity. Business goals represent the ultimate *why*, the deepest motivation for elements of the strategy for the business solution (Policy Charter).

Business Goals vs. Project Objectives

A *project objective* is a specific, measurable target that a project is tasked with attaining, often but not always time-based, which disappears when the project terminates. As the comparison in Table 3-2 shows, business goals and project objectives are *completely* distinct.

Table 3-2. Business Goals vs. Project Objectives

	Business Goals	Project Objectives
What do they represent?	effects that the strategy for the business solution must satisfy in the best possible way	what the overall change produced by the project can be expected to achieve for the business
What are they used for?	to gauge the continuing success of the future-form business capability once rolled out	to judge the one-time success of the project
When do they go away?	never (for as long as the business capability lasts)	when the project is over

 Once a business capability is operational, business goals play an important role in assessing never-ending changes to **business rules**. Business goals provide a basis to answer the crucial question: *Does every proposed change to* **deployed business rules** *make good business sense?*

To illustrate the differences between business goals and project objectives, let's return to the future-form business capability for the large bank:

Business mission: *To offer a retirement savings plan product to customers of all ages*

Table 3-3 shows some possible business goals and project objectives.

Table 3-3. Business Goals vs. Project Objectives for the Large Bank Example

Business Goals	Project Objectives
■ *To satisfy the individual, evolving needs of customers.* ■ *To support a personal relationship with customers.* ■ *To comply with government regulation.* ■ *To yield a profit.*	■ *To become operational by 1Q 2015.* ■ *To recover costs in 2 years.* ■ *To achieve a 10% profit level from the third year on.* ■ *To identify information required to comply with government regulations.*

The distinct focus of business goals vs. project objectives should be readily apparent in their expression. Table 3-4 explains how you highlight the distinction.

Table 3-4. How to Highlight the Differences Between Business Goals and Project Objectives

	Business Goals	Project Objectives
What should you emphasize?	ongoing operation of the future-form business capability	one-time change to create the future-form business capability
What kind of verb should you use?	verbs conveying a clear sense of *continuous* activity	verbs conveying a clear sense of *change*
Examples	to maintain, to support, to manage, to sustain, to satisfy, to conserve, to protect, to supply	to improve, to develop, to create, to become, to upgrade, to build, to re-engineer, to correct, to integrate

Should Business Goals Be Measurable?

Business goals should always be *inherently* measurable, but they should not include explicit measurement criteria (a.k.a. *metrics*). Until you develop the Policy Charter, there's simply no way to be sure what's truly important to measure in what way.

Metrics for business goals are developed as one of the final parts of the business model. Example: Metrics for the business goal *To keep customers satisfied* might include: *rate of repeat business, number of complaints, number of referrals,* etc. For more, refer to Chapter 16.

Common mistakes in expressing business goals:

Mistake #1. Addressing improvement in internal workflow as a business goal instead of a project goal. Examples: *To streamline clerical operations. To create better performance metrics.* Such effects are about change, so they are project objectives.

Mistake #2. Addressing IT infrastructure as a business goal instead of a project goal. Example: *To build an integrated, shared database.* Again, project objective.

Mistake #3. Explaining the consequence or business risk if the business goal is not met. Example: *To maintain a high-level of customer satisfaction because we are losing customers to the competition.* The phrase *because we are losing customers to the competition* identifies a consequence of not achieving the business goal. That part should be omitted. Business risks will be developed as part of the Policy Charter.

It's best to verbalize business goals using the infinitive form of the verb.

You should specify both *enterprise goals* and *business goals*. Enterprise goals apply to the business as a whole and are normally fixed (not subject to change by the project). Business goals apply specifically to the business capability.

A question to test each business goal: *Can the business goal be achieved by doing the business mission?*

   Example business mission: *To sell high-quality pizzas to customers city-wide.*

Proposed business goal: *To be the best source in town for tomato consumption.* No, you cannot achieve this business goal by doing the business mission.

Proposed business goal: *To keep customers satisfied.* Yes, you can achieve this business goal by doing the business mission.

Enterprise goals should not simply be repeated as business goals, but rather translated as appropriate. Example of an enterprise goal for a publishing company: *To yield a profit.* Corresponding business goal for a business capability providing order fulfillment services: *To be cost-effective.* The business capability has no direct ability to yield a profit so the enterprise goal is translated to a more appropriate counterpart.

Business Goals, Trade-Offs, and Business Strategy

Real-life business problems *never* involve only a single business goal. Suppose the only business goal were: *To keep customers satisfied*. As a means to achieve that business goal, you suggest locating an employee at every customer site worldwide. Customers might be delighted, but the expense could cause the business to fail overnight.

Business goals must be balanced. Architectural scope always includes one or more *balancing* business goal(s), which generally pertain to conserving valuable business resources (time, money, people, etc.).

If you go deep enough, business goals *always* conflict. Establishing optimal trade-offs is the very heart of excellent strategy. The next Chapter explains.

Avoid *and's* and *but's* in expressing business goals. For example, the same business goal should not say *effectively and profitably*. These effects could easily conflict.

Who: Principal Business Actors

Principal business actors are real-world people and organizations of primary importance in achieving business goals. Examples: *customers, suppliers, government bodies, unions, retail outlets,* etc. Every principal business actor must be somehow involved in some operational business event.

In specifying principal business actors, the focus is external. Organizational sub-units supporting the business capability either should not be listed, or listed collectively as a single item.

In sizing a project, the more principal business actors the longer the information-gathering and review work will probably take.

Generally, a software system is not considered a principal business actor. In sizing a project, however, the need for significant interaction with some existing major system(s) (e.g., SAP) should definitely be taken into account.

When: Operational Business Events

An *operational business event* is an **event** requiring the business to respond in a non-trivial way and often following some pattern of activity developed in advance, for example, a business process model. Such events fall into three categories:

Category	Example
actor event	*Customer places order*
temporal event	*Time to invoice customers*
spontaneous event	*Upon recognition of low inventory status*

Actor events are the most common as scope items.

These examples follow our conventions for naming operational business events. Refer to Chapter 6 for discussion.

In sizing a project, the more operational business events the bigger the project will likely be.

Operational business events treated as scope items should be:

External. *What from the outside kicks off business activity inside?*

Initiating. *Is this an original event, or one that results from some other event(s)?*

Important. *Does the event relate directly to achieving business goals? Does it require substantial work and/or* **know-how**? *Does it impact finances or other resources?*

Factored Analysis of Business Complexity

A large consulting company recently conducted an assessment of the IT development approach followed by one of our clients that uses our approach for business analysis. The consulting company judged the approach highly effective (even for prototyping) because the approach is 'componentized'. The consulting company meant that business rules are treated as a component; business processes are treated as a component; business vocabulary is treated as a component; etc.

'Componentized' may or may not be the right description, but the consulting company hit upon an important point. Most IT methodologies for requirements development today make no attempt to examine the fundamental questions *what, how, where, who, when,* and *why* individually and selectively. That omission is odd to say the least. Those six questions are ones all of us ask and answer every day in real life. The six question words are very basic to our language.

Instead, most methodologies today are *centric*. They are *process*-centric or *data*-centric or *interaction*-centric (read *use-case*-centric) or sometimes even *rule*-centric or *decision*-centric. A *centric* approach requires force-fitting some or all elements of a solution into a single mold that distorts and submerges other elements. Worse, a *centric* approach does little to avoid elements being neglected or omitted altogether.

Business problems are inherently complex and multi-faceted, as are their solutions. So we make every effort to ensure our approach to business analysis is well-factored and balanced — that is, *non-centric* — right from the start in creating architectural scope.

A non-centric approach doesn't make developing winning business solutions harder, just the opposite. By addressing business complexity head on — as naturally factored in the real world — top-quality business solutions are far easier to attain. Experience proves it time and time again.

What: Core Business Concepts

A *core business concept* is a base thing, resource, or construct in the future-form business capability that is relevant to satisfying business goals, coordinating day-to-day operational activity, or expressing necessary **know-how**. Examples: *customer, vessel, service order, certification, rental, account transaction, claim.*

A core business concept should never designate a business process, business task, operational business event, or organizational sub-unit.

Is It an Entity?

In a business context *business entity* is naturally taken to mean a real-world business or other external organization (perhaps a principal business actor). A *data entity* might play a part in a **system model,** but not a business model. We find the term *entity* is too broad (and too vague) to be of much use for business analysis.

Identifying and discussing core business concepts should quickly give you a feel for whether everyone is on the same page. Problem terms and differences of opinion often surface quickly (e.g., what is really meant by *customer*).

In creating ballpark scope, lack of agreement over the intuitive meaning of core business concepts is the best indicator of problems ahead, both for the business model in general and the structured business vocabulary (**fact model**) in particular. If you can't be reasonably sure what key terms mean when business leads (and Business Analysts) use them, what *can* you really be sure of?!

 In sizing a project, the more disagreement over the meaning of core business terms the longer developing an effective business solution is likely to take. Allow adequate time to resolve conflicts — **semantic** disconnects frequently have deep and difficult roots.

How: Central Business Processes

A *central business process* is a **business process** that produces results of foremost importance, complexity, or value. Examples: *Take Customer Order, Adjudicate Claim.*

Central business processes should be named from an *internal*, rather than external, point of view. For example, *Take Order* instead of *Place Order*. Think of *Take Order* as designating the business tasks done *internally* to satisfy the operational business event *Customer places order*.

 In sizing a project, identifying central business processes often provides some intuitive sense about the complexity of related business rules. For example, *Take Order* is likely to involve business rules less complex than *Pay Employee*, which is likely to involve business rules less complex than *Adjudicate Claim*.

In naming central business processes, avoid implicit bias toward current mechanisms or infrastructure. For example, *Charge Customer* is probably better than *Invoice Customer*. (Who knows whether 'invoices' will literally be created and sent in the future?) Additional naming guidelines for business processes are discussed in Chapter 6.

Where: Business Locations

A *business location* is any physical or logical place where some principal business actor is located, some operational business event occurs, or some central business process takes place. Examples: *regional office, warehouse, web site.*

 In sizing a project, the number of business locations often gives some initial sense of probable diversity in central business processes, business vocabulary, and business know-how. A many-location project generally proves more time-consuming.

Standardizing Know-How

All elements of the business solution, including structured business vocabulary (**fact model**) and **business rules**, will need to be standardized within the boundaries set by architectural scope. Standardization is required, however, only *within* that scope. In other words, architectural scope establishes the outer boundary of guaranteed consistency, share-ability, and reusability. The same boundary will also apply to supporting software and data.

Consistency, share-ability, and reusability are good things, of course, but they can also be expensive, time-consuming, and organizationally challenging. Balancing these conflicting goals is the central trade-off in architectural scope. Starting off *smaller but not necessarily small* (as we put it in Chapter 1) is the prudent course. Remember, many people have yet to **see the elephant**.

Sizing the Project

The scope lists provide an initial basis for project planning, including resource requirements, budget, and schedule. The Policy Charter will provide a far more concrete basis.

 A certain amount of redundancy across the scope lists may be evident, as well as some differences in 'leveling'. For ballpark scope such problems are usually not significant so don't spend too much time trying to resolve them.

The scope lists represent pure business perspective. They should *not* address any software development concerns or IT technology requirements. *Separately* from the scope lists and business model, however, the project *should* address those concerns and requirements — and do so *up-front*.

 IT technology requirements involve the necessary hardware/software infrastructure to support the future-form business capability — e.g., database management, communication networks, **rulebook management**, business rule engines, etc.

The project should be sized first in terms of architectural scope and then in terms of resources required (e.g., time, cost, people, etc.). Other concurrent projects and their resource requirements must be considered as well. Not infrequently, architectural scope must be modified as a result.

Managing Architectural Scope

Once the business model has been completed, architectural scope should remain relatively stable throughout the project. Changing the scope becomes progressively more expensive and risky as the project continues.

Factors may emerge during any of phase of project activity that impact architectural scope. For example, additional business innovation may be suggested and judged worthwhile. Or non-architectural factors (e.g., budget cutbacks, schedule overruns, etc.) may force reduction in scope. Since any change in architectural scope can impact the project's resource requirements, budget, and schedule, such changes *must be managed.*

Architectural scope should be treated as a real living-and-breathing thing. When such factors emerge, scope must be revisited and revised as appropriate. All revisions should be handled consistently following a formal amendment process.

 We recommend using the scope lists as a continuing point of coordination for architectural scope. Once the business capability is deployed, however, any change in architectural scope must be handled by a *new* project.

Disappearing Acts

Sometimes a clever business model or system model allows some scope item(s) to be eliminated from business operations altogether. The project's resource requirements, budget, and schedule should be adjusted accordingly. Architectural scope, however, need *not* be amended, a good way of disproving any neglect.

Summary

A business model is a blueprint for creating a business capability. A business model defines architectural scope, which includes everything needed to operate the business capability in future form. Although architectural scope exerts considerable influence on project definition, architectural scope and project definition are entirely distinct.

Project definition is about getting the business from its current business capability ('point A') to the future-form business capability ('point B'). In other words, projects are about managing change in the organization, not architecture per se.

The first step in creating a business model is to establish a ballpark view of architectural scope. This ballpark view is based on six quick lists of scope items needed for the future-form business capability. Ballpark scope lets you manage scope on a sound business basis right from the start. It also leads quickly to the Policy Charter, the heart of the business solution.

CHAPTER 4

Strategy for the Business Solution

The Policy Charter

The very large majority of IT-based methodologies have no real foundation in business strategy and business policy. One reason is that programming and system development have traditionally been deeply **procedural**.

Another reason is more obvious — they are about building systems, not creating business solutions. As discussed in Chapter 2, the price for that failure has been very high.

About Strategy

Your business solution needs to be based on a **strategy**. That strategy will precipitate many **business rules**.

The key word in understanding strategy is *motivation*. Sound strategy has to be based on strong motivation.

Motivation means *why* we do what we do. For a business solution, motivation involves establishing *ends* the business wants to achieve, **business goals** in particular, and the appropriate *means* to achieve those ends. Included among the means are **business tactics** and **business policies**, which play the central role in mitigating business risks.

A conversation about the elements (ends and means) of a strategy for the business solution is exactly the conversation that business leads are looking to have. It is how Business Analysts can ensure they're talking about what's really important for the business. *It's about how Business Analysts can get quality time and quality insight from the business leads.*

 A **Policy Charter** is the deliverable in our approach that presents the complete strategy for the business solution in a trim, easy-to-digest form, including the motivation for each element. The approach is easy to understand and provides a powerful thinking tool.

The Battle Plan for the Business Solution

We often think of a Policy Charter as a 'battle plan'. You don't want the troops storming the beaches until you've adequately assessed operational feasibility, identified significant risks, and chosen the best means to minimize those risks. If the battle plan were to fail, the costs could be quite high. If the battle plan is deemed too risky, you can assess other opportunities.

The top brass (read *business sponsors*) are quite busy, so you want to take as little of their time as possible. They nonetheless need to grasp the plan fully (**see the elephant**) and 'own' the plan. And, by the way, after all is said and done it also wouldn't hurt if you got a promotion as a result of the plan's success.

 Techniques for creating strategy can be applied to many areas of business activity. The Policy Charter specifically addresses the engineering of a future-form **business capability**.

Here's a comment we receive time and time again: "Our organization does develop strategies for business solutions but we've never done it in a structured, pinpoint fashion like this." *Structure* is exactly what's been missing.

 A **ballpark view** of **architectural scope** is provided by **scope lists,** as discussed in the previous Chapter. Be sure this ballpark view has been created before beginning work on the strategy.

Creating the Strategy

Business strategy is about knowing where you will play and how you will win. The five essential questions in Figure 4-1 provide a structured approach for creating a winning strategy for the business solution.

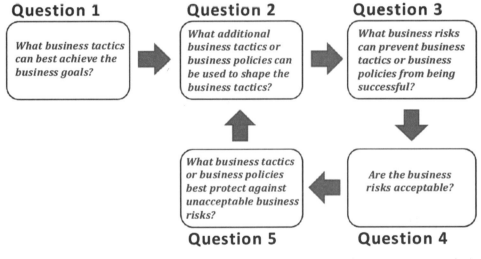

Question 1

What business tactics can best achieve the business goals?

Question 2

What additional business tactics or business policies can be used to shape the business tactics?

Question 3

What business risks can prevent business tactics or business policies from being successful?

Question 5

What business tactics or business policies best protect against unacceptable business risks?

Question 4

Are the business risks acceptable?

Figure 4-1. Five Questions for Creating a Winning
Strategy for the Business Solution

These five questions touch on the four key elements of strategy in a Policy Charter: *business goals, business tactics, business policies,* and *business risks.* Business goals were discussed in the previous Chapter. The other three elements are discussed below. Elements of all four kinds will be woven into a coherent structure that is self-explanatory with respect to motivation.

 Well-considered business goals are essential in developing a winning strategy for the business solution.

Strategy Has Inherent Structure

Many people think of strategy as ideas and plans without much structure. *Not so.* Strategy has inherent structure based on **ends** and **means**. The structure is easy to understand and provides both business leads and Business Analysts with a powerful *thinking tool*.

The *why* question of the **Zachman Architecture Framework** concerns motivation and strategy. The generic model it gives for answering the *why* question is *ends-means-ends*. What *ends* will you try to achieve? What *means* will you employ to achieve those ends?

This structure is bare-bones, pinpoint, and very business-friendly. It forms the heart of the **Business Motivation Model**, the industry standard for organizing **business strategy**.

Question 1. *What Business Tactics Can Best Achieve the Business Goals?*

A *business tactic* is a means that involves some particular characteristic(s), feature(s), or use(s) of one or more **scope items**.

The easiest way to think about a business tactic is as a *course of action* that can be followed to meet some business goal(s). A course of action has no steps or sequence; it's just a first, brief description of some element of a business solution.

A pizza business, for example, might have the business tactic *Deliver pizzas to the customer's home or office.* This business tactic addresses the business goal *To keep customers satisfied.* This motivation connection is illustrated in Figure 4-2.

Figure 4-2. Graphical Depiction of Business Tactic Addressing a Business Goal

We usually prefer to present the elements of the strategy graphically. *Strategy diagrams* are friendly and self-explanatory.

A business tactic must be based on some scope item(s). For example, the business tactic above might be based on the scope item (central business process) *Deliver pizzas.*

 A business tactic that needs some item not in architectural scope produces your first scope issue. The disconnect can and should be addressed immediately.

When development of the Policy Charter commences, scope items have only been listed, not defined, described or elaborated. A business tactic therefore gives some initial form, fit, or function for the scope item(s) as needed for the business solution.

Question 2. *What Additional Business Tactics or Business Policies Can Be Used to Shape the Business Tactics?*

A *business policy* is guidance representing a critical *do* or *don't* in day-to-day operation of the future-form business solution. A business policy always indicates some degree of operational freedom (usually some reduction) appropriate to meet business goals.

Here is an example of a business policy for a pizza business: *Pizzas should be delivered within one hour.* In the pizza business this business policy (illustrated in Figure 4-3) indicates the degree of freedom appropriate to meet business goals.

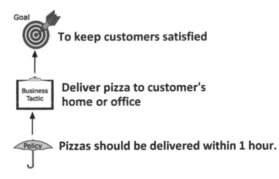

Figure 4-3. A Business Policy Indicating a Degree of Freedom to Shape a Business Tactic

 Strategy diagrams are always oriented vertically, rather than horizontally, to avoid any suggestion of flow or sequence (as in a model of business process). Strategy diagrams always portray only *motivation* connections.

Business Policy vs. Business Tactic

The key question for distinguishing business policies from business tactics: *Does it touch on some tangible degree of operational freedom?*

　　Example:　*Keep prices competitive.*

This item is a business tactic because the range of 'competitive' prices is huge. What's 'competitive' is completely subject to interpretation. Contrast that expression with the business policy: *Prices should be kept lower than the competition's.* This expression clearly indicates a tangible reduction of operational freedom, *lower than the competition's.*

　　Example:　*Provide customer-friendly service.*

This item is a business tactic because what qualifies as 'customer-friendly' is again completely subject to interpretation. Opinions could vary widely. Contrast that expression with the business policy: *Delivery personnel should wear uniforms.* This expression clearly indicates a tangible reduction of operational freedom.

Question 3. *What Business Risks Can Prevent Business Tactics or Business Policies from Being Successful?*

Risks of course are everywhere you look — **business risks**, project risks, IT risks, professional risks, and more. Which kinds of risks should you consider in creating a strategy for the business solution? Let's be very clear on this point: *Not* project risks.

Business Risks vs. Project Risks

Business risks and project risks are completely distinct. As an example, suppose a business capability for a large bank has the business mission: *To offer a retirement savings plan product to customers of all ages.*

Business risks must be addressed continuously in the day-to-day operation of the future-form business capability. Examples: *Early withdrawal of funds. Loss of customer involvement. Low return in the early years.*

A project is about *developing* a future-form business capability — that is, bringing about change within the organization. Project risks represent impediments or barriers to achieving those changes successfully. Examples: *In-house resources might be inadequate for putting together an experienced and highly skilled team. The database administrator is currently involved in 20 projects and might not be available when needed.*

A *business risk* is an exposure arising in day-to-day business activity that can:

- Preclude or complicate satisfaction of some business goal(s).

- Imperil or subvert one or more business tactics or business policies.

Such exposure can arise either from inadequate internal resources or external factors beyond the control of the endeavor. For each business tactic and business policy we ask: *What could prevent this means from producing the desired effects?*

The pizza business has the business goal *To keep customers satisfied.* Hungry customers will clearly not be satisfied if pizzas take too long to arrive. *Taking too long* represents a business risk. Mitigating this business risk is the purpose of the business policy *Pizzas should be delivered within one hour.*

Then we should ask: *What could prevent pizzas from being delivered within one hour in day-to-day operation of the future-form business capability?* Traffic congestion during rush hours certainly could (and, unfortunately, *has* where I live!). So as illustrated by Figure 4.4 *traffic congestion* is a business risk that imperils the business policy about one-hour delivery.

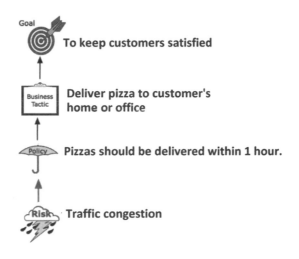

Figure 4-4. A Business Risk for One-Hour Pizza Delivery

Question 4. *Are the Business Risks Acceptable?*

When Gladys was a child, her grandfather taught her always to think through risks. When you want to take on something big, he said, think of every risk you can and how you would handle it. Only when you have decided you can live with all remaining risks should you actually do whatever it is. All the remaining risks must be acceptable to you.

Question 5. *What Business Tactics or Business Policies Best Protect Against Unacceptable Business Risks?*

What (within our power) can be done to address an unacceptable business risk?

Figure 4-5. Drill-Down to Equip Drivers with Traffic-Aware GPS

For the pizza business, one suggestion might be the business tactic *Equip drivers with traffic-aware GPS.* That way drivers can avoid areas of heavy congestion. The business leads will want to discuss the idea. The strategy diagram in Figure 4-5 graphically depicts the *drill-down.*

Is the proposed business tactic *Equip drivers with traffic-aware GPS* a good one to address the business risk *Traffic congestion?* Is it economically feasible for a pizza business? Does it engender too much risk (e.g., distracted drivers, theft, etc.)? The business leads must decide.

You have two options if the business leads can't resolve an issue: Kick it up to the sponsor(s) or task a Business Analyst (or other staff) to go do some digging.

Another important point: *Traffic-aware GPS* is probably not on any of the scope lists. So if deemed acceptable, architectural scope needs to be adjusted right away. By exploring the business means to achieve desired ends, the Policy Charter helps solidify architectural scope deftly and rapidly. *It works!*

Adjusting and Fine-Tuning the Strategy

The Policy Charter is your battle plan. It should be reviewed and fine-tuned to ensure we 'win' the battle. The success of a business solution depends largely on its strategy.

For example, pizza businesses are very competitive. At some point the owner of the business decides that in order to stay competitive, pizzas need to be delivered in 30 minutes instead of 1 hour. Figure 4-6 illustrates his rethinking on questions 2, 3, and 4. He doesn't proceed because he perceives the risk (undercooked order items) to be unacceptable.

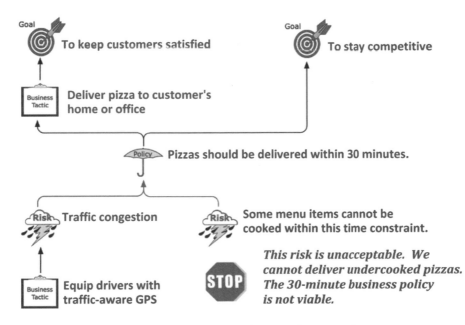

Figure 4-6. Policy Charter for 30-Minute Delivery for the First Company

Where the first pizza company sees unacceptable risk, a competitor looks harder and sees opportunity. Figure 4-7 illustrates that company's finer-edged strategy.

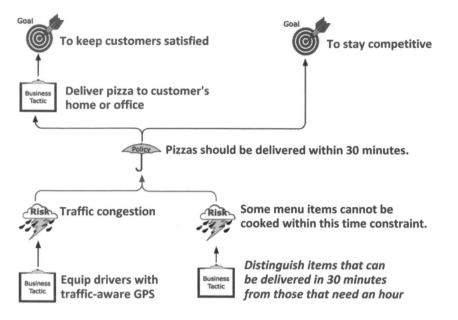

Figure 4-7. Policy Charter for 30-Minute Delivery by the Competitor

The competitor sees 30-minute delivery for some menu items as a new offering. As illustrated by Figure 4-8, drilling down even more he arrives at a new business policy for question 5.

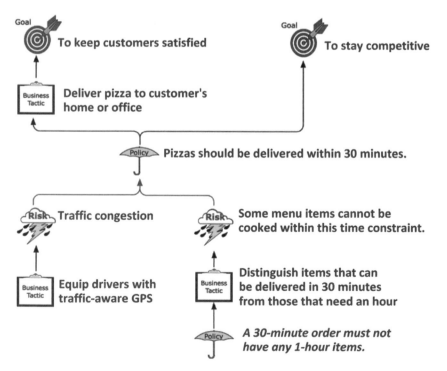

Figure 4-8. More Drill-Down in the Competitor's Strategy

Key Point: You shouldn't start developing a complete business model — and certainly not design or develop any systems — until all business questions like these have been resolved. It's just common sense.

High-Impact Sponsorship

The Policy Charter supports *high-impact sponsorship*, a distinguishing characteristic of our approach. Benefits for the sponsor(s):

- Maximum leverage for controlling the business direction of a project with a *minimum investment of time*.

- The ability to manage projects *by business benefit*, rather than simply or primarily by cost. As Gladys famously puts it, "Cost overruns are manageable if worthwhile business benefits are achieved; however, failing to meet business goals is always unacceptable."

The Policy Charter enables sponsor(s) to monitor a project closely with minimal investment of time. The Policy Charter equips the sponsor(s) with:

- An up-front opportunity to directly assess the overall strategy for the business solution, identify holes, and provide pin-point feedback.

- A clear, concise, and continuing framework to understand how business goals are met by the business model and subsequent design and development of a system.

- A way to detect easily and early in the project life cycle if the project strays from original business intent so appropriate action can be taken in timely fashion.

Conflicts, Trade-Offs, and Risk Brackets

Consider the drill-down depicted graphically in Figure 4-9 in the strategy of a business solution supporting order fulfillment.

Business goals in this drill-down: *To stay competitive. To keep customers satisfied. To make a profit.* A business lead indicates a necessary business tactic *Accept orders on credit.* The business tactic addresses two of the three goals: *To stay competitive. To keep customers satisfied.*

Associated with the business tactic is an obvious business risk *Non-payment of purchases made on credit.* This business risk imperils the third business goal *To make a profit.* So a **conflict** arises among the business goals. How is the conflict best resolved?

**Figure 4-9. Strategy diagram illustrating
a Drill-Down for Order Fulfillment**

The business leads decide that orders over $1,000 present an unacceptable level of business risk. To address the business risk the business leads formulate a business policy *Orders on credit over $1000 should be credit checked.*

We often refer to a delimiter such as the $1,000 in this business policy as a *threshold of pain*, a specific limit in the degree of risk the business can tolerate.

Where does that leave things? The business leads have decided that orders up to $1,000 don't merit credit checks; that is, an *acceptable* business risk is: *Orders up to $1,000 on credit without a credit check.* Some important observations:

- **Tight lips.** A threshold of pain can represent sensitive information. In the wrong hands, it could threaten the very success of the strategy for the business solution. *A Policy Charter, like any battle plan, should be treated as confidential.*

- **Metrics.** A threshold of pain represents a clear danger point in day-to-day operation of the future-form business capability. How do you determine whether the business policy is being subverted? The answer is metrics — *key performance indicators* — aimed around the threshold of pain. Strategy-based metrics are critical. To differentiate them from other kinds of metrics (e.g., metrics for business processes) we call them *key **strategy** performance indicators.*

Until the business model nears completion, delineating metrics is premature. We'll return to this important topic in Chapter 16.

■ **What's better left unsaid.** Documenting why business leads deem business risks acceptable is optional — *not* necessary. Tread carefully here. For example, suppose business leads deem the following business risk to be acceptable: *Failure to comply with regulations might result in a fine.* It turns out the cost of compliance far exceeds the amount of any potential fines. Also, the chances of getting caught are slim. In creating Policy Charters, situations like this one fortunately don't arise often, *but they can.*

Remedies

Sometimes, a business risk simply cannot be overcome in all cases by any reasonable means. Then the right question to ask becomes: *How can we make the best out of a bad situation?*

For example, suppose that despite all best efforts by the pizza business, traffic congestion is sometimes so heavy that deliveries can't be made in an hour (or 30 minutes). No matter whose fault, hungry customers are still likely to be unhappy. What can be done in those cases to achieve the business goal *To keep customers satisfied*?

One idea might be to offer the customer a free-pizza coupon. Some restrictions (read *business rules*) would naturally have to apply, but those can be worked out later. The new business policy *Customers should be offered free-pizza coupons when pizzas cannot be delivered within one hour.* A business policy like this one provides a *fall-back position* or **remedy** when all else fails.

Remedies can go too far, of course. Suppose the tardy-pizza customer were given free pizzas for a month. Turns out the customer has a household full of teenagers. You can see that situation could get out of hand very quickly. Always keep *balancing* business goals in mind — for example, *To make a profit.*

The key to excellent business strategy is optimizing trade-offs when business goals conflict. Remember, at some level of drill-down, business goals *always* conflict.

Risk Brackets

Optimizing trade-offs sometimes requires calibrated responses to a business risk. By distinguishing **risk brackets**, each threshold of pain can be addressed selectively by an appropriate business policy.

For example, a business capability supporting purchasing identifies the business risk *Wasteful or fraudulent expenditures.* Addressing this business risk in optimal fashion requires calibrated trade-offs between two business goals: *To protect financial resources* and *To ensure efficient operations.* Selective business policies for different risk brackets are presented in Table 4-1.

Table 4-1. Selective Business Policies for Different Risk Brackets

Risk Bracket	Selective Business Policy	Calibration
1. Expenditures under $10,000	Expenditures under $10,000 may be processed by operations staff without any approval.	This level of risk is deemed acceptable. The business goal *To protect financial resources* is preempted in favor of *To ensure efficient operations.*
2. Expenditures from $10,000 up to $100,000	Expenditures from $10,000 up to $100,000 should be approved by a supervisor.	The conflicting business goals are balanced against each other, but more in favor of *To ensure efficient operations.*
3. Expenditures from $100,000 up to $1,000,000	Expenditures from $100,000 up to $1,000,000 should be approved by a regional manager.	The conflicting business goals are balanced against each other, but more in favor of *To protect financial resources.*
4. Expenditures over $1,000,000	Expenditures over $1,000,000 should be approved by the president.	This level of risk is deemed unacceptable. The business goal *To ensure efficient operations* is preempted in favor of *To protect financial resources.*

Best Practices for Policy Charters

Best Practice 1: *A business tactic should never be expressed as a sequence of actions.*

A business tactic is a *course* of action, not a *series* of actions. *Important difference!* Avoid getting bogged down at this point in process flow.

Wrong way to express a business tactic: *A repair shop continues to create supplements for an estimate, and the estimator approves or denies. The estimator returns to the Claims Office where supplements are keyed into the estimating pad. A copy of the new original estimate is sent to the repair shop.*

Good expression of a business tactic: *Provide estimators with the ability to perform on-site supplement reviews when an estimating pad is unavailable.*

Best Practice 2: *A lousy business tactic is a lousy business tactic, not a business risk.*

Lousy business tactic: *Piece-meal billing on an individual order-by-order basis.*

If a customer receives a hundred separate invoices for $10 each, that's asking for trouble. But what's the true business risk?

True business risk: *Unhappy high-volume customers.*

The lousy business tactic forces customers to process a great many invoices each month, resulting in frustration and wasteful use of resources.

Perceiving business risks correctly is an essential step in finding suitable resolutions. Possible replacement business tactic: *Monthly billing on an account basis.*

Best Practice 3: *Be alert for motivation gaps.*

A publishing company has the business goal *To make a profit.* The business tactic in Figure 4-10 is proposed: *Offer discounts to intermediary companies.*

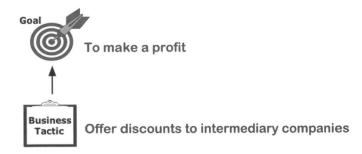

Figure 4-10. Motivation Gap

The motivation for the business tactic is not obvious. How can offering discounts result in boosting profits? Something seems to be missing.

Between the business goal and the original business tactic lurks an unstated business tactic. Figure 4-11 reveals that business tactic and clarifies the motivation.

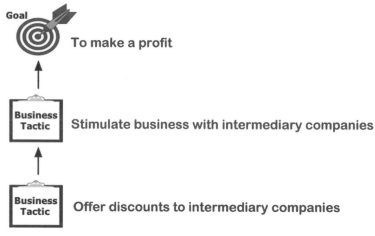

Figure 4-11. Filling in Motivation Gaps

The new business tactic has been added in: *Stimulate business with intermediary companies.* Now the motivation for the discounts is clear. They will stimulate business with intermediary companies, resulting in a greater volume of business. The greater volume will presumably more than compensate for the discounts, thereby boosting overall profits.

 Figure 4-11 includes a drill-down from one business tactic to another business tactic. 'Decomposing' business tactics in this fashion often proves useful.

Best Practice 4: *Be on the lookout for missing business goals.*

Business goals for a prison system: *To rehabilitate offenders. To punish offenders. To protect society.* Someone proposes the business policy *A non-violent inmate should not be housed with a violent inmate.* Assuming the business policy is appropriate, its motivation is problematic. The business policy doesn't clearly address any of the business goals. Perhaps a business goal is missing: *To protect the physical welfare of the offender while in prison.*

If so, architectural scope must be adjusted right away; the new business goal needs to go onto the appropriate scope list. Here again we see the Policy Charter ably serving a secondary purpose — to solidify architectural scope as early in the game as possible.

More on the Role of Business Policies in Strategy

Business policies are crucial for defining the fine-weave of a strategy for the business solution. They are how you win the business battle.

My Favorite Business Policy

Any customer can have a car painted any color that he wants so long as it is black.

Henry Ford, *My Life and Work*, 1922, Chapter IV

Henry Ford developed a successful strategy to create a mass market for automobiles. His strategy included such well-known innovations as assembly lines (in strategy terms, a business tactic) and wages high enough so workers could buy cars (a business policy). To create the mass market, prices had to be kept low (a business tactic). Among the business policies adopted to support low prices was the one above (here reworded): *All cars should be painted black*. No variation in color equaled lowest possible cost.

Let's review some additional roles that business policies play.

Identify mission-critical business rules.

Business policies provide the basis for the most critical business rules in the future-form business capability, *core business rules.* As discussed in the next Chapter, we think of a business policy as *some business rule(s) in the making.*

Disallow business tactics or business policies.

Business Policy: *We will not make on-site visits.*

This business policy precludes any business tactic prescribing on-site visits. (Perhaps on-site visits are too expensive and time-consuming or set the wrong expectations.) Suppose a business goal is: *To stay in close contact with customers.* Even though business tactics involving an on-site visit might prove effective in achieving that business goal, they cannot be admitted to the strategy. On the other hand, a business tactic involving sending holiday courtesies by mail would be acceptable. It involves no on-site visits.

Business policies can also protect against inappropriate *reduction* of operational freedom. Example for an international bank: *Accounts may be held by a person of any age.* No business policies placing restrictions by age alone in holding accounts are permitted.

Govern business processes.

Business policies shape both the form and operation of **business processes** within the future-form business capability. Refer to Chapter 6 on modeling business processes.

At the extreme, business policies (or their absence) can even preclude the need for some business process(es). For example, if there were no business policy that you need a driver's license to drive, there would be no process for getting a driver's license(!). *Hold on though.* Isn't requiring a driver's license a law rather than a business policy? Yes, but with respect to strategy and motivation, it doesn't matter. Laws work essentially the same for societies as business policies do for businesses.

Think about the motivation (goals) for the driver-license law: *To ensure public safety on public roads. To identify drivers and their driving history uniquely. To certify knowledge of traffic laws.* Operating any complex capability implies strategy, whether for societies or for business capabilities. By the way, a *bad* strategy, or a strategy by *default*, is still a strategy!

Gob-Smacked: A Case Study

In the U.K. a large pharmaceutical company sought to integrate four lines of business that had previously been stovepipes. At the same time they wanted to open a new channel for their offerings via the web. Very complicated stuff, with delicate business trade-offs to consider. They asked us to conduct facilitated Policy Charter sessions.

On Monday morning, the room filled quickly with more and more people — about triple the number expected. As the meeting progressed we found out why. The various business managers from the four lines of business had brought their operational staff. The managers had become accustomed to IT requirements sessions asking questions only their operational staff could answer.

At the end of the first day's session, the managers told their operational staff not to come back the next day. The managers caught on quickly what the discussion was about and that they themselves needed to participate.

During Policy Charter sessions, we like to use different colored sticky notes on the walls for each component of strategy — that is, different colors for business goals, business tactics, business risks, and business policies. We use red or pink for the risks so they stand out.

It startled us a bit when we entered the room the next morning and all we could see was seemingly a sea of red, all these risks bleeding out of the walls. Gladys shook her head and walked out of the room to get some coffee. The project manager ran after her and said, "Gladys, this is good stuff!" Gladys gave him a look like, *'Were you in the same room I was?!'*

The feedback from the managers was very positive. The previous day's discussion was simply the first time they'd ever talked through the business risks face-to-face. The project manager said he could already see they were saying many of the same things, just using different words. He turned out to be right. By the end of the second day, the sea of red had shrunk considerably.

The group went on to do some great thinking. Originally the sessions had been planned for three days. They were so pleased with the progress, however, that at the end of the third day they asked us to return the next day for more. Whenever did you ever hear of business managers asking for *more* time to spend in 'requirements' sessions?!

Several years later we learned that the manager had received a worldwide award for the project. They determined that the project had saved the company some £80 million.

About a month after the sessions, Gladys received an email from one of the manager participants. The very first line said, "We were gob-smacked." *Gob-smacked?!* What's that?! Had something horrible happened? What had we done?!

She called me immediately to find out what it meant. I didn't know either. After a flurry of emails another Brit finally assured us it was highly complementary. Loosely translated he was simply saying they were *blown away* by the sessions.

No Policy Charter? *Take this Two-Part Test!*

Do you find yourself in the middle of a project that didn't create an up-front Policy Charter? Here's a two-part test to determine how much trouble you might be in.

1. See if you can pull together all the elements of your *implicit* strategy for the business solution (i.e., business goals, business tactics, business risks, and business policies) into a coherent document of modest size. Be sure not to include any elements of project definition (e.g., project objectives, project risks, etc.).

2. See if you can summarize the strategy as an 'elevator pitch'. The sponsor should be able to absorb the key points, ask an intelligent question or two, and give an informal thumbs-up or thumbs-down in one elevator ride.

If you truly understand the business solution, you shouldn't find these tests too hard and they shouldn't take very long. You'll end up with excellent new communication tools.

If you *can't* document the implicit strategy for the business solution with reasonable effort and summarize it coherently, yes, you could indeed be in trouble. Storming the beaches without a battle plan won't make up for hard work and good intentions. Think seriously about lobbying for a freeze on further development. Quickly set about undertaking some Policy Charter sessions. The time and energy couldn't be better spent! Remember, it's all about the best possible business solution!

How Long Does It Take to Create a Policy Charter?

With the right people in the room (*major* caveat), good facilitation, and a solid ballpark view of scope, creating a Policy Charter in draft form doesn't take that long at all — sometimes as little as a half-day.

In the gob-smacked case study above, the sessions took 4 half days with the business leads, the last half-day at *their* request. The strategy was for an altogether new business capability. We've proven time and time again it's possible to create a Policy Charter that fast (or faster). It's simply not as hard as you might think — again, *if* you have the right people in the room and the right approach.

Why? The appropriate business leads have already been thinking about new and better ways of conducting business. Intuitively they understand what business risks and trade-offs are involved. Remember it's not about IT, so it's natural for them. The Policy Charter simply provides *structure* so they can lay out their thoughts clearly and work through problem areas. *Strategy is exactly the conversation the business leads want to have!*

Another caveat: If the strategy for the business solution requires approval beyond the sponsor(s), more time may be required. One Policy Charter we did involved a new business policy that literally had to be approved by the U.S. Congress. That one took a while(!)

When is the Strategy 'Done'?

Work on the Policy Charter should continue as long as business leads or sponsor(s) can think of additional business risks. Each business risk deemed unacceptable must be addressed by one or more business tactics and/or business policies. In addition, no business tactic or business policy can rely on any item not in architectural scope. Either the item must be brought into architectural scope or the strategy for the business solution modified.

The Policy Charter is complete when all remaining business risks are deemed *acceptable*. Then the business sponsor(s) must sign off. Their approval may take several iterations.

 The actual size of individual Policy Charters can vary depending on architectural scope, level of drill-down, and presentation style. Short and concise is always best. Remember, no **fluff** allowed!

Sample of a Real-Life Strategy Drill-Down

The strategy diagram in Figure 4-12 shows a drill-down (one-page) from a real-life Policy Charter we helped facilitate for one of our clients.

Background: A primary goal for this insurance company is to be recognized as providing the best customer service in the industry. The drill-down in Figure 4-12 addresses the new business tactic of providing after-hours claim support via a call center. In the past, claims have been assigned to an adjuster exclusively responsible for interacting with the claimant. The new business tactic means that people other than adjusters will now interact with claimants. This new mode of business operation entails business risks. The drill-down indicates how some of these business risks are to be addressed.

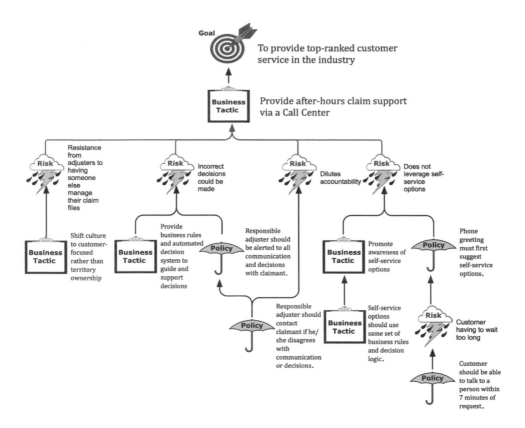

Figure 4-12. A Real-Life Drill-Down from a Client Policy Charter

 Strategy is never static for an organization. It must be periodically revisited. What better means than by retaining and revising the Policy Charter?!

Summary

A conversation about strategy is exactly the one your business leads are looking to have. A Policy Charter gets right down to business — *literally*. It addresses two fundamental questions, two sides of the same coin.

- *Looking down from business goals.* What are the best business tactics and business policies to achieve the business goals, and how are the associated business risks addressed?

- *Looking up toward business goals.* What is the business motivation for each of the business tactics and business policies, and why are they appropriate?

To achieve true **business alignment**, your approach to business requirements needs to be based on a Policy Charter. And as discussed in Chapter 16, the performance of the business capability, once deployed, should be measured according to the key elements of the strategy.

Here's a final thought for you (not original). The person who knows *how* will always have a job; the person who knows *why* will always be his boss.

CHAPTER 5

Business Rules

Basic Principles and Pattern Questions

A **Policy Charter** can be an important source for harvesting **business rules**. Their capture occurs in two essential ways. First, **business policies** are further refined. Second, business tactics and business policies are analyzed to identify what additional guidance is needed.

Basic Principles for Business Rules

Before harvesting business rules, you should be aware of some basic principles and absorb them into your practices.

The techniques described in this Chapter can be used even if no formal Policy Charter has been created. You will (or should) have other sources for business policies. Also, the pattern questions presented later in this Chapter apply almost anywhere.

First, *all* business rules are subject to change, including (and perhaps especially) business rules derived directly from business policies. The ability to change and redeploy business rules is essential to **business agility**.

> **Basic Principle for Business Rules:** *No business rule is ever set in stone.*

 Across industries, we've found that typically only 30-45% of all business rules change rapidly. Some of those though change *quite* rapidly.

A business rule must make sense for *all* stakeholders, business tasks, and operational business events within the **business capability**.

The resulting mindset is quite different from traditional requirements methodologies. In those approaches, especially ones centered on use cases, the focus is local to individual roles and interactions. The issues of business agility, compliance, and **know-how,** however, are global for the business capability. **See the elephant!**

> **Basic Principle for Business Rules:** *A business rule must make global sense across architectural scope.*

There is no such thing as an **implicit business rule** in any **business model**. Assuming that other people share intuitive understanding about some unexpressed business rule(s) usually leads to big trouble downstream. We like to say that if a business rule isn't explicit it doesn't exist.

> **Basic Principle for Business Rules:** *There are no business rules until you say there are.*

Making business rules explicit puts a premium on the words you use to express them. Sooner or later you'll find you need a structured business vocabulary (**fact model**).

> **Business Rules vs. Choices Made in Designing Systems:**
> ***Not the Same Thing!***
>
> A colleague and I were recently discussing business rules. In the course of conversation he used this example: *A customer may have only one address.*
>
> *Hold on!* That's not a business rule. Rather, it's a *design decision* (probably a poor one) some IT person made in creating a **system model**. The business wouldn't (and couldn't!) make a real-world business rule about customers having only one address. But a design decision might be made *to record* only one (in a system).
>
> Eventually we agreed the desired business rule probably was: *A customer may have only one __preferred__ address*.

Expressing Business Rules

As discussed in Chapter 8, a fact model defines shared business concepts. The meaning of these concepts is given by definitions. When you look at a fact model you should see a structured business vocabulary that includes both nouns (terms) and verbs (wordings). These nouns and verbs are used directly in expressing business rules.

Sample business rule: *A customer must be assigned to an agent if the customer has placed an order.*

Figure 5-1 shows the relevant terms and wordings for this sample business rule.

Figure 5-1. Terms and Wordings for the Agent-Assignment Business Rule

The sample business rule directly uses the fact types worded *customer places order* and *customer is assigned to agent*, with only minor adjustments in tense as appropriate for English grammar. As this example illustrates, every business rule can be expressed as a complete sentence that includes a sense of obligation or necessity for relevant fact types.

Business capabilities often involve hundreds or even thousands of business rules. Achieving consistency and coherence across so many business rules requires a blueprint. A structured business vocabulary (fact model) is indispensable for *scaling up*.

Basing verbalizations directly on wordings for fact types is a key feature of business-oriented notations for business rules such as **RuleSpeak**, our notation for business rules used throughout this book.

Are Your Legacy Business Rules Right?

A Business Analyst at a major insurance company recently said this: *"When we looked hard at business rules currently implemented in existing systems, we found at least 30% were flatly wrong. That's a very conservative estimate: the actual figure was probably much higher. IT told us they couldn't solve the problem because it was a business issue not a software issue. And they were absolutely right about that."*

The thing about business rules is you never know who will read them or what background or purpose the reader may have. So every business rule (including '**exceptions**') must be understandable *out of context*. The words you use must have clear definitions; the expression must include everything needed to interpret it correctly.

Basic Principle for Business Rules: *A business rule means exactly what the words you use to express it mean — nothing more and nothing less.*

Turning Business Policies into Core Business Rules

A business policy is guidance representing a critical *do* or *don't* in day-to-day operation of a business capability. The ongoing success of a business capability is largely determined by its business policies.

A *core business rule* is a business rule derived directly from a business policy. Like the business policy on which it is based, it too is make-or-break for the business capability.

We estimate that only 2-3% of all business rules are derived directly from business policies crucial to the strategy for the business solution. These select business rules should be crafted and managed with extra-special care.

Think of a business policy as some *business rule(s) in the making.* A business policy always provides guidance, but rarely in a form ready to deploy to business people or machines. Additional analysis and refinement is required first.

Sample business policy: *Pizzas should be delivered within one hour.*

A Business Analyst should ask:

- When does the clock *start* ticking? *The time of the order? When the pizza is taken from the oven?*

- When does the clock *stop* ticking? *Arrival at the customer's? When the customer signs for the pizza?*

At issue is whether the guidance is **practicable**: *Could a person who knows about the guidance and who understands the business vocabulary observe a relevant situation including his or her own behavior and decide directly whether or not the business was complying with the business rule or applying it properly?*

> **Basic Principle for Business Rules:** *A business rule is always practicable.*

Business policies fail the *practicable* test. As expressed by the **Business Motivation Model**, compared to a business rule, a business policy tends to be less structured, less discrete, less atomic, less compliant with standard business vocabulary, and less formally articulated.

Example: The core business rule derived from the one-hour pizza delivery policy might be: *A pizza order delivered off-premises must be handed-off to the customer within one hour from the time the pizza order is taken.*

Example: The core business rule derived from Henry Ford's paint-color policy in the previous Chapter (*All cars should be painted black.*) might be: *The chassis of an automobile must be painted coal black.*

 Practicable business rules should be developed only after the Policy Charter is completed and approved.

Use Your Time with Business Leads Wisely

Business leads usually have only limited time to review business rules, so use their time wisely. In addition to core business rules, pay special attention to business rules that:

- Support the business mission or central business process(es)
- Address compliance with law, regulations, etc.
- Enforce contracts, agreements, and deals
- Maintain appropriate or desired quality of service
- Define escalation criteria (service level agreements)
- Establish business priorities
- Reflect business culture or philosophy
- Improve (or lower) productivity significantly
- Ensure operational business activity remains within supportable limits

General Pattern Questions for Harvesting Business Rules

Basic business rules can be captured from a Policy Charter and many other sources using the general **pattern questions** presented below. These pattern questions focus directly on the **basic engineering questions** *what*, *how*, *where*, *who*, *when*, and *why*, plus exceptions. Applying these pattern questions represents an important step in externalizing **semantics** from other parts of a business model, especially business process models.

General Pattern Question for 'What'

Pattern Question G1: What
   What computed or derived facts does a business capability require? What criteria should be used to compute or derive the facts?

Sample business tactic:
   Base large deals on an established risk management scheme.

Ask specifically:
   What criteria should be used to decide whether a deal is a large one?

Sample business rule specifying a criterion:
   A deal must be considered a large deal if the total cost of the deal is over 150% of the average deal size for the given region.

General Pattern Question for 'How'

Pattern Question G2: How
What method is appropriate for doing something? How
should some action be done? Is there a particular way
in which a business tactic or core business rule needs to be
performed or carried out?

Sample business tactic:
Give customers proof of purchase for each purchase.

Ask specifically:
What method should be used to give proof of purchase?

Sample business rule specifying a method:
A paper receipt must be given for each purchase.

General Pattern Question for 'Where'

Pattern Question G3: Where
Does a business tactic or business policy need to be
performed at a particular place? Are there business
rules pertaining to transport, connectivity, or linkage??

Sample business tactic:
Minimize transport costs for components to be assembled.

Ask specifically:
Where should assembly of components be located to minimize
transport costs?

Sample business rule specifying a location:
The assembly of the components included in a finished product
must be located at the source of the heaviest component.

General Pattern Question for 'Who'

Pattern Question G4: Who
Who is responsible or authorized for what? Is there a particular party (e.g., person, role, organization, etc.) that should (or should not) be involved in a business tactic or business policy?

Sample business tactic:
Large orders from new customers must be individually approved.

Ask specifically:
Who should approve a large order from a new customer?

Sample business rule specifying a party:
An order on credit over $50,000 from a new customer must be approved by a Director.

General Pattern Question for 'When'

Pattern Question G5: When
When should something occur? What deadline or limit on cycle time applies? What timing criteria apply to a business tactic or business policy?

Sample business tactic:
Fill orders from good customers before other orders.

Ask specifically:
How fast should orders from good customers be filled?

Sample business rule specifying a timeframe:
An order placed by a good customer must be filled within 2 days.

General Pattern Question for 'Why'

Pattern Question G6: Why
Do priorities need to be established when business
goals, business tactics, or business policies cannot be
completely satisfied? What tie-breakers apply?

Sample business policy:
Particular car models may be requested in making car rental
reservations.

Ask specifically:
If we don't have enough cars of a certain model, which rental
requests have priority?

Sample business rule specifying priorities:
The priority of rental requests for the same car model must be
determined as follows:

- First, by the current membership level of the customers
  who made the rental requests.
- Then, by the earliest date the membership level was attained.

General Pattern Question for Exceptions

Pattern Question G7: Exceptions
What exceptions should be made? Who or what is
exempt from a business tactic or business policy?

Sample business policy:
Particular car models may be requested in making car rental
reservations.

Ask specifically:
Is anyone excluded from requesting a particular car model in
making car rental reservations?

Sample business rule specifying an exception:
An employee must not request a particular car model in making
a rental request.

'**Exceptions**' to business rules simply imply more business
rules.

How the Policy Charter and Business Rules Support Each Other

A Policy Charter provides an authoritative framework for on-going assessment about whether emerging business rules align with the strategy for the business solution. If not, the business rules can be revised until suitable.

Occasionally an emerging business rule highlights some omission or weak spot in the strategy for the business solution. With the help of Business Analysts, adjustments should be made as quickly as possible by the appropriate business leads and sponsor(s).

Summary

Business rules offer a powerful tool for Business Analysts to improve communication with business leads (and IT) and to come to grips with real-life complexity. The basic principles and techniques of business rules are relatively straightforward. It's all a matter of getting started and then *practice, practice, practice.*

CHAPTER 6

Business Processes

Better with Business Rules

Your business solution will include one or more operational business processes. Each business process will involve many business rules.

The key word in understanding business processes is *transformation*. A business process takes operational business things as inputs and *transforms* them into outputs. These outputs might be the same operational business things in some new state, or altogether new operational business thing(s). For example, a business process might take raw materials and transform them into finished goods. A successful transform creates or adds value, though not always in a direct way.

Thou Shalt Not Kill

Could anyone possibly mistake that Commandment for a process?!

Analysis

- The *process* of murder transforms a live person into a dead person by killing them.

- The *concept* of murder is defined as the act of killing someone.

- The *rule* about murder is that there shouldn't be any of them.

The first is about *doing*; the second is about *knowing*; the third is about *prohibiting*. Three very different things. **Walk the walls!**

What a Business Process Is

The best definition of **business process** we have come across to date is Janey Conkey Frazier's from one of the very first Business Rule Forum conferences in the late 1990s: *the [business] tasks required for an enterprise to satisfy a planned response to an operational business event from beginning to end with a focus on the roles of actors, rather than the actors' day-to-day job.*

We especially like that part about *a planned response to an operational business event.* It raises a very interesting question: Can you possibly predict all the **operational business events** that might happen in your business and all the circumstances under which those operational business events might occur? What do you do about the ones you *can't* predict? Be thinking about those questions. We'll come back to them later.

Here are key points about business processes that Roger Burlton makes. A business process:

- Is triggered by an external event involving a stakeholder.

- Is comprised of all the actions necessary to provide the appropriate business outcomes.

- Transforms inputs into outputs, according to guidance (**business policies**, standards, procedures, **business rules**, etc.) employing resources of all types.

- Contains logical steps that usually cross functions and often organizational units.

- Delivers a product or service to an external stakeholder or other internal process.

Much has been written about how to model business processes. In this Chapter, we simply ensure you can create business process models that are friendly to business people and business rules. Our focus throughout is on *operational* business processes.

Just in case we need to say it, business processes and business rules are *not the same*. In fact, they are fundamentally different. Specifically, a business process *transforms* something, always. Business rules properly expressed in **declarative** form do not transform anything, *ever.* (The *evaluation* of business rules might result in something being transformed, but that's a different matter.)

So if there is any doubt, you *do* need both business processes and business rules, not just one or the other. The trick is not to get them entangled, to stay clear about which is which. This Chapter and the next will show you how. By following these prescriptions you can improve your business process models dramatically.

Are Your Business Process Models Too Complicated?
Take the Business Rules Out!

One of our clients, a major pharmaceutical company, called us with a significant problem. They had created a business process model some 28 pages long. No one could follow it, and everyone was confused.

The problem was clear to us immediately — business rules embedded in the flow. We extracted all the business rules, reducing the business process model to just four pages! Now everyone could understand the business process. In the bargain, they could also now clearly see the business rules and which ones needed to be modified. There is nothing unusual or exceptional about this story — *it happens all the time*. **See the elephant!**

The Elements of a Business Process Model

Always keep in mind that the things found in a business process model refers to real things (activities) in day-to-day operations of the business, not to how those things are represented or coordinated in a system. *Big difference!* A business process model, for example, should have no tasks whose sole purpose is updating stored data.

What notation you should use for modeling business processes? Use your own judgment. We'll briefly apply and explain a notation we often use, but just for the sake of illustration.

The basic rule of thumb for modeling business processes is *keep the notation simple.* To explore how value-add is created cross-functionally at the business level and to discuss it with business people, you don't need fancy event symbols and such. In fact, they'll work against you. And they're mostly not necessary for business rules anyway.

For the kind of work typically done by Business Analysts, we find a swim-lane format usually works best. Figure 6-1 shows a very simple business process model from an insurance company using a swim-lane format.

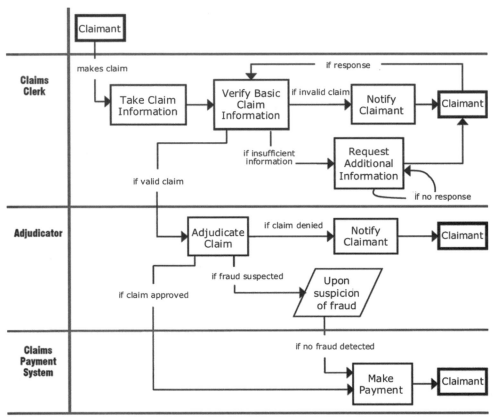

Figure 6-1. Business Process Model for an Insurance Company in Swim-Lane Format

 Showing swim lanes in early versions of a business process model may prove less desirable if the scope is particularly large, if there is considerable leeway for business re-engineering, or if significant organizational pushback can be expected early on.

Business Tasks

The larger boxes in this business process model represent *business tasks* to be performed. We always use a two-part *verb+noun* format to name business tasks. This verb-in-front notation helps distinguish boxes in a business process model from 'thing' boxes in structured business vocabularies (**fact models**).

- The noun part of the name for a business task (often compound) should generally designate some item within scope. For example, for *Make Payment* we should find "payment" in scope. Applying this test can lead to a more accurate name, for example, *Make <u>Claim</u> Payment*. That particular kind of payment might be the only kind in scope.

- The verb part of a business task name should indicate some discrete action (e.g., "notify") rather than some continuous responsibility (e.g., "manage"). This guideline emphasizes that business tasks are discrete transforms.

 A test for whether the name for a business task is a good one is to flip it around. The result should always reflect the completed transform. For example, for *Notify Claimant* the completed transform is appropriately designated *claimant notified*. Note how flipping around *Manage Staff* to *staff managed* represents a 'transform' that's *never* really completed(!).

How Business Process Models, Fact Models, and Business Rules Relate: *It's All About What State You're In*

Business Process Models: A completed transform often achieves a business milestone and a new state for some operational business thing(s). Example: *claimant notified.*

Fact Models: In **fact models** such states are represented by fact types, for example, *claimant <u>is</u> notified* (or *claimant <u>has been</u> notified*, if you prefer). A fact model literally represents what things the business can know (remember) about completed transforms and other operational business events.

Business Rules: Business rules indicate which states are allowed or required. They should not reference business processes or business tasks by name, just the states they try to achieve. For example, a business rule might be: *A claimant may <u>be notified</u> that a claim has been denied only if the specific reason(s) for denial have been determined.*

 Business rule statements should always be based directly on fact types. The sample business rule above, for example, is based on the fact type *claimant is notified*. English grammar requires just a small tweak: *<u>is</u> notified* becomes *<u>may be</u> notified*. Since **RuleSpeak** is simply structured English, RuleSpeak naturally follows this basic rule of English grammar.

Business tasks need to be individually documented. Until you describe what a business task represents, a box with a name on it is just a box with a name on it. Some aspects we document about business tasks are outlined below.

Documenting a Business Task

- Specify the inputs and what different forms they can take.
- Specify the outputs and what different forms they can take.
- Document the transform(s).

 A business task can have multiple transforms for each form of input and/or output, or for different scenarios.

- Define the source for each input, which can be from:
    (a) Outside the business process.
    (b) A previous business task in the business process.
    (c) Evaluation of **decision rules**.

 Some business tasks in a business process model are likely to require extensive **know-how**, for example *Adjudicate Claims.* Such *decision tasks*, which can be the source of a great many business rules, require special analysis techniques. Refer to Chapters 12 and 13 on **decision analysis**.

Flow Arrows

The arrows in a business process model represent flows; therefore they are always unidirectional. Loops (iterative flows) are commonplace; things don't always get done, or done right anyway, in a single try(!).

You should never think of the arrows as data flows; a business process model is *not* a data flow diagram. (Data flow is about how the logic of a procedural program works.) With state-of-the-art database systems and network communications, operational data these days can be just about anywhere as soon as you need it. It doesn't really need to flow *anywhere*.

Instead, think of each arrow as a hand-off of work between business tasks, possibly to a different actor. Output(s) from one or more previous business tasks become input(s) to some other business task.

As above, these inputs and outputs are not data, not information *about* operational business things. They represent the *actual things themselves*. A business process model is a form of business model; business models are always about real-world things. Of course, that line gets a bit fuzzy when the things the business works with are intangible (e.g., insurance policies, financial products, tax, etc.); nonetheless, since the customer thinks about those things as very real, real they are.

Collectively, the boxes and arrows in a business process model represent management's blueprint for understanding, coordinating, and revising how operational work in the organization gets done — that is, how value add is created. Consequently:

- Responsibility for performing business tasks can be re-allocated (or automated) as appropriate.

- Bottlenecks can be identified and corrected.

- Appropriate business rules can be applied to ensure work is done correctly.

Some FAQs about Business Process Models

Can flows be conditional?

Yes. In fact, conditional flows are one of the most important features of a business process model. The example above includes multiple conditional flows — e.g., *if valid claim, if claim approved, if fraud suspected*, etc. A conditional flow simply means that work follows the given path only if the condition is satisfied for a given **case**.

The secret of effective business process modeling with business rules is: *Never embed the criteria used to evaluate a conditional in the conditional itself.* Instead, just name the conditional using an adjective (e.g., *valid*) or **past participle** (e.g., *approved*). The criteria for evaluating conditionals should always be expressed separately as business rules. Fortunately there's nothing particularly hard about that.

Following this best practice is how you keep a business process model simple — often by an order of magnitude or more! Frankly, most business processes aren't nearly as complicated as people think. What's complicated is the **know-how** needed to perform the business process correctly. That know-how should be represented by business rules.

What if an actor's work cannot be re-engineered?

For external actors in particular, how work gets done is essentially unknowable, or at least cannot be re-engineered — rather, the actor's involvement sits more or less like a black box in the midst of the flow.

In such cases, we often do not give the actor a swim lane, but rather simply indicate the actor's involvement directly in the flow wherever it happens to pop up (using a box with heavy dark lines). For example, the actor *customer* appears four times in Figure 6-1 above. In one appearance, the flow goes right through it. Using this flow-through technique avoids line crossings (to reach another swim lane), which can make the diagram hard to follow.

 These days, emphasis is often placed on extended value chains and cooperative interaction. In such cases, the external actor's work *is* to be re-engineered. If so, give the actor his own swim lane.

Can an application system be shown as an actor?

Judgment call. We say if you already know that a legacy system (e.g., *Claims Payment System* in Figure 6-1) is not to be reengineered — but does play a significant role in the work — show it. It can either be given its own swim lane (as in Figure 6-1) or be shown using heavy-dark-line boxes (as for *customer*).

Can one business process re-use another business process?

Yes. Note the parallelogram labeled *Upon suspicion of fraud* in Figure 6-1. That's another business process that's being invoked (re-used) at that point in the flow. Modular construction of business processes is generally a good thing.

How many initiating events should a business process model have?

If possible, just one. The initiating **event** in Figure 6-1 is claimant makes claim.

What kinds of initiating event can there be?

Generally three.

■ An *actor event* is when an actor does something — for example, *claimant makes claim* (as for Figure 6-1).

- A *temporal event* is when the time comes to do something — for example, *time to make payments*. You will need some business rule(s) to specify when the "time to ..." is.

"Time to ..." is literally how we designate a temporal event.

- A *spontaneous event* (or *conditional event*) is when certain circumstances arise — for example, *upon recognition of low inventory*. You will need business rules to specify what these relevant circumstances are.

"Upon recognition of ..." is literally how we designate a spontaneous event.

How should you name a business process model?

As for business tasks, we recommend the verb+noun format. The business process model above, for example, is named *Process Claims*. Note that name takes an internal view of the initiating event *claimant makes claim.* The correspondence is deliberate. The name given to a business process should reflect what work the business needs to do "internally" to satisfy the initiating event.

Is There *Always* a Process?

A restaurant sometimes allows members of a party to split the bill for a meal so each person can pay just part.

> Business Rule: *The amount paid for a meal may be split among the members of the party served the meal only if all the following are true:*
> - Each member initials his or her portion of the amount paid on the bill for the meal.
> - Each member provides the room number in which he or she is currently registered in the hotel.

Does the restaurant have some business process for collecting payment? *Of course.* The bill for meals usually does get paid (usually involving a transform of my personal financial resources!). But that's not the right question.

The real question is whether the business process is simply *ad hoc,* or *modeled and prescribed* (or somewhere in between). No matter, the business rule always applies. That's important because there will always be at least *some* **ad hoc business activity** — and perhaps quite a lot.

Should business rules appear on your business process model?

Generally, no. The purpose of the business process model is to provide a management blueprint for how work gets done. Showing business rules just clutters that picture. There will be lots of business rules — which ones will you show? Better to **walk the walls**!

What if business practices for some business process vary extensively across organizational or geographical units?

Think business milestones. Developing business rules for business milestones ensures that basic imperatives for all variations of the business process can be identified and coordinated. Then local variations of the business process can be created as (and if) needed. Refer to Chapter 10.

How Does the Policy Charter Help?

Often, initiatives featuring business process models start off great guns. Everyone is excited to be involved and to see some 'big picture' emerge, possibly for the first time. Things go well for a while but then start to bog down, sometimes fatally. Why? There are many reasons, but three stand out that you can do something about.

- **Business rules are embedded in the flows.** We've already warned you about this one. Just don't do it. It won't scale. As you consider and incorporate more and more scenarios, the complexity of the business process model compounds itself. As business people mentally drop out, IT takes the helm. *Not what you want!*

- **Organizational politics kick in.** Managers start silently assessing what the emerging to-be model means to their area's head count and budget. If they feel they're likely to lose out, they understandably start to politically drop out. To counteract this response as soon as it kicks in, something needs to be already in place.

- **Unanswered questions surface about critical business practices and trade-offs.** Such questions typically pertain to tricky or risky or difficult scenarios. Maybe *black swans*. Maybe day-to-day operational issues. Maybe showstoppers. Since you probably started modeling with the **happy path** (recommended), little or no thinking may have been devoted to these other issues.

The solution to the last two problems is to create a strategy for the business solution (**Policy Charter**) *before* you start modeling the business process(es). Without a strategy to address significant business risks and set key business policies, it's hardly a surprise things can go awry. In essence, you're trying to develop a management blueprint for how work is done without having established key parameters about the shape of the business solution. First, **see the elephant**!

A Father's Story

My three children are grown now, but when they were young, Friday was 'pancake night' at IHOP, our family's special time just to talk. The kids would discuss whatever was happening at school or with sports and friends (and, of course, video games). I would talk about work some. *Really!* Sometimes I would even try out new lecture material. Kids are just full of surprising responses.

In those days, Gladys and I had just started doing Policy Charters. We often used a pizza business as a case study. I told my kids the pizza business wanted to deliver pizzas *within five minutes*. I thought it would stump them.

"No problem!" they replied. "We'll operate a fleet of helicopters 24x7 with radio dispatch. We'll put the ovens right on board the helicopters [*big* helicopters!], all the ingredients, everything, so as soon as we get an order we'll send the helicopter right toward the person's house. We'll bake the pizza in route ... and check their credit, of course. After all, we *do* want to get paid for that $15[!] pizza. Upon arrival, the customer can come out into their front yard [where we live, everybody has yards] and we'll *parachute* the pizza down to them." Then my older son (now a lawyer) spoke up, "And we'll get liability insurance in case the parachute doesn't open and the pizza hits them on the head and knocks them out."

Then I radically changed the business policy: Pizzas must be delivered *within seventy-two hours.* They weren't nearly as interested in that one. They said, "Aw, we'll just mail them the pizza!"

Then I set the business policy to *within one hour.* I should have known what was coming. Almost immediately they launched into when they would be getting their own cars. Wouldn't I be just *so pleased* they could earn money by delivering pizzas in their own cars as soon as they started driving?! (*Not!*)

The serious point behind the story is this. The process of flying helicopters to deliver pizzas is very different from handing off pizzas to the postal service, which is very different from dispatching owner-operated vehicles. *Until you establish the basic business policies, how can you model the business process?!*

The content of the Policy Charter helps shape the business process model in at least three specific ways.

Business tasks that need to be done. Suppose the Policy Charter includes the business policy: *A receipt should be given to a customer for every purchase.* This business policy addresses three business goals: *to facilitate return of goods, to keep the customer satisfied,* and *to minimize insider theft.* The implication is that a business task *Generate receipt* needs to be included in the business process model.

Allocation of responsibility to actors. Suppose the Policy Charter includes the business policy: *An order that exceeds the customer's credit limit by more than $50,000 must be approved by the owner.* This business policy addresses two business goals: *to minimize financial exposure* and *to encourage large sales.* (The customer might be an old golf buddy of the owner.) The implication is that the business task *Approve order* must be assigned to the actor *owner* (e.g., included in the owner's swim lane).

Evaluation of conditionals. Suppose the Policy Charter includes the following three business policies: (1) *An order that exceeds the customer's credit limit by more than $50,000 must be approved by the owner.* (2) *An order that exceeds the credit limit of a long-time customer must be approved by the owner.* (3) *A rush order placed by a new customer not yet given a credit limit must be approved by the owner.* In Figure 6-2, these business policies determine when a case is to follow the conditional flow *if owner approval required* between the business task *Take order* and the owner's business task *Approve order.*

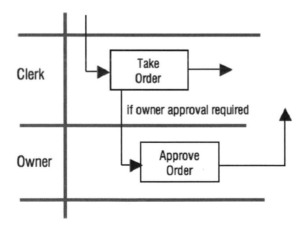

Figure 6-2. Conditional Flow in a Business Process Model

Are You Sure You Have a Business *Process* Problem?

Case Study: An organization runs public conferences. In reaching an agreement with a hotel, it must commit to a room block of a certain size. If the conference does not fill the room block, it must compensate the hotel. The amount of the compensation is roughly equivalent to the cost of the number of room nights not filled. So it's prudent to always guesstimate on the low side.

Sometimes conference attendance exceeds expectations. If the hotel is already heavily booked for the conference dates (e.g., for other conferences), attendees will not be able to secure a hotel reservation. Not having a hotel room may naturally discourage them from coming. So it's wise to constantly monitor the number of hotel reservations vs. the size of the room block. Once exceeded, provisions should be made immediately to secure more hotel rooms for attendees, often at a nearby hotel.

Analysis: Business process problem? *No.* This problem is really an **operational business event** — in particular, a **spontaneous event**.

■ The operational business event is *when hotel room block is exceeded*.
■ A business rule could be specified defining the appropriate conditions producing the operational business event.
■ An appropriate response to the operational business event might be *Notify conference organizer*.

If detecting the spontaneous event via testing of the business rule and notifying the conference organizer can all be automated, fine. If not, monitoring the hotel room block should be assigned as a job responsibility for staff, possibly just one of many 'checklist' items to perform daily.

Does a to-do item constitute a business process? *No.* A to-do item — or even a whole checklist — is *not* a business process! Each item is what it is, simply a job responsibility. Simply notifying the conference organizer is not a business process either. It needs to be something more substantial, like *Secure additional hotel rooms*.

 To be a business process it's not enough for someone to be informed, something must be *transformed*.

After-the-Fact Settlement: What happens if the hotel registration overflow is *not* detected in real time? Nothing good! Suppose the hotel continues to accept reservations knowing they can be accommodated at near-by hotels. Now you need an additional business process: *Handle hotel registration overflow*. It's one you'd rather not have.

Transferring registrations to other hotels entails significant work and communication, leaving some registrants inevitably unhappy. Clearly you need a 'fairness' rule for who gets transferred — probably *first-come, first-serve*.

The bottom line: Failure to detect operational business events in real time can result in highly undesirable 'settlement' problems downstream. Use business rules in real time to detect out-of-tolerance business transactions whenever you can.

 In creating the business model, stay alert for business processes involving after-the-fact settlements. Could real-time reaction to operational business events eliminate them?

When is the Business Process Model 'Done'?

A common device used in modeling business processes is **scenarios**, which assist with:

- Getting started (usually using the **happy path**).
- Easing gradually into more complex and organizationally-challenging areas.
- Pursuing completeness.

Can a business process model (or set of them) ever *really* be complete? Earlier we asked whether you can possibly predict all the operational business events that might happen in your business and all the circumstances under which those operational business events might occur. You obviously can't. You could model scenarios from now until you retire and still probably not cover them all.

A key question then is which scenarios *should* you model, and which ones *not*? Generally, you should probably model a scenario if it's high frequency or involves a large number of employees doing the same kind of work. You probably *shouldn't* if it's low frequency and involves only a small number of employees.

That answer is more subtle than it seems. Suppose the large majority of claims submitted to an insurance company are for less than $10,000. One day a claim arrives for $10,000,000 (fortunately, a very rare event). Only a few people in the whole company are qualified to handle such a claim.

So should you model that rare scenario? What happens to scenarios left *un-modeled*?

A claim of such magnitude clearly presents a significant business risk to the insurance company. Where are such risks addressed? *The Policy Charter.* Appropriate business policies should have already been developed to protect the company. A business process is not the solution. You need a good strategy for the business solution!

If you develop strategy beforehand, and then specify all the know-how separately as business rules, what does a business process model really do for you? Think back to the earlier definition of *business process,* which described it as *a planned response to an operational business event.* That's spot on. A business process model is a management blueprint that that provides a focal point for coordinating highly repetitive work.

Summary

What do business rules do for business processes? Roger Burlton says it this way: "If you separate the business rules, you can develop remarkably stable business processes." If you're looking to manage business activities on a business-process basis, stability is key. Burlton goes on to say, "The really rapid change is in the business rules, not in the business processes." *Exactly!*

How do business rules and business processes relate? Burlton observes that business processes "... transform inputs into outputs according to guidance — policies, standards, business rules, etc. ...." The key phrase in that is *according to guidance*. Critical guidance and know-how is exactly what business rules provide. **See the elephant!**

CHAPTER 7

Business Rules From Business Process Models

Pattern Questions

Think of a business process model as a recipe. I'm no cook, so if I want to bake a cake, I'd better follow the recipe. The great chefs of Paris don't need to though. As long as they produce outstanding results and follow all the rules about health and sanitation, *so what?!*

A model of a **business process**, like a recipe, is a task-by-task blueprint for performing repetitive work. A recipe doesn't imply any particular rules, and a rule doesn't imply any particular recipe.

(A rule might effectively disallow some recipes, but that's a different matter.) A recipe and a rule are simply different.

What do **business rules** do for business processes? Collectively, business rules provide guidance and **know-how.** They shape judgments and **operational business decisions** in day-to-day business activity. With business rules you can create **smart business processes**.

Basic business rules can be captured from business process models using the **pattern questions** presented and illustrated in this Chapter. Use of these pattern questions represents an important step in externalizing **semantics** from business process models.

Reminder: A business model should never assume any **implicit business rule.** There are no business rules until you say there are.

Remember that each **behavioral business rule** needs to be satisfied only to the **level of enforcement** specified for it.

Conditional Flows

Pattern Question for Conditional Flows

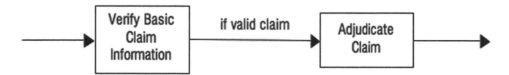

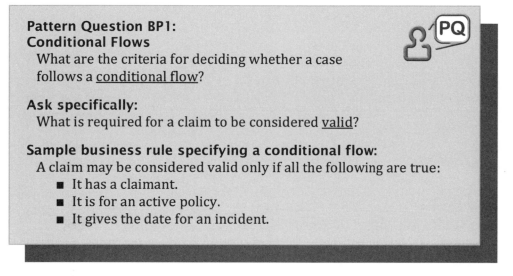

Figure 7-1. Partial Business Process Model to Illustrate Pattern Questions about Conditional Flows

Pattern Question BP1:
Conditional Flows
What are the criteria for deciding whether a case follows a <u>conditional flow</u>?

Ask specifically:
What is required for a claim to be considered <u>valid</u>?

Sample business rule specifying a conditional flow:
A claim may be considered valid only if all the following are true:
- It has a claimant.
- It is for an active policy.
- It gives the date for an incident.

This first pattern question is fundamental in externalizing business rules from business process models in an organized and intelligible way. As the example illustrates, the conditional flow is named, but the criteria for deciding whether any given case follows the conditional are not embedded within the business process model itself. Instead, some separate business rule(s) express the criteria. This approach simplifies the business process model dramatically and permits the business rule(s) to be revised independently.

 A conditional should be expressed using an adjective (e.g., *valid*) or a **past participle** carefully chosen for the purpose. Consistent use is critical for coordinating business rules with the business process model(s). The words might also appear in the structured business vocabulary (**fact model**) and/or a **business milestone** model. Adjectives and past participles are literally the verbal glue that holds the business model together as you **walk the walls**.

Production and Use of Outputs

Figure 7-2. Partial Business Process Model to Illustrate Pattern
Questions about Production and Use of Outputs

Pattern Question for Existence of Prior Output

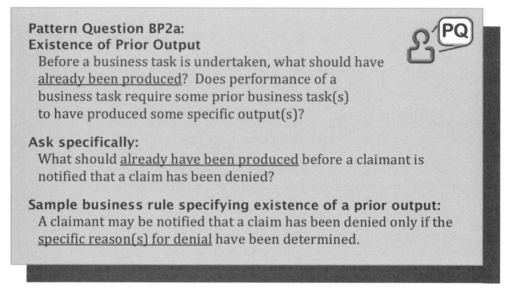

Pattern Question BP2a:
Existence of Prior Output
  Before a business task is undertaken, what should have
  already been produced? Does performance of a
  business task require some prior business task(s)
  to have produced some specific output(s)?

Ask specifically:
  What should already have been produced before a claimant is
  notified that a claim has been denied?

Sample business rule specifying existence of a prior output:
  A claimant may be notified that a claim has been denied only if the
  specific reason(s) for denial have been determined.

Presumably, reason(s) for denial is an output of the business task
Adjudicate Claim. The business rule indicates the business task
Notify Claimant may be performed for a **case** (i.e., some claim)
only if *Adjudicate Claim* has produced some reason(s) for denial
for that case.

Business rules about outputs are not limited only to
those business tasks leading directly into the targeted
business task.

Production of some output does not necessarily mean the
business task that produced it is complete. A business task
is over only when its whole transform finishes and results
in some recognizable **state**. If a business rule actually requires a state
to have been achieved, rather than simply some output produced,
refer to Chapter 10 on analysis of business milestones.

Pattern Question for Specific Use of Prior Output

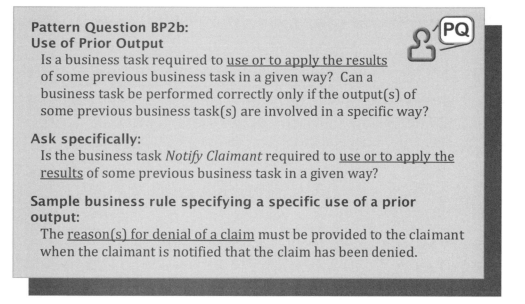

Pattern Question BP2b:
Use of Prior Output
Is a business task required to <u>use or to apply the results</u> of some previous business task in a given way? Can a business task be performed correctly only if the output(s) of some previous business task(s) are involved in a specific way?

Ask specifically:
Is the business task *Notify Claimant* required to <u>use or to apply the results</u> of some previous business task in a given way?

Sample business rule specifying a specific use of a prior output:
The <u>reason(s) for denial of a claim</u> must be provided to the claimant when the claimant is notified that the claim has been denied.

As before, reason(s) for denial is presumably an output of the business task *Adjudicate Claim*. The business rule indicates that the follow-on business task *Notify Claimant* must use those reason(s) in a specific way (present them to the claimant) in each case of notification about a claim being denied.

To use or apply an output in a specific way, it obviously must have been produced. So this pattern question is actually a stronger version of the previous one.

Inter-Task Timing

Pattern Question for Immediate Inter-Task Timing

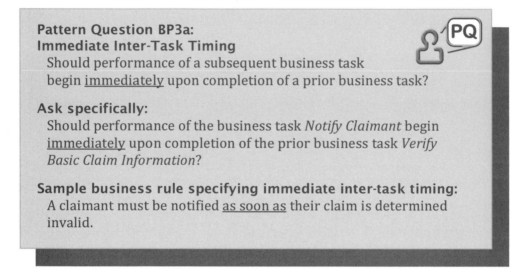

**Figure 7-3a. Partial Business Process Model to Illustrate
Pattern Questions about Immediate Inter-Task Timing**

Pattern Question BP3a:
Immediate Inter-Task Timing
   Should performance of a subsequent business task
   begin <u>immediately</u> upon completion of a prior business task?

Ask specifically:
   Should performance of the business task *Notify Claimant* begin
   <u>immediately</u> upon completion of the prior business task *Verify
   Basic Claim Information*?

Sample business rule specifying immediate inter-task timing:
   A claimant must be notified <u>as soon as</u> their claim is determined
   invalid.

An arrow represents a hand-off of work between business tasks. This
pattern question asks whether the follow-on business task is to be
initiated for a case immediately upon hand-off from the previous
business task.

 Often immediate initiation isn't necessary or even
desirable, so no business rule like the one above
would be needed.

Pattern Question for Maximum Inter-Task Timing

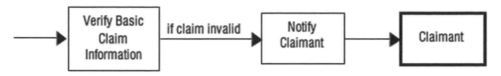

Figure 7-3b. Partial Business Process Model to Illustrate
Pattern Questions about Maximum Inter-Task Timing

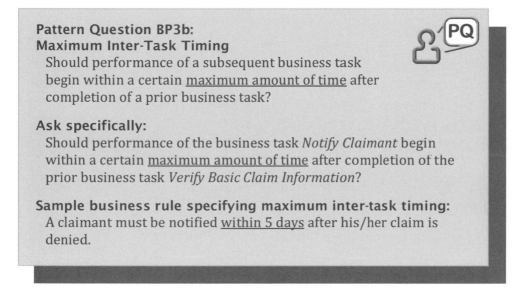

Pattern Question BP3b:
Maximum Inter-Task Timing
  Should performance of a subsequent business task
  begin within a certain <u>maximum amount of time</u> after
  completion of a prior business task?

Ask specifically:
  Should performance of the business task *Notify Claimant* begin
  within a certain <u>maximum amount of time</u> after completion of the
  prior business task *Verify Basic Claim Information*?

Sample business rule specifying maximum inter-task timing:
  A claimant must be notified <u>within 5 days</u> after his/her claim is
  denied.

Maximums and minimums represent distinct business rules, so we
separate the related pattern questions and address them in pairs as
above and below.

 A maximum timing criterion is not limited only to business
tasks that lead directly into the targeted business task.

 If an external actor is involved (as in this example) you
can think of the maximum timing criterion as defining a
service commitment.

Pattern Question for Minimum Inter-Task Timing

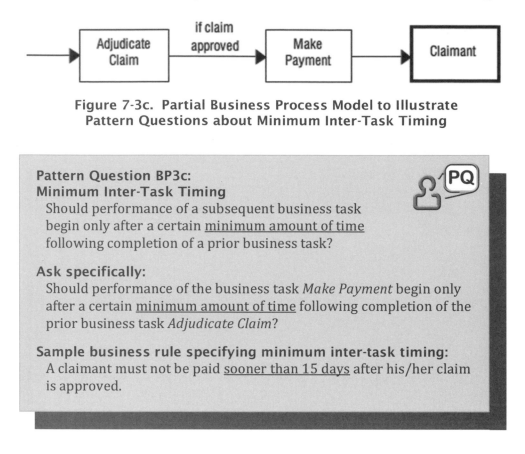

Figure 7-3c. Partial Business Process Model to Illustrate Pattern Questions about Minimum Inter-Task Timing

Pattern Question BP3c:
Minimum Inter-Task Timing
  Should performance of a subsequent business task begin only after a certain <u>minimum amount of time</u> following completion of a prior business task?

Ask specifically:
  Should performance of the business task *Make Payment* begin only after a certain <u>minimum amount of time</u> following completion of the prior business task *Adjudicate Claim*?

Sample business rule specifying minimum inter-task timing:
  A claimant must not be paid <u>sooner than 15 days</u> after his/her claim is approved.

As for a maximum timing criterion, a minimum timing criterion is not limited only to business tasks that lead directly into the targeted business task.

You can think of a minimum timing criterion as allowing the business some 'float' time, especially if money or other valuable resource will be handed off.

Timing and Iteration for Loops

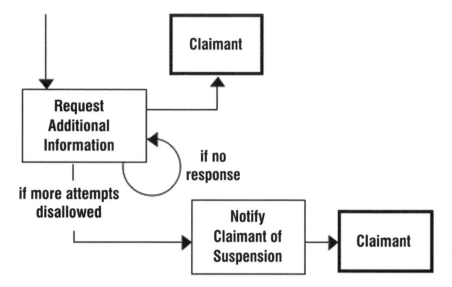

Figure 7-4. Partial Business Process Model to Illustrate Pattern Questions about Timing and Iteration for Loops

The partial business model involves a loop (a 'pig's ear') on the business task *Request Additional Information*. Such loops enable iteration for any given case, which could potentially go on endlessly. The business rule provides a way 'out' of the loop.

Pattern Question for Maximum Timing between Iterations

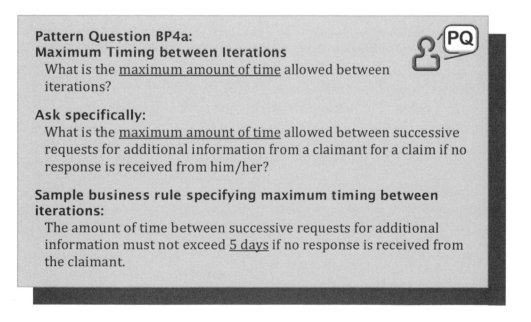

Pattern Question BP4a:
Maximum Timing between Iterations
   What is the <u>maximum amount of time</u> allowed between iterations?

Ask specifically:
   What is the <u>maximum amount of time</u> allowed between successive requests for additional information from a claimant for a claim if no response is received from him/her?

Sample business rule specifying maximum timing between iterations:
   The amount of time between successive requests for additional information must not exceed <u>5 days</u> if no response is received from the claimant.

We use the keyword phrase *if more attempts disallowed* for a conditional flow as a standard device to exit a loop. As always, business rules provide the criteria for deciding when the condition *more attempts disallowed* becomes true for a given case.

Pattern Question for Minimum Timing between Iterations

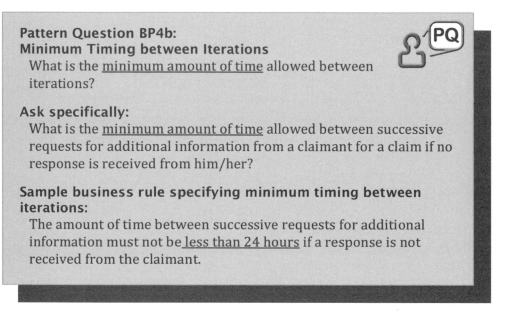

Pattern Question BP4b:
Minimum Timing between Iterations
 What is the <u>minimum amount of time</u> allowed between iterations?

Ask specifically:
 What is the <u>minimum amount of time</u> allowed between successive requests for additional information from a claimant for a claim if no response is received from him/her?

Sample business rule specifying minimum timing between iterations:
 The amount of time between successive requests for additional information must not be <u>less than 24 hours</u> if a response is not received from the claimant.

RuleSpeak prescribes that whenever a business rule counts or measures something in order to constrain it, that something should be indicated as the subject of the sentence. In the example above, *the amount of time between successive requests for additional information* is being measured and constrained. Following this guideline as a best practice is highly recommended.

Pattern Question for Maximum Iterations

Pattern Question BP4c:
Maximum Iterations
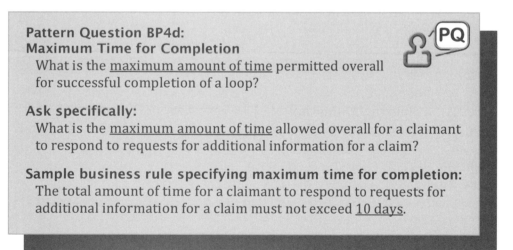
   What is the <u>maximum number of iterations</u> permitted
   overall?

Ask specifically:
   What is the <u>maximum number of requests</u> for additional
   information from a claimant for a claim allowed overall if no
   response is received from him/her?

Sample business rule specifying maximum iterations:
   The total number of requests made for additional information for a
   claim must not exceed <u>10</u>.

This pattern question, like all others, is really about
working with business people to establish an optimal
business policy on the matter.

Pattern Question for Maximum Time for Completion

Pattern Question BP4d:
Maximum Time for Completion
   What is the <u>maximum amount of time</u> permitted overall
   for successful completion of a loop?

Ask specifically:
   What is the <u>maximum amount of time</u> allowed overall for a claimant
   to respond to requests for additional information for a claim?

Sample business rule specifying maximum time for completion:
   The total amount of time for a claimant to respond to requests for
   additional information for a claim must not exceed <u>10 days</u>.

Think about the clock ticking while we might try and try
again. The business can wait only so long for something
to happen.

Events Initiating a Process

Pattern Question for an Actor Event Initiating a Process

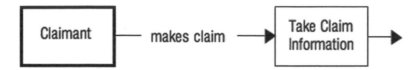

Figure 7-5a. Partial Business Process Model to Illustrate Pattern Questions about an Actor Event Initiating a Business Process

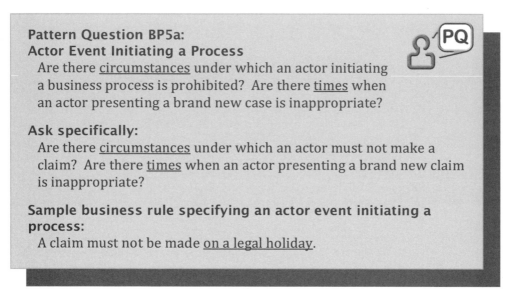

Pattern Question BP5a:
Actor Event Initiating a Process
  Are there <u>circumstances</u> under which an actor initiating
  a business process is prohibited? Are there <u>times</u> when
  an actor presenting a brand new case is inappropriate?

Ask specifically:
  Are there <u>circumstances</u> under which an actor must not make a
  claim? Are there <u>times</u> when an actor presenting a brand new claim
  is inappropriate?

**Sample business rule specifying an actor event initiating a
process:**
  A claim must not be made <u>on a legal holiday</u>.

If an actor is permitted to present a new case (e.g.,
a claim) at any time, no business rule like this one is
needed. A case can be made (or received) at any time.
Whether the business will do anything about a new case in the
same timeframe (i.e., work on it) is a different matter. If not,
other business rules should be specified.

Pattern Question for a Temporal Event Initiating a Process

Figure 7-5b. Partial Business Process Model to Illustrate Pattern Questions about a Temporal Event Initiating a Business Process

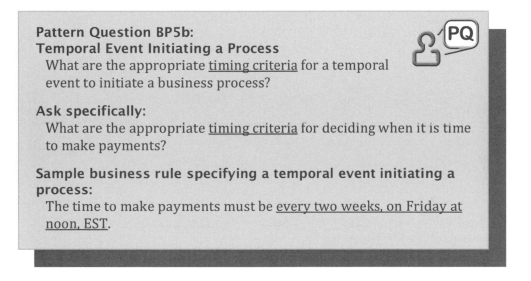

> **Pattern Question BP5b:**
> **Temporal Event Initiating a Process**
> What are the appropriate <u>timing criteria</u> for a temporal event to initiate a business process?
>
> **Ask specifically:**
> What are the appropriate <u>timing criteria</u> for deciding when it is time to make payments?
>
> **Sample business rule specifying a temporal event initiating a process:**
> The time to make payments must be <u>every two weeks, on Friday at noon, EST</u>.

In a temporal event, no actor has to do anything to kick-start the business process. So business rule(s) are needed to express relevant timing criteria. The same is true about spontaneous events, as illustrated below, except that the criteria need not pertain to timing.

Pattern Question for a Spontaneous Event Initiating a Process

Figure 7-5c. Partial Business Process Model to Illustrate Pattern Questions about a Spontaneous Event Initiating a Business Process

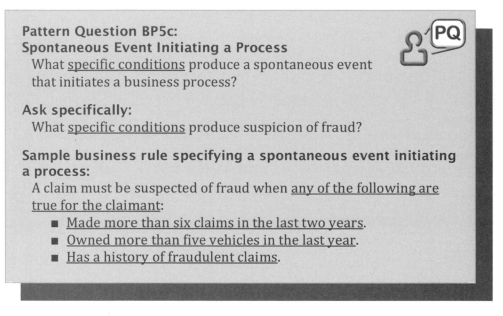

Pattern Question BP5c:
Spontaneous Event Initiating a Process
  What <u>specific conditions</u> produce a spontaneous event
  that initiates a business process?

Ask specifically:
  What <u>specific conditions</u> produce suspicion of fraud?

Sample business rule specifying a spontaneous event initiating a process:
  A claim must be suspected of fraud when <u>any of the following are true for the claimant</u>:
  - <u>Made more than six claims in the last two years</u>.
  - <u>Owned more than five vehicles in the last year</u>.
  - <u>Has a history of fraudulent claims</u>.

Whether a claimant has a *history of fraudulent claims* probably requires additional rule analysis.

Summary

Business rules offer a powerful tool for Business Analysts to simplify business process models and improve their quality. Pattern questions assist not only in capturing related business rules, but also in discussing related business issues with business leads.

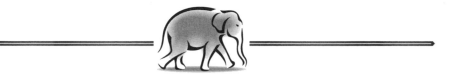

CHAPTER 8

Structured Business Vocabulary

The Fact Model

Your business solution will include exactly one business vocabulary. A business vocabulary allows you to communicate (talk and write) about operational business things in a consistent manner. The business vocabulary will support a great many business rules.

The key word in understanding a business vocabulary is *structure*. That's why we prefer to say *structured* business vocabulary, not just "business vocabulary." A structured business vocabulary provides the two basic ingredients needed to communicate effectively:

- *Terms* — the nouns and noun phrases used to designate operational business things.

- *Wordings* — the verbs and verb phrases that allow you to express what you know about those things in a consistent manner.

You need wordings to write complete sentences — for example, business rule statements. A sentence represents a complete thought. Sentences are what you (the reader) and I are using right now to 'talk' with each other, even though displaced in time and space.

That's the thing about **business rules** — they *will* be read by people you personally haven't met, in circumstances you might never have anticipated. Best to mean the words you say and to say exactly what those words mean.

About Structured Business Vocabularies (Fact Models)

We define a **structured business vocabulary** as *the set of terms and their definitions, along with all wordings, that organizes operational business know-how.* If operational business know-how were simple and limited, there might be no need for a structured business vocabulary. But the know-how is *not*. Not by a long shot. To scale in today's world, you need a structured business vocabulary.

Business Vocabulary — Requirement?

Ask people what they mean by *requirements* for developing software systems and typically you get answers centered on functions to be performed or on the look-and-feel of user interfaces. Maybe use cases, perhaps data models. "Business vocabulary" is almost never among the responses.

Technically, that omission is correct. A business vocabulary is *not* a requirement for developing systems. It's part of the **business model**, which you need to conduct day-to-day business operations. Structured business vocabulary is a critical part of the business model, though, the part that holds things together and allows you to express (and retain) business **know-how**.

Does a business vocabulary play a role in business requirements? *Yes,* of course. It ensures your business requirements can be expressed coherently and understood by others. It's *literally* how you can make sure you always know exactly what you're talking about.

Terms and wordings can be organized into a graphical **fact model**. We'll get to an example later. Given the focus on expressing business rules and other know-how, a better name for 'fact model' would probably be **verbalization model**. Think of a fact model as a *verbal* model, one serving for effective verbalization of operational business know-how. Since *fact model* has been used widely, however, we'll stick with that term here. Fact models (and verbalization) are backed by a powerful standard, **SBVR**.

 Remember that the terms and wordings in a fact model do not represent data or information *about* operational business things. They represent *the actual things themselves* out in the real world. That distinction can get a bit fuzzy when the things the business works with are intangible (e.g., insurance policies, financial products, tax, etc.); nonetheless, since the customer thinks about those things as very real, real they are.

About Operational Business Things

A *term* is a noun or noun phrase that workers recognize and use in day-to-day **business communications**, including business rules, to refer to an operational business thing. A term carries a particular meaning for the business, which should be unambiguous given a particular context of usage. Some examples:

customer	employee name	date
prospect	delivery date due	high-risk customer
shipment	manager	employee
order	gender	line item
invoice	status	quantity back-ordered

Our meaning of *term* comes straight from Merriam-Webster's Unabridged Dictionary [MWUD]: *a word or expression that has a precisely limited meaning in some uses or is peculiar to a science, art, profession, trade, or special subject.* The key words in the definition are *precisely limited meaning.*

The particular noun or noun phrase selected as a term for an operational business thing represents merely the tip of the iceberg with respect to meaning. More fundamental is the business *concept* for which the noun or noun phrase stands.

This concept *must* be defined. That is, the concept a term represents should never be taken for granted. As one practitioner put it, *"The more self-evident the meaning of a term is, the more trouble you can expect."* As an example, another practitioner from a medium-sized company rattled off six different (and conflicting!) definitions of *customer* from different parts of his organization.

Every use of a term will depend on the meaning provided by its **definition**. Here is a good sample definition for *customer*, straight from MWUD: *one that purchases some commodity or service; especially, one that purchases systematically or frequently.*

 Definitions should always be business-friendly and free of any IT jargon. Always define the real thing as it appears to the business, not as represented or viewed as data (e.g., as a data element). Giving (and retaining) examples always proves very useful in reinforcing the intended sense of a definition. And short is good — but be aware of the important role of **definitional rules**.

Core terms in your fact model represent types (or *classes*) of things in the business, rather than *instances* of those classes. For example, a business might have 10,000 customers, but they are represented by the single term *customer*.

 In creating a fact model, a term's singular form is preferred over its plural form. Plural forms sometimes suggest flow or sequence, as in a **business process** model. Connections in a fact model are always structural.

Generally, business rules address classes rather than instances. But business rules can address instances too — for example, a business rule might apply to one country, say *The Netherlands*, and not another country, say *Belgium*.

About Structure: Verb Concepts

Structural connections between noun concepts are generally expressed using verbs and verb phrases relating appropriate terms. These noun-and-verb constructions are called *wordings* — phrases of predictable types that permit sentences, especially expressing business rules, to be made about business know-how. The wordings represent *fact types*.

Examples of wordings for fact types are given in Table 8-1. Note that each wording involves a verb or verb phrase (italicized in the Table) to connect relevant terms.

Table 8-1. Sample Wordings for Fact Types

Wording for a Connection Between Noun Concepts	Sample Business Rule Statement Using the Wording
customer *places* order	A customer must *place* at least one order.
shipment *is approved by* employee	A shipment must *be approved by* at least two employees.
shipment *includes* order	A shipment must not *include* more than 10 orders.

 Selection of the best verbs and verb phrases to succinctly represent the meaning of connections between noun concepts in a standard, easy-to-understand way is fundamental to expressing business rules, especially *at scale*.

Wordings extend the business vocabulary in important ways. Most obvious is that wordings add standard verbs and verb phrases.

Equally important is that by connecting terms they bring *structure* to the business vocabulary. For this reason, we like to say *structured* business vocabulary.

Since a fact type is always worded with a verb or verb phrase (wording), fact types are often called *verb concepts*. That's one reason fact models can be described as *verbal* or **verbalization models**.

Facts, Fact Types, and Predicates

The sample wordings in Table 8-1 represent types of connections, *fact types*, rather than individual connections, *facts*. For example, for the fact type *customer places order* an actual fact might be *Global Supply, Inc. has placed the order A601288*. Developing a structured business vocabulary generally focuses on fact types, not facts per se.

In formal logic, each wording represents a *predicate*. More precisely, a wording represents the *meaning* of a predicate.

In English and other languages, every wording follows a strict subject-verb-object structure — for example, *customer places order*. The wording thus provides a building block for constructing unambiguous sentences of arbitrary complexity.

A fact type does not imply or establish any business rule on its own, nor does any associated wording. For example, the wording *customer places order* creates no business rule. It would be inappropriate to express a wording as: *A customer must place at least one order*. This latter statement is more than a fact type — it expresses a business rule pertaining to the fact type.

Verbs (e.g., *places*) used in wordings do not represent or label any action, transform, or task per se (e.g., *Place order*). Think of a structured business vocabulary as providing the most appropriate way to organize what can be known as a *result* (or potential result) of such operations. More broadly, a business vocabulary organizes what we can know as the result of operational business processes, **ad hoc business activity**, and **operational business events**. That way you can talk about results **declaratively** (rather than **procedurally**) and independently of any specific method of origination.

A majority of connections of core interest for structured business vocabularies involve exactly two terms — e.g., *customer places order*. In other words, such connections are *binary*. Connections involving more than two terms, however, are sometimes appropriate (e.g., person *visits* city *on* date). So are wordings that concern only a single term (e.g., order *is completed*). The latter, which represent *unary* fact types, are prevalent in modeling **states** and **business milestones**. Refer to Chapter 10 for discussion.

> **Spotlight on Verbs**
>
> Without plunging too deeply into philosophical questions, every verb generally has two sides. Most obvious is that a verb designates some action. But you can also think of a verb as designating something you can know. Take, for example, the verb *to place* as in a *customer placing an order*. You can look at *to place* from two perspectives, both valid:
>
> - There is something a customer can *do* — i.e., place an order. That's an action you would expect some business task in a business process model to support.
>
> - There is something that *can be known* — i.e., that a customer can place an order. That's a fact type you would expect to see in a fact model.
>
> The first perspective, of course, is very important. No one is saying you shouldn't model business processes(!). But the second is also crucial, more so every day, for business rules and other business communications.

Special-Purpose Elements of Structure

Table 8-2. Special-Purpose Elements of Structure

Special-Purpose Element of Structure	General Form	Example	Use in a Sample Business Rule Statement
categorization	(Class of thing$_1$) *is a* **category** *of* (class of thing$_2$).	'Corporate customer' *is a* **category** *of* 'customer'.	A customer must be considered corporate if the customer is not an individual person.
property association	(thing$_1$) *has* (thing$_2$)	order *has* date taken order *has* date promised	An order's date promised must be at least 24 hours after the order's date taken.
whole-part (or **partitive structure**)	(whole) *is composed of* (parts) (part) *is included in* (whole)	chair is composed of: ■ legs ■ seat ■ back ■ armrests	A chair must not be ordered without a seat.
classification	(Instance) *is classified as a* (class of thing).	Canada *is classified as a* country. Canadian dollar *is classified as a* currency.	An order may be priced using the currency 'Canadian dollar' only if the customer placing the order is located in Canada.

Certain important kinds of structural connections between noun concepts come in handy, *pre-defined* 'shapes' courtesy of **SBVR**. These special-purpose elements of structure, presented in Table 8-2, extend the reach and precision of the structured business vocabulary significantly. For additional discussion refer to *Business Rule Concepts*, 3rd ed., Chapter 6.

 Developing a shared, well-structured business vocabulary means capturing the essential meaning of business concepts for business-side workers and managers. The verbal and analytical skills needed to distill and express such meaning require the ability to abstract and conceptualize. To some extent those abilities come naturally for Business Analysts. To do fact modeling well, though, requires training and constant practice. To be frank, it's probably the hardest part of creating any business model.

Using Graphical Fact Models

You might have noticed that even though fact models are often rendered graphically, we've been concentrating in this Chapter so far on definitions, terms, wordings, and structure. This focus is not because diagrams are not useful. Just the opposite is true; they are *very* useful.

Rather, we wanted to emphasize that a structured business vocabulary is first and foremost about what we can *know*, and about how we can *communicate* about what we can know. Knowledgeable workers on the business side must originate and understand the vocabulary.

Getting all the terms and wordings in a vocabulary to fit together as if in some large jigsaw puzzle can be hard. That's where a graphical fact model plays an important role.

When creating a blueprint for remodeling your house, you can quickly see when the pieces are not fitting together. The eye often spots the problems quite easily. A graphical fact model serves a similar purpose in developing a business vocabulary.

 Sponsors and business workers should sign off on the vocabulary — the terms, definitions, and wordings — *not* on any diagram per se.

Figure 8-1 presents a simple fact model in graphical form, following our conventions. (SBVR does not standardize notation.) The various connections in this fact model are listed below it. The list includes several that are unlabeled in the diagram — these connections are based on the special-purpose elements of structure mentioned earlier.

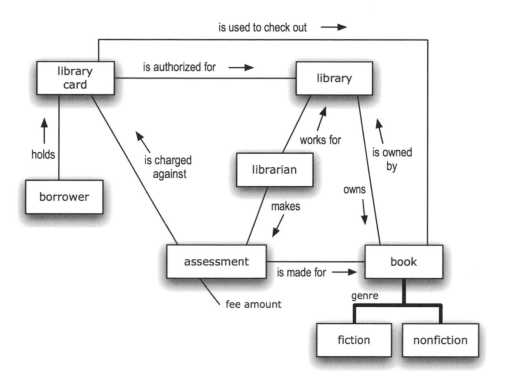

Figure 8-1. Sample Fact Model for a Library

Connections in Figure 8-1:

Explicitly-labeled
- library card *is used to check out* book
- library card *is authorized for* library
- library *owns* book (book *is owned by* library)
- librarian *works for* library
- librarian *makes* assessment
- assessment *is made for* book
- assessment *is charged against* library card
- borrower *holds* library card

Unlabeled, based on connector type
- fiction *is a category of* book
- nonfiction *is a category of* book
- assessment *has* fee amount

When is the Fact Model 'Done'?

The fact model is 'done' only when each concept has a term acceptable to the business and a clear, concise business definition. In addition, no additional concept needs to be referenced (talked about), where such concept:

- Is at the day-to-day operational level of the business.
- Cannot be derived or computed from other concepts.
- Is within scope of the **business capability**.

If some distinction about things in the business is worth mentioning in a business rule (or other business communication), then you need a way to talk about it, no matter how fine-grained it is. If you *never* need to make the distinction in any business rule, then you don't need the concept in the fact model. By the way, *concept* here refers to both noun concepts and verb concepts (fact types).

A structured business vocabulary establishes the full scope of potential discourse about operational business activity in a very fundamental way. If a business worker or Business Analyst needs to express know-how about some concept *not* in the vocabulary, and wants to communicate or share that know-how in a standard and consistent fashion, you're dead in the water. End of story. Do some more fact modeling.

How far? Should you go beyond business rules in assessing the completeness of your fact model? Judgment call, but our feeling is that *all* operational business communications should use standard business vocabulary. (What are we missing?!) Fortunately, rarely do you come across an operational business thing not referenced by any business rule at all.

How large? Your fact model will be large, perhaps ultimately hundreds of terms. But not *impossibly* large. After all, we're just talking about standard business terms (and wordings) for basic concepts used in business operations day-in and day-out. If you don't have words for those things, how can you really manage them anyway?!

How stable? Structure is the hardest (and most expensive) part of any business solution to change. (Think remodeling your house.) Fortunately when fact models are done correctly they tend to be very stable. The reason is simple. Any business practice subject to change is treated as a business rule and externalized from the fact model, *not* embedded within it.

How Long Will Your Fact Model Last?

In early 2011, one of our first business-side clients from the 1990s called out of the blue. We last worked with them in 1998, helping first to create a **Policy Charter** and future-form business process model, then a fact model for an entire line of business. We had since lost touch, so they brought us up to date.

In 1998 and 1999 they built a completely new system (largely in an early version of Java) based on our work together. The system had supported worldwide business operations quite well until just recently. In the past year or two, though, the business had expanded both in volume and variety, and the existing system architecture had simply maxed out.

A pleasant surprise awaited me when I went for an on-site visit a few days after the call. Sitting on the conference room table in front of the business managers was a large plot of the 1998 fact model! They said, "The fact model is still about 90% accurate. We've determined it's really the only thing we can salvage from the legacy environment. It's our business blueprint for a next generation of software." Although lots had changed in their dynamic business space through the intervening years, the core concepts *had remained 90% the same*.

Then they explained why they had called. The 1998 fact model focused on a single line of business. Their other major line of business had sadly opted not to use the relevant portions of the fact model or follow the approach. (They estimated about 60% overlap between the lines of business.) In the dozen years since, this other line of business abundantly demonstrated the business (and software) pitfalls of not having done so. Side-by-side comparisons of key business concepts highlighted the shortcomings.

Recently the organization had acquired a third line of business, also inter-related. Management understood they needed an integrated, holistic view of the business. Expanding the fact model to include the other two areas was the obvious path forward.

Your fact model is about the business and its core concepts, *not IT*. That's why it will stand the test of time. **See the elephant**!

Once a fact model is well-structured, new concepts can often be added with minimal disruption. It's *changing* concepts already in it that can have big ripple effects. Let's be very clear here though. Put aside all derived and computed concepts — you have business rules for those. The fundamental concepts in your fact model, the ones needed for day-to-day business activity, really don't change very often. If they do, you're really moving into a whole new business space, aren't you?!

 Any business practice subject to change should be treated as a business rule, not embedded in a definition. For the full meaning of concepts you also need **definitional rules**.

Summary

A fact model represents a structured business vocabulary, a key component in a business model whose purpose is to organize meaning (**semantics**). Each noun and verb concept in **know-how** supporting day-to-day business activity within scope should be represented in the fact model.

Terms and wordings should be selected carefully and with sensitivity, both to existing terminology and subtle differences in usage. Good definitions are essential.

A single, unified fact model (no duplication) is a prerequisite for creating a *scalable*, multi-use body of business rules. A good business vocabulary permits business rules and other forms of business communication to be expressed precisely, consistently, and without ambiguity. No form of business rule expression or representation, including **decision tables**, is viable or complete if not based on a well-defined, well-structured business vocabulary.

It almost goes without saying that you must know exactly what the words mean in all parts of your business model. In running a complex business (and what business *isn't* complex these days?!) the meaning of the words can simply never be taken as a 'given'.

Some IT professionals believe that if they can adequately model the behavior of a business capability (or more likely, some information system to support it), structural components of the know-how will somehow fall into place. That's naïve and simply wrong. Business can no longer afford such thinking. **See the elephant!**

Business Rules from the Fact Model

Pattern Questions

A structured business vocabulary (**fact model**) is fundamental to analyzing and managing business **know-how**. The fact model represents what can be communicated about basic day-to-day business activity in a standard, consistent way. All expression of business rules should be based on the fact model.

Basic business rules can be captured from fact models using the **pattern questions** presented and illustrated in this Chapter. Use of these pattern questions represents an important step in ensuring the validity of what the business knows about its day-to-day business activity.

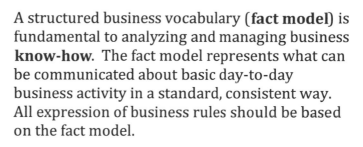

Reminder: A **business model** should never assume any **implicit business rule.** There are no **business rules** until you say there are.

Remember that each **behavioral business rule** needs to be satisfied only to the **level of enforcement** specified for it.

Categories

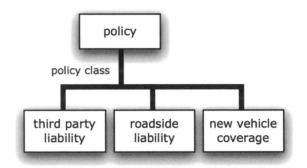

Figure 9-1. Partial Fact Model Used in Illustrating Pattern Questions about Categories

Pattern Question for Mandatory Categorization

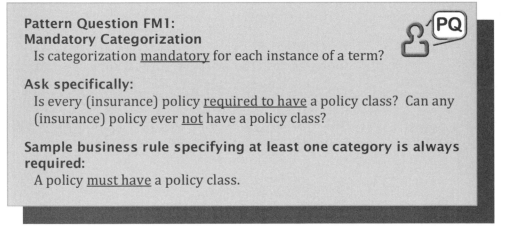

Pattern Question FM1:
Mandatory Categorization
   Is categorization <u>mandatory</u> for each instance of a term?

Ask specifically:
   Is every (insurance) policy <u>required to have</u> a policy class? Can any (insurance) policy ever <u>not</u> have a policy class?

Sample business rule specifying at least one category is always required:
   A policy <u>must have</u> a policy class.

If this business rule were not specified, policies could exist that have no policy class.

Pattern Question for Mutually-Exclusive Categorization

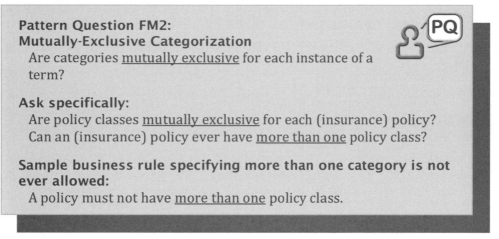

Pattern Question FM2:
Mutually-Exclusive Categorization
  Are categories <u>mutually exclusive</u> for each instance of a term?

Ask specifically:
  Are policy classes <u>mutually exclusive</u> for each (insurance) policy?
  Can an (insurance) policy ever have <u>more than one</u> policy class?

Sample business rule specifying more than one category is not ever allowed:
  A policy must not have <u>more than one</u> policy class.

If the business rule were not specified, policies could exist that have multiple policy classes.

 If each instance of a term must have at least one category, but not more than one, a single business rule can be expressed using *exactly*. For example: *A policy must have <u>exactly</u> one policy class.*

Connection Counts

Pattern Question for Minimum Connection Count

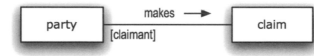

Figure 9-2. Partial Fact Model Used in Illustrating Pattern Questions about a Minimum Connection Count

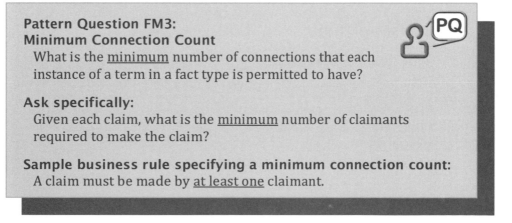

Pattern Question FM3:
Minimum Connection Count
  What is the <u>minimum</u> number of connections that each instance of a term in a fact type is permitted to have?

Ask specifically:
  Given each claim, what is the <u>minimum</u> number of claimants required to make the claim?

Sample business rule specifying a minimum connection count:
  A claim must be made by <u>at least one</u> claimant.

If this business rule were not specified, claims could exist without any claimant.

Counting connections as in this pattern question is more or less the business-level equivalent of *cardinality* or *multiplicity* in data modeling.

Roles — Noun Concepts Whose Meaning Is All Tied Up with Verbs

Business people often have a special term for a noun concept they use only in the context of some particular fact type. Figure 9-2, for example, includes the noun concept *claimant,* which is meaningful only in the context of the fact type: *party [claimant] makes claim*. The term *claimant* is simply a more specific term used to refer to a *party* when the *party* is one that makes a *claim*. Such a *role* name designates what part (or *role*) the concept plays in the context of the fact type.

Roles are not the usual kind of noun-ish things IT professionals generally expect; that is, they are not 'normal' entity types or classes as understood in data models or class diagrams. Rather, the meaning of these noun concepts is inextricably tied to the meaning of some verb (e.g., *makes*).

Role names are a particularly good way to handle terms that directly reflect the particular choice of verb in the wording of a fact type. For example, Figure 9-3 shows a role name *owner* that directly reflects the verb of choice, *owns*.

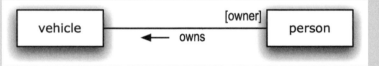

Figure 9-3. Fact Model Showing a Verb-Reflecting Role Name

Like any other term, a role name is frequently relevant to expressing business rules. Example: *A parking citation may be issued only to the owner of a vehicle.*

The verb "owns" from the fact type *person owns vehicle* is absent from this business rule statement. Does this absence result in ambiguity? *No.* Inclusion of a role name always *implies* the associated fact type.

You never need to ask about a minimum connection count for a role (e.g., *owner*). By definition, using a role name to designate something in the real world presumes at least one connection exists for the something. For example, a *person* is an *owner* only if the *person owns* at least one *vehicle*; otherwise, the *person* is not an *owner*.

Pattern question FM3 should be asked for each term involved in the fact type. Starting from the other 'end' of the fact type we can ask: *Given each instance of party, what is the minimum number of claims the party is allowed to make?* Presumably the business will be involved with parties who have made *no* claims (e.g., agents, new insureds, etc.) so probably no business rule is appropriate in this respect.

Pattern Question for Maximum Connection Count

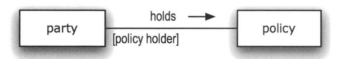

Figure 9-4. Partial Fact Model Used in Illustrating Pattern Questions about a Maximum Connection Count

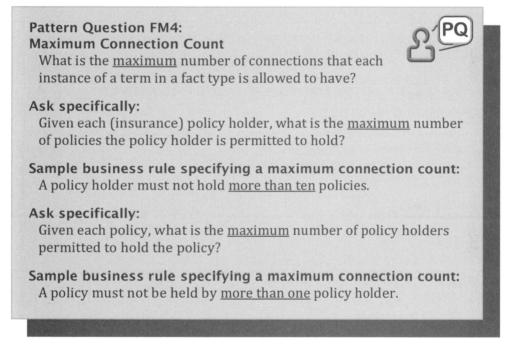

Pattern Question FM4:
Maximum Connection Count
  What is the <u>maximum</u> number of connections that each instance of a term in a fact type is allowed to have?

Ask specifically:
  Given each (insurance) policy holder, what is the <u>maximum</u> number of policies the policy holder is permitted to hold?

Sample business rule specifying a maximum connection count:
  A policy holder must not hold <u>more than ten</u> policies.

Ask specifically:
  Given each policy, what is the <u>maximum</u> number of policy holders permitted to hold the policy?

Sample business rule specifying a maximum connection count:
  A policy must not be held by <u>more than one</u> policy holder.

This pattern question has been applied to both terms involved in the fact type *'policy holder holds policy'*. Maximum connection counts have been given as business rules for both.

 If each instance of a term in a fact type has both a maximum and a minimum connection count and the counts are the same, a single business rule can be expressed using *exactly*. For example: *A policy must be held by <u>exactly</u> one policy holder.*

Maximum and minimum connection counts are not meaningful for a **unary fact type**. By definition, unary fact types are always simply true or false.

Conditional Connection Counts and Restrictions on Facts

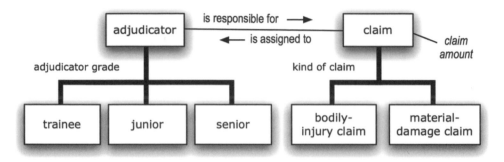

Figure 9-5. Partial Fact Model Used in Illustrating Pattern Questions about Conditional Connection Counts and Restrictions on Facts

Pattern Question for Conditional Minimum Connection Counts

Pattern Question FM5:
Conditional Minimum Connection Counts
  Given an instance of a term, if some <u>specific condition or qualification</u> holds true is there a minimum number of connections required for a fact type?

Ask specifically:
  Given each claim, is there a specific condition or qualification that requires the claim to be assigned to some <u>minimum</u> number of adjudicators?

Sample business rule specifying a conditional minimum connection count:
  A claim <u>over $500</u> must be assigned to an adjudicator.

A claim $500 or less need not be assigned to an adjudicator. Any claim over $500, however, *does* need to be assigned to at least one adjudicator. In other words, the fact type *is assigned to* is *conditionally* mandatory for claims.

The business rule as expressed above does not indicate what the $500 specifically refers to. Presumably, the $500 refers to the property *claim amount* included in Figure 9-5. In general, omitting fact types in expressing business rules invites ambiguity and misinterpretation. A better version: *A claim <u>that has a claim amount</u> over $500 must be assigned to an adjudicator.*

Why So Much Ambiguity and Miscommunication in Requirements?

Let us share something we've learned from our work on business rules. The world's leading cause of ambiguity in expressing business rules is *missing verbs*.

Consider this sample business rule: *An order must not be shipped if the outstanding balance exceeds credit authorization.* As a first-cut statement, that's perhaps not bad. The more you read it, however, the more ambiguity you'll find. Clearly, important ideas are hidden or missing. For example: The outstanding balance *of what*? ...order? ...customer? ...account? ...shipment? The credit authorization *of what?* ...order? ...customer? ...account? ...shipment?

The hidden or missing ideas are all verb-related. To eliminate the ambiguity, the relevant verb concepts — i.e., *fact types* — must be discerned; then the original business rule restated. Suppose the relevant fact types can be worded:

customer *places* order
customer *has* credit authorization
customer *holds* account
account *has* outstanding balance

Using **RuleSpeak** the business rule can now be restated: An order must not be shipped if the outstanding balance <u>of</u> the account <u>held</u> by the customer that <u>placed</u> the order exceeds the credit authorization <u>of</u> the customer.

Although the resulting statement is a bit wordier, it is far less likely to be misunderstood, misapplied, or misimplemented. It is now *enterprise-robust*. The key insight: Wordings for relevant fact types should always appear *explicitly* in expression of business rules. For that matter, wordings should appear explicitly in *any* form of **business communication** you want to be understood correctly — *including business requirements.*

You probably noticed use of the preposition *of* in the revised business rule. Stand-in prepositions for fact types are considered *lazyman's verbs*. (Literally, you can't make complete sentences with only prepositions!) Yes, you can use a preposition to stand in for a full wording, but do so with caution. As a rule of thumb, prepositions are safe only for two cases: (1) properties (e.g., *credit authorization* and *outstanding balance* as above), and (2) role names (e.g., *owner* as in the earlier example, *owner <u>of</u> a vehicle*).

Pattern Question for Conditional Maximum Connection Counts

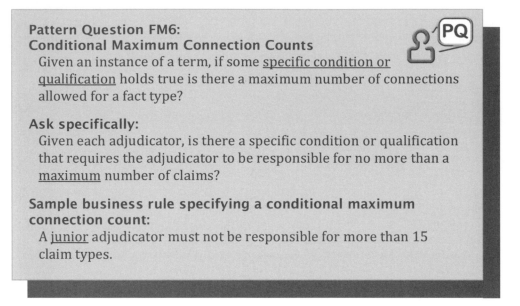

Pattern Question FM6:
Conditional Maximum Connection Counts
  Given an instance of a term, if some <u>specific condition or qualification</u> holds true is there a maximum number of connections allowed for a fact type?

Ask specifically:
  Given each adjudicator, is there a specific condition or qualification that requires the adjudicator to be responsible for no more than a <u>maximum</u> number of claims?

Sample business rule specifying a conditional maximum connection count:
  A <u>junior</u> adjudicator must not be responsible for more than 15 claim types.

If an adjudicator is not junior, there is no maximum number of claims the adjudicator can be responsible for. For any adjudicator who is junior, however, the maximum permitted is 15.

There is no need to express the following: *An adjudicator who is not junior may be responsible for any number of claim types.* Unless some other business rule takes that degree of freedom away, such permission is simply assumed.

Advice (Non-Rule)

Suppose someone does express the statement: *An adjudicator who is not junior may be qualified to assess any number of claim types.* Because the statement removes no degree of freedom, under **SBVR** it does not express a business rule. So what does the statement represent? Literally, it expresses something that is a *non-rule* — a.k.a. an **advice**.

Pattern Question for Restriction on Connections by a Category

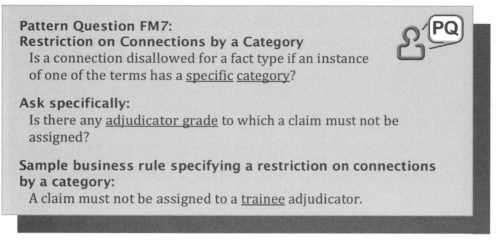

Pattern Question FM7:
Restriction on Connections by a Category
Is a connection disallowed for a fact type if an instance of one of the terms has a <u>specific</u> <u>category</u>?

Ask specifically:
Is there any <u>adjudicator grade</u> to which a claim must not be assigned?

Sample business rule specifying a restriction on connections by a category:
A claim must not be assigned to a <u>trainee</u> adjudicator.

This business rule expresses a business practice that claims are not be assigned to trainees.

Disallowing a connection is the same as expressing a maximum connection count of zero.

Pattern Question for Restriction on Connections by a Combination of Categories

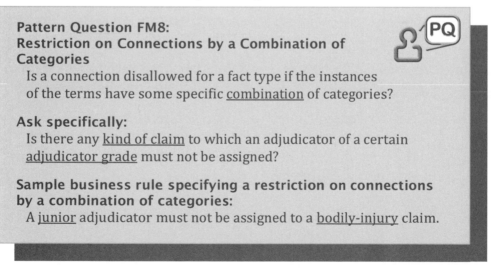

Pattern Question FM8:
Restriction on Connections by a Combination of Categories
Is a connection disallowed for a fact type if the instances of the terms have some specific <u>combination</u> of categories?

Ask specifically:
Is there any <u>kind of claim</u> to which an adjudicator of a certain <u>adjudicator grade</u> must not be assigned?

Sample business rule specifying a restriction on connections by a combination of categories:
A <u>junior</u> adjudicator must not be assigned to a <u>bodily-injury</u> claim.

This business rule indicates a business practice that bodily-injury claims are not be assigned to junior adjudicators. This business rule naturally raises the question: *Why does the fact model provide for a possibility that a business rule prohibits?*

Fact Models, Business Rules, and Business Agility

Business practices change, faster every day. The business practice today might be that bodily-injury claims are not to be assigned to junior adjudicators. Tomorrow that business practice could be modified or even eliminated altogether.

The secret to **business agility** is isolating basic things that seldom or never change from things that can change relatively fast. The fact model represents the former; business rules are for the latter. *Let business rules handle changing business practices!*

 To engineer the best possible **business capability**, Business Analysts should look carefully at creating a more general fact model than current business practices necessarily require. Be reasonable though. What does *reasonable* mean? *Reasonable* means that there is a chance the business practice *will* change. If the business practice will almost certainly never change (as long as you stay in the same business), then generalizing the fact model to accommodate such possibility is *not* reasonable.

Specific Instances

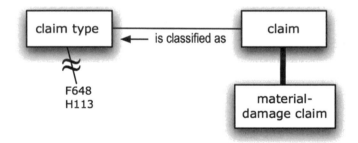

Figure 9-6. Partial Fact Model Used in Illustrating Pattern Questions about a Restriction on Connections by Specific Instances

 Double squiggly lines on a connection indicate the connection represents a classification. The two things on the bottom, *F648* and *H113,* represent instances of the term on the top, claim type.

Pattern Question for Restriction on Connections by Specific Instances

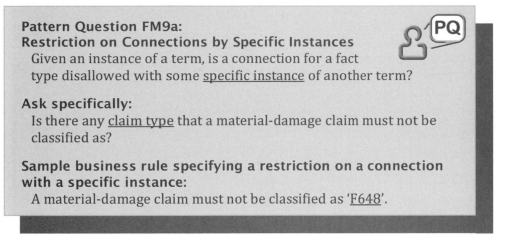

Pattern Question FM9a:
Restriction on Connections by Specific Instances
   Given an instance of a term, is a connection for a fact
type disallowed with some <u>specific instance</u> of another term?

Ask specifically:
   Is there any <u>claim type</u> that a material-damage claim must not be
classified as?

**Sample business rule specifying a restriction on a connection
with a specific instance:**
   A material-damage claim must not be classified as '<u>F648</u>'.

This business rule references an instance, 'F648'. The business rule
naturally raises the question: *What is an 'F648'?*

Let Things Speak for Themselves

Businesses have codes for things. *Lots of them.* That's fine if everybody
already knows the codes. And if none of the codes ever changes to mean
something other than what it did before. And if everyone uses the codes
properly. And if you never hire anyone new.

How often can you really ensure all that?! In writing business rules, use the
real names of things whenever you can. Actually, that's why the things have
the real names in the first place(!).

Pattern Question for Restriction on Connections with a Combination of Specific Instances

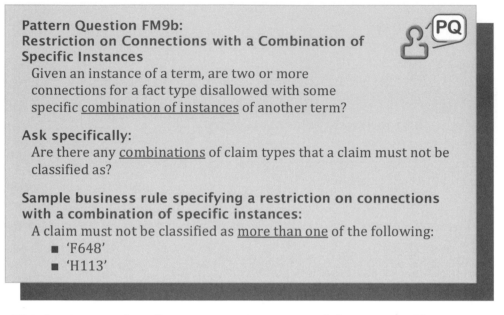

Pattern Question FM9b:
Restriction on Connections with a Combination of Specific Instances

Given an instance of a term, are two or more connections for a fact type disallowed with some specific <u>combination of instances</u> of another term?

Ask specifically:

Are there any <u>combinations</u> of claim types that a claim must not be classified as?

Sample business rule specifying a restriction on connections with a combination of specific instances:

A claim must not be classified as <u>more than one</u> of the following:

- 'F648'
- 'H113'

This business rule references two instances of claim type. The same claim must not be classified as both at the same time.

A business rule that references multiple things (instances, classes, conditions, etc.) is often best expressed using a list of bullet items. **RuleSpeak** recommends using the keywords *the following* along with an explicit threshold (e.g., *more than one*) for each such list.

Mutually-Exclusive Connections and Connection Cycles

Pattern Question for Mutually-Exclusive Connections

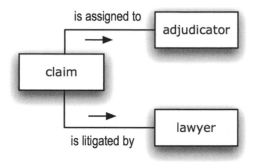

Figure 9-7. Partial Fact Model Used in Illustrating Pattern Questions about Mutually-Exclusive Connections

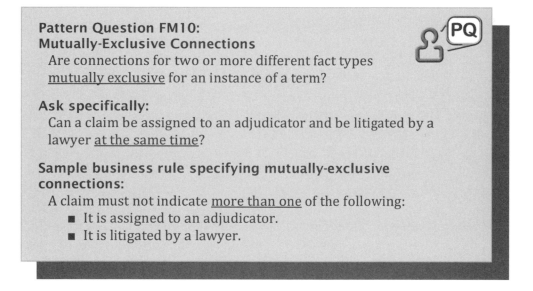

Pattern Question FM10:
Mutually-Exclusive Connections
   Are connections for two or more different fact types
<u>mutually exclusive</u> for an instance of a term?

Ask specifically:
   Can a claim be assigned to an adjudicator and be litigated by a
lawyer <u>at the same time</u>?

Sample business rule specifying mutually-exclusive connections:
   A claim must not indicate <u>more than one</u> of the following:
     ■ It is assigned to an adjudicator.
     ■ It is litigated by a lawyer.

If the business rule were not specified, connections of both types
could exist for a claim at the same time.

Pattern Question for Restrictions on Connection Cycles

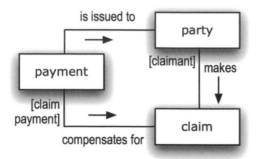

Figure 9-8. Partial Fact Model Used in Illustrating Pattern Questions about Restrictions on Connection Cycles

 The fact types *is issued to*, *makes*, and *compensates for* form a recursive structure of fact types. A *connection cycle* is a set of connections for a recursive structure, one connection per fact type, that begins and ends with the same instance of a term (e.g., a given payment).

Pattern Question FM11:
Restrictions on Connection Cycles
  Is a connection for a fact type allowed only if two or more <u>other connections in a recursive structure</u> complete (or do not complete) a connection cycle?

Ask specifically:
  Can a claim payment be issued to some party other than a claimant that makes the claim for which the claim payment compensates?

Sample business rule specifying a cycle restriction:
  A claim payment may be <u>issued</u> only to a claimant who <u>makes</u> the claim for which the claim payment <u>compensates</u>.

You can't just pay *any* party a claim payment. A claim payment is acceptable only if it is issued to a claimant for the given claim. Remember, there are no business rules until you say there are.

 Business rules about connection cycles are far more common than you might think.

> **Go Verbal!**
>
> Verbs are so crucial to effective business communication of all kinds, you might wonder why data models and class diagrams haven't focused more directly on them in the past. The answer, quite simply, is that those techniques weren't created for that purpose. They are first and foremost *design* tools for IT professionals.
>
> What do IT professionals design? In general, they are focused on implementing data containers (e.g., tables) or software objects. That focus leaves the data models and class diagrams noun-ish, but not also verb-ish. The price we are paying for that shortfall in poor business communication practices is huge. **See the elephant!**

Volume Limits

Pattern Question for Volume Limits

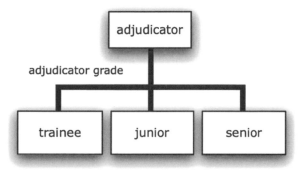

Figure 9-9. Partial Fact Model Used in Illustrating
Pattern Questions about Volume Limits

> **Pattern Question FM12:**
> **Volume Limits**
>   Is there an upper limit on the <u>number of instances</u> of a term that may exist at any one time?
>
> **Ask specifically:**
>   What's the <u>absolute limit</u> on the number of trainees at any one time?
>
> **Sample business rule specifying an absolute volume limit:**
>   The total number of trainee adjudicators <u>must not exceed 100</u>.
>
> **Ask specifically:**
>   How many trainees are allowed at any one time <u>relative to</u> the number of senior adjudicators?
>
> **Sample business rule specifying a relative volume limit:**
>   The total number of trainee adjudicators <u>must not exceed the total number of senior adjudicators</u>.

If these business rules were not specified, there would be no absolute or relative limits on the total number of trainees.

 Volume limits on terms are one of the few pattern questions involving no fact types.

Summary

Business rules offer a powerful tool for Business Analysts to ensure the highest possible quality of structured business vocabularies (fact models). Pattern questions assist not only in capturing related business rules, but also in discussing related business issues with business leads.

CHAPTER 10

Business Milestones

The Life of Operational Business Things

Your business solution will identify many business milestones. A business milestone usually involves many business rules.

The key words in understanding business milestones are *event* and *state*. An **event** is simply something that happens. A **state** is simply a condition or form of being. When an event happens, *something* always goes into a new state.

In day-to-day business activity that something is usually an instance of an operational business thing. For example, we might say a *received* order is now *credit-checked*. If the business cares about the events and states for some operational business thing, each instance of the operational business thing is said to have a **life**.

Two things are implied by an instance of an operational business thing achieving a new state in its life:

- Some business action (transform) has completed successfully. For example, if we say an order is now *credit-checked* it might mean the business task *Check credit* has finished successfully.

- All **business rules** applicable to the new state have been satisfied. For example, if we say an order is now *credit-checked* it means that all business rules pertaining to *credit-checked orders* have been satisfied at that point in time.

Each recognized state in the life of an operational business thing has a starting point called a **business milestone**. For any instance of an operational business thing moving into a recognized state, achieving the business milestone for that state specifically implies (a) a business action has just completed successfully, and (b) all relevant business rules have just been satisfied. The state itself can last an arbitrary amount of time thereafter.

The State of *What*?

For IT professionals the state of *processes* has always reigned supreme. In **procedural** approaches the internal state of a process is represented by some **token**. Most computer languages use that approach (the token generally falls through lines of code sequentially). Many current approaches to business process modeling do as well, at least implicitly.

But why should business people care about the internal state of any process? For example, if a business person asks *How far along are we in processing this order?* the person is really asking: *Has the order been credit-checked? Has it been filled? Has it been shipped?* (etc.). In business operations it's the state of each operational business thing that matters.

True **business agility** cannot be achieved so long as business processes are perceived as managing state internally (privately). That's a fundamentally flawed paradigm for **business operation systems**.

Instead, business processes must **externalize semantics** so business people can understand and manage the state of operational business things directly. Externalizing semantics is accomplished by means of **SBVR**-style structured business vocabularies (**fact models**) and **single-sourced** business rules.

Rule independence allows business actions (transforms) and **business rules** to be analyzed separately, simplifying and sharpening both. Transforms are often (but not always) included in some **business process** model. Analysis of business milestones is an excellent tool for capturing and analyzing business rules in their own right, separately from transforms.

 Just because business rules are satisfied for an instance of an operational business thing at a business milestone does not mean the business rules automatically remain satisfied thereafter for the full duration of the state. Continuing satisfaction of business rules is a matter of proper on-going enforcement, taking into account that most business rules have multiple flash points. Refer to Chapter 14.

The Happy Life

Operational business things such as orders have a life that encompasses an overall regime, a set of states that start with origination and end with final resolution. If all goes well (from the business point of view) this regime represents a *happy life,* and each state within it a *stage.* Figure 10-1 illustrates a happy life informally for orders.

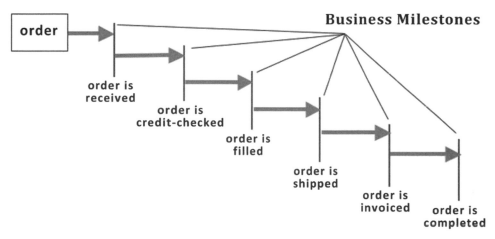

Figure 10-1. Informal Representation of the Happy Life of Orders

This happy life of orders involves six business milestones. At each business milestone, an instance of order enters a new stage, each closer to final resolution. The arrows represent the operational business events (successfully completed transforms) that get individual orders into the next stage.

Note that each stage is expressed using a **past participle** (e.g., *received, credit-checked, filled,* etc.). In English, a past participle represents a completed action, so stages are always designated in this fashion. The past participle selected to designate any particular stage should be one that is natural for business people.

Remember that for business people and customers, even intangible business things (e.g., insurance policies, financial products, etc.) are quite real. They too can have a life.

Using Fact Types and Roles to Represent States

Past participles represent a form of verb. In fact models, verbs represent fact types. A state can be represented by a very simple fact type since:

- Only one operational business thing (term) is involved (e.g., *order*).

- For any given instance of this operational business thing, the action designated by the past participle either has been completed or it has not (e.g., an order either has been *shipped* or it has not).

Such true-or-false questions about a single thing are handled by *unary* fact types. Any set of states (e.g., stages in a happy life) requires an equivalent number of unary fact types. Figure 10-2 illustrates for the happy life of *order*. (SBVR does not standardize notation — the graphic conventions are ours.)

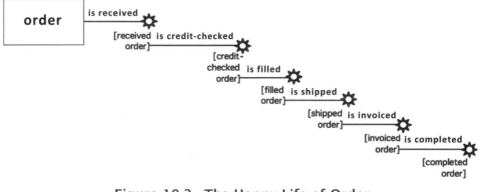

**Figure 10-2. The Happy Life of Order
Represented by Unary Fact Types**

The six stages in the happy life of *order* are represented by six unary fact types, each designated by an appropriate past participle. Also shown are six roles (in brackets), one for each of the six stages. Now we can talk about (e.g., write business rules about) the happy life of *order* using standard, business-friendly terms. We'll look at some business rules shortly.

The business milestone model above has been organized such that each unary fact type after the first is dependent on the role in the previous unary fact type. This configuration represents the dependencies appropriate for a happy life:

- Only a *received* order (i.e., an order that *is received*) can be *credit-checked.*

- Only a *credit-checked* order (i.e., an order that is both *received* and *credit-checked*) can be *filled*.

- And so on.

At finalization of the happy life, the only orders that can be *completed* are ones that have been *received, credit-checked, filled, shipped*, and *invoiced*.

Unhappy Business Milestones

In real life, unfortunately, things don't always have a happy life. For example, an order might be *cancelled* somewhere along the way. Best practices in developing business milestone models include:

- Developing the happy life as fully as possible *before* addressing any unhappy states. Following this best practice will help you get started much easier.

- *Segregating* states that are very unhappy (ones that are undesired and preclude successful termination). This approach enhances clarity and avoids conflicts among business rules.

Figure 10-3 illustrates *cancelled order*, a new state separated completely from the happy life of *order*.

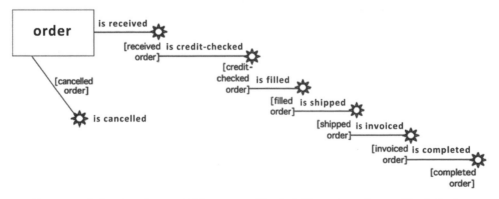

Figure 10-3. Business Milestone Model Showing Cancelled Order

Other states are also unhappy, but not so severely as *cancelled*. As illustrated by Figure 10-4 they might represent:

- A prudent course of action taken to mitigate some risk (e.g., a *received* order is *rejected* because of poor credit).

- An interlude while the company gets its act together (e.g., a *credit-checked* order is *back-ordered*).

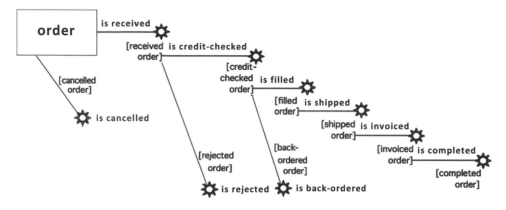

Figure 10-4. Business Milestone Model Showing Rejected and Back-Ordered Orders

Expressing Business Rules for States

Having developed appropriate business vocabulary for the life of an operational business thing, now you can write business rules. Some examples:

Business rule: A rejected order must not be credit-checked.

Business rule: A cancelled order must not have been shipped.

More examples are presented in the next Chapter. Remember that any such business rule applies to *all:*

- Business processes within **architectural scope**, not just one.

- Business tasks within each of those business processes (as relevant).

- Ad hoc business activity (as relevant).

By defining and managing all business rules separately from business processes and business tasks you achieve **thin processes**.

When are Business Milestone Models 'Done'?

Analysis of business milestones should be undertaken for each operational business thing within **architectural scope** that has a happy life.

Other operational business things can have life too. An employee, for example, might be *active* or *retired*. Where there's life, there are probably business rules.

A business milestone model is not complete as long as there is any state some business rule needs to single out (reference).

Summary

A business milestone implies an action that completed successfully during the life of an operational business thing significant to the business. A business milestone also signals the beginning of a new state that can last an arbitrary amount of time.

States are represented by unary fact types with appropriate wordings and roles. This special business vocabulary permits business rules and other forms of **business communication** to be expressed in a standard, precise, business-friendly manner.

Some operational business things have a happy life with predictable stages of completion. A business milestone model for a happy life usually includes unhappy states as well, states by the wayside into which instances of the operational business thing sometimes fall. These unhappy states can be temporary (e.g., *back-ordered*) or possibly permanent (e.g., *cancelled*).

Business rules provide the means to organize and coordinate the life of operational business things in a direct, consistent manner. The **single-sourced** business rules apply no matter how many business processes and business tasks are involved and how much ad hoc business activity occurs.

CHAPTER 11

Business Rules from Business Milestone Models

Pattern Questions

When an **operational business event** happens in day-to-day business activity, an instance of an operational business thing can enter a new **state**. The initial point in that state is called a **business milestone**. Achieving a business milestone means that every relevant **business rule** has just then been satisfied for that instance.

Many business rules can be captured from business milestone models using the **pattern questions** presented and illustrated in this

Chapter. Use of these pattern questions represents an important step in **externalizing semantics** from business process models.

Reminder: A **business model** should never assume any **implicit business rule.** There are no business rules until you say there are.

Remember that each **behavioral business rule** needs to be satisfied only to the **level of enforcement** specified for it.

When is a Business Process or Business Task Over?

The production of some output(s) does not necessarily reflect completion of a business process or a business task. A **business process** or a **business task** is over when some specific business milestone that reflects completion of the transform is achieved. That business milestone might be undesirable but, even so, that's how the business process or business task signals "I'm finished."

Of course, a business process or a business task does not *literally* signal "I'm finished." Instead, it asserts a fact for the appropriate state so it can share that fact with business people and with other business activity.

One consequence of this approach is that in capturing business rules from business process models, we don't ask: Does a business task require some prior business task(s) to have been completed? Instead we ask: Does a business milestone require some prior states(s) to have been achieved? That way of asking the question is the right one for **externalizing semantics**.

To achieve any given business milestone, all relevant business rules must have been satisfied. If the business process or business task cannot satisfy all relevant business rules, it simply leaves the instance of the operational business thing in the original state.

If leaving the instance of the operational business thing in its original state 'hides' something that business people need to know, or that some business rule needs to reference, some *other* state is missing in the business milestone model.

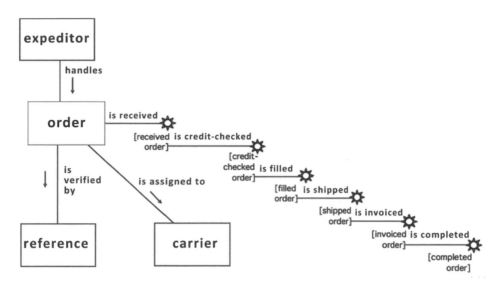

**Figure 11-1. Business Milestone Model to Illustrate
Basic Pattern Questions for Business Milestones**

Pattern Question for Milestone Imperatives

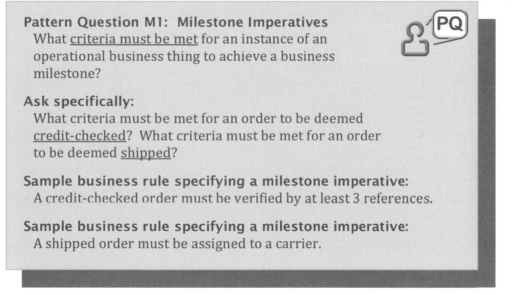

Pattern Question M1: Milestone Imperatives
  What criteria must be met for an instance of an
  operational business thing to achieve a business
  milestone?

Ask specifically:
  What criteria must be met for an order to be deemed
  credit-checked? What criteria must be met for an order
  to be deemed shipped?

Sample business rule specifying a milestone imperative:
  A credit-checked order must be verified by at least 3 references.

Sample business rule specifying a milestone imperative:
  A shipped order must be assigned to a carrier.

Any business rule that must be satisfied for an instance of an
operational business thing to achieve a business milestone is called a
milestone imperative. This first pattern question is basic to
externalizing business rules from business process models in an
organized and intelligible way.

States are represented using unary fact types, then the associated role
names (e.g., *credit-checked order, shipped order,* etc.) are used directly
in capturing milestone imperatives. This approach helps simplify the

business process model dramatically and permits the business rule(s) to be revised independently.

 If a milestone imperative is meant to be applied only when a business milestone is first achieved, not continuously thereafter for the state, the business rule must be written that way. Event-specific applicability is never the default. In **RuleSpeak**, the keyword *when* is used for that purpose. Example: Suppose the business intends the first business rule above to be applied *only* at the business milestone, not thereafter. In that case the business rule should be written: A credit-checked order must be verified by at least 3 references <u>*when*</u> *the order is credit-checked*.

 Remember that the **happy life** of *order* has been modeled such that each state is dependent on the previous one having been achieved. So any business rule that applies to *credit-checked orders* also applies to *filled orders, shipped orders,* etc. Any given business rule should therefore always be associated with the first (earliest) state in the happy life to which the business rule applies.

Pattern Question for Spontaneous Behavior

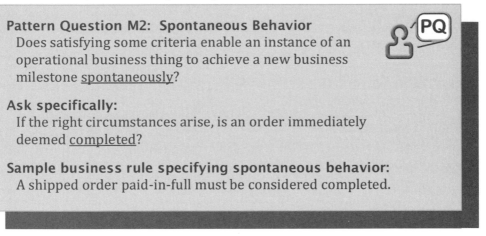

Pattern Question M2: Spontaneous Behavior
Does satisfying some criteria enable an instance of an operational business thing to achieve a new business milestone <u>spontaneously</u>?

Ask specifically:
If the right circumstances arise, is an order immediately deemed <u>completed</u>?

Sample business rule specifying spontaneous behavior:
A shipped order paid-in-full must be considered completed.

The business milestone *completed* is spontaneously achieved if an order is both *shipped* and *paid-in-full*. Whether an order is *paid-in-full* might be derived by a set of computational business rules.

 Be careful about conflicts that might arise if other business rules (milestone imperatives) pertaining to *invoiced* and *completed* orders are not satisfied.

About the Very First Business Milestone in Life

It frequently proves useful to specify some first state (e.g., *received order*) in a happy life to which few if any business rules apply. **Events** *do* happen that the business needs to know and talk about even though they satisfy virtually no business rule (e.g., the placing of an incomplete or poorly-done order).

Also, you need to be able to distinguish between orders that have been *credit-checked* from ones that have not. Simply saying *order* doesn't suffice because any given order might be in any of the other states.

The solution is to ensure that every order is considered (at the least) a *received* order – that is, the unary fact type *is received* is true for every order. Specify a business rule for that purpose: *An order must be considered a received order.* This business rule illustrates one of several ways in which the life of an operational business thing can be selectively regulated. Indeed, with appropriate specification all instances can be required to follow a carefully governed **life pattern.**

Pattern Question for Suspense Criteria

Pattern Question M3: Suspense Criteria
Is there a <u>time limit</u> for how long an instance of an operational business thing can remain in the same state?

Ask specifically:
How long can an order be <u>shipped</u> without being <u>invoiced</u>?

Sample business rule specifying a suspense criterion:
An order may be shipped but not invoiced for only a week.

Sometimes an instance of an operational business thing gets hung up at a state. A business rule specifying a suspense criterion indicates how long is *too* long for the business to stand idly by (i.e., tolerate the instance remaining there).

What if a suspense criterion is exceeded? The appropriate reaction should be specified as a **violation response** for the business rule. (Refer to Chapter 15 for discussion.)
For example, the appropriate response for the sample business rule above might be another business rule: *... must be handled by an expeditor.* (Since this new business rule is a violation response, its subject is understood to be *an order shipped but not invoiced for more than a week.*)

If a suspense criterion involves a happy path (as above), *two* states are usually referenced (e.g., *shipped* and *invoiced*), not just one. Caution should be exercised in specifying a suspense criterion that references just one state. The business often needs to talk about, or to write business rules about, whatever it is that hasn't been accomplished.

Figure 11-2 serves to illustrate additional pattern questions useful in capturing business rules from business milestone models.

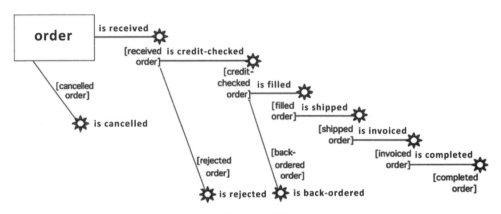

Figure 11-2. Business Milestone Model to Illustrate Additional Pattern Questions

Pattern Question for Prohibited Antecedents

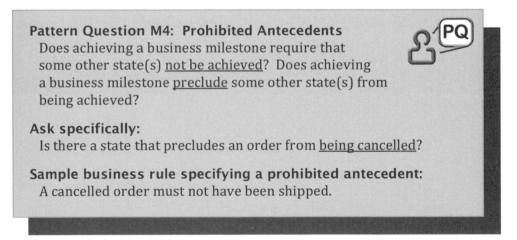

Pattern Question M4: Prohibited Antecedents
Does achieving a business milestone require that some other state(s) <u>not be achieved</u>? Does achieving a business milestone <u>preclude</u> some other state(s) from being achieved?

Ask specifically:
Is there a state that precludes an order from <u>being cancelled</u>?

Sample business rule specifying a prohibited antecedent:
A cancelled order must not have been shipped.

The state *shipped* must not be antecedent to (have been achieved before) the business milestone *cancelled* for any given order.

Remember to model severely unhappy states (such as *cancelled*) outside the happy life. Otherwise, **anomalies** (e.g., **conflicts**) among the business rules almost always result.

Be sure not to embed constraints about prohibited antecedents in any business process. Such business rules apply to *all* business activity, and like all business rules, might change. **Single-source** them!

Pattern Question for Interruptions in Life

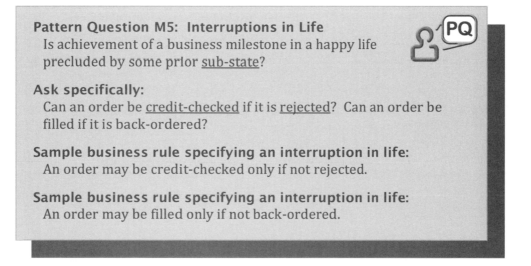

Pattern Question M5: Interruptions in Life
Is achievement of a business milestone in a happy life precluded by some prior <u>sub-state</u>?

Ask specifically:
Can an order be <u>credit-checked</u> if it is <u>rejected</u>? Can an order be filled if it is back-ordered?

Sample business rule specifying an interruption in life:
An order may be credit-checked only if not rejected.

Sample business rule specifying an interruption in life:
An order may be filled only if not back-ordered.

These business rules enforce possible interruptions in the life of individual orders.

An interruption in the life of an operational business thing is not permanent unless a business rule in its life pattern makes it so. For example, unless specified otherwise, once an order is *un*-rejected it can then move forward. Once an order is *un*-back-ordered it too can move forward.

Messages or Business Rules?

A tax collection agency has the business process *Post tax returns*. This business process can encounter the following situation. A tax return from one year can elect a credit based on a tax return from a previous year that has not yet been posted. In response, the former tax return needs to be placed on hold because it cannot be fully processed. So as the business process handles one case it must somehow know about something having arisen from the handling of another case.

One approach is for the process to send itself a message. Sounds simple enough until you try to model it, then it quickly becomes complex. One such model we saw featured the exotica 'pools'. It was pretty much incomprehensible, even to its author (who was seeking help).

Such 'solutions' represent classic cases of not **externalizing semantics**. And wouldn't you think *business people* would also like to know that a tax return has been placed on hold?! Issues like this one are not just about software design; they are about building effective **business operation systems.**

A better approach is to view the problem as a case of *interrupted life*. At the appropriate point in the happy life of tax returns (oxymoron?), the sub-state *is placed on hold* is specified. The appropriate business rule then is:

> Business Rule: *A tax return must be placed on hold if it elects a credit based on a tax return for a previous year that has not been posted*.

For any *on-hold* tax return, the next state in the happy life is disallowed (by another business rule) until such time as the hold is discontinued. This solution is simple and business-friendly and in the bargain, externalizes all the semantics.

Pattern Question for Afterlife

Pattern Question M6: Afterlife
Are there any time limits on how long an instance of an operational business thing must or must not be <u>retained</u> once some terminal business milestone is achieved?

Ask specifically:
How long must a <u>completed</u> order be retained?

Sample business rule specifying a retention criterion:
A completed order must be retained for 7 years.

The business rule is meant to ensure the business will not 'forget' about a completed order for at least 7 years. The motivation might be that some external tax authority requires organizations to keep business records for at least that long.

> Be sure that the motivation for such a business rule arises from the business, and is not simply a choice made by IT in designing or optimizing a system.

Summary

Business rules offer a powerful tool for Business Analysts to understand and orchestrate business things with **life**. Pattern questions pertaining to business milestone models assist not only in capturing related business rules, but also in discussing and resolving related business issues with business leads.

Decision Analysis

Capturing Decision Logic

Your business solution will include some, perhaps many, **operational business decisions**. Each operational business decision will involve many **business rules,** called *decision rules,* usually best represented in the form of decision tables.

The key word in understanding an operational business decision is *question.* An operational business decision considers cases arising in day-to-day business activity and answers the question definitively for each case by choosing among potential outcomes. Examples of such questions: *Should this insurance claim be accepted, rejected, or examined for fraud? Which resource should be assigned to this task? Which service should be used to ship this package?*

Operational business decisions based on questions like these are very common in operational business processes. In the next Chapter we'll discuss a technique called **Question Charts (Q-Charts**™) for analyzing and modeling such questions. This Chapter provides background.

What Decision Analysis Is

We define **decision analysis** as identifying and analyzing key questions arising in day-to-day business activity and capturing the decision logic used to answer the questions.

> A **decision** is a determination requiring **know-how**; the resolving of a question by reasoning.

> An *outcome* is an answer to such a question; that is, some result from making a decision.

> A *decision task* is a business task or action in which some decision is made.

Decision analysis focuses selectively on **operational business decisions**, ones that involve bringing the know-how of the business to bear to make the best or optimal choice for a given situation at a particular point in time.

Whose Decision Is It Anyway?

An important question for **decision analysis** is: *Whose decision is it?* Let's take an example. Suppose your organization has the business rule *A domestic flight must not be booked for an employee in first class or business class while on company business.*

As an individual actor (i.e., as a human), you always have a choice about whether to obey a behavioral rule. Because choice is involved, there *is* a decision. But it's your *personal* decision, not an operational business decision.

To be perfectly honest, organizations generally don't really care very much about how you make your personal decisions. In this example, the business intent of the organization, in fact, is clearly that you *not* have any decision to make about your ticket class.

Business rules always take the organizational view. Although you *personally* can decide to violate a business rule such as the airfare-class rule, that's *your* business. (Of course if the company catches you, then it becomes their business too.) In decision analysis when we say *decision* we really mean *operational business decision*, never some personal decision.

The end-product of decision analysis is **decision logic** in the form of decision structures, **decision tables**, and business rule statements.

This answer-oriented decision logic is rendered in a form that is **practicable**, enterprise-robust, and business-friendly.

 Every Business Analyst should be familiar with creating decision tables for representing decision logic. For a complete discussion, see *Decision Analysis Using Decision Tables and Business Rules* on www.brsolutions.com/b_decision.php (free), starting with Part 5.

More About Decision Rules

Operational business decisions appropriate for decision analysis are ones that resolve some answer-oriented business question by identifying the correct or optimal choice. The choice is always based on decision rules, a special kind of **definitional rule**.

Evaluation of any definitional rule, including all decision rules, always classifies or computes something using known facts. Consider the example: *A customer must be considered a gold customer if the customer places more than 12 orders during a calendar year*. Evaluation of this definitional rule for any given customer indicates whether the customer is or is not *gold* given known facts. In other words, the evaluation indicates whether the customer is or is not a member of a certain class (i.e., the class *gold customer*).

Definitional rules and **behavioral rules** are fundamentally different. Definitional rules simply produce answers; behavioral rules indicate what you must or must not do. Unlike definitional rules, behavioral rules always carry the sense of *obligation* or *prohibition*. Refer to Chapter 14 for additional discussion.

 Decision analysis should not be used for discovering behavioral rules. Use pattern questions instead. Avoid force-fitting a decision-oriented approach to every business rule problem. It simply won't work.

Decision analysis is not appropriate for decisions that are:

- Removed from day-to-day business activity or abstract. Examples: *Are we following our business rules correctly? Is our business process optimized or well-coordinated? Are we aligned with our* **business strategy**? Decisions appropriate for decision analysis are always directly in-line to a **business process** (whether modeled or not).

- Ones that can be resolved or predicted by a formula or calculation — i.e., by some equation(s). Examples: *How much is owed for an order? How much business has a customer done in the last 12 months? What is a student's cumulative grade point average?* Decisions appropriate for decision analysis generally do not have outcomes that can be calculated mathematically based on circumstances or cumulative history.

The Basic Elements of Operational Business Decisions

The basic elements of operational business decisions are represented in Figure 12-1.

A **case** is some particular matter or situation arising in day-to-day business activity and requiring consideration. Example: *John Smith*, an ordinary applicant in terms of income, employment, and experience, applies for auto insurance. Such a case requires an operational business decision to be made.

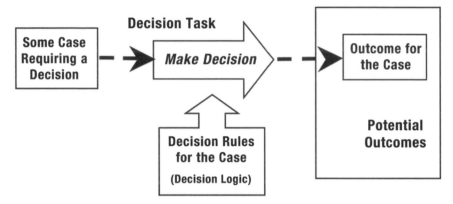

Figure 12-1. Basic Elements of Operational Business Decisions

A *potential outcome* is some result, conclusion, or answer that might be deemed appropriate for a case. An operational business decision must always have at least two potential outcomes. Depending on the decision, potential outcomes might be:

- some form of yes/no (e.g., *eligible/ineligible*), which can be expressed as a unary fact type

- some quantities (e.g., *dollar amounts*) that cannot be resolved or predicted by a formula or calculation

- some categories (e.g., silver, gold or platinum customer)

- some real-world instances (e.g., employees who are candidates for representing a gold customer)

- some courses of action (e.g., on-site visit, teleconference, telephone call, email, FAX)

 Always be very clear about potential outcomes. Shape and define them early; make sure they are not hazy or fuzzy; revisit and challenge them often.

The *outcome* is the result, conclusion, or answer deemed appropriate for a *given* case. Example: *John Smith*, an ordinary applicant in terms of income, employment, and experience, is deemed *eligible* for auto insurance (but could have been deemed *ineligible*).

A **decision rule** is a business rule that links a case to some appropriate outcome. Example: The decision rule that links the case of an ordinary applicant like *John Smith* to the outcome *eligible*.

The **decision logic** is the set of all decision rules for cases in scope of a given decision. Decision logic should be represented **declaratively** in the form of **decision table(s)**, business rule statement(s), or some combination thereof. Example: The decision logic for the eligibility decision would include all the business rules for whether an applicant is eligible for auto insurance.

A *decision task* corresponding to this decision logic might be *Determine eligibility of applicant for auto insurance.* Quite possibly this decision task is embedded in some business process model(s), just one of many business tasks. As Figure 12-1 illustrates, decision logic should always be externalized from such decision tasks.

About Decision Tasks

Decision tasks, like all tasks, are **procedural**. A decision task *does* something; specifically, it makes an operational business decision. Without some decision task, nothing happens — that is, no decision is made.

The decision logic, in contrast, should be purely **declarative**. It indicates only what the outcome (answer) for each possible case *should* be; the decision logic cannot actually make the decision. So there *always* has to be some task(s) or action(s) to make a decision.

In decision analysis we take the necessity for such task(s) or action(s) to actually make a decision as a given. From this point forward on we'll focus exclusively on declarative analysis of the operational business decision itself. *Yes, such analysis is possible, and yes, it produces great results!*

 A decision task always involves a determination of some kind, so we recommend using the convention *"Determine ..."* to name a decision task.

Externalizing decision logic from decision tasks, a form of **rule independence**, produces simple (or *thin*) decision tasks, which in turn produces **thin processes**. It also results in decision logic that is far more accessible, adaptable (easier to change), and re-usable (e.g., in other business processes).

Naming Operational Business Decisions

An operational business decision must be named. The best, most business-friendly way to name it is using the business question it answers. Example: *Is an applicant eligible for insurance?* Naming an operational business decision according to the question it answers:

- Assists in delineating scope. For example, the decision logic addressing the question above might not be about *all* kinds of insurance, perhaps just *auto* insurance. If so, the question can be sharpened to: *Is an applicant eligible for auto insurance?*

- Provides a continuing checkpoint for testing what the operational business decision is really about.

- Serves as a constant reminder that decision analysis produces declarative answers, not procedural results. The focus is *not* on how work is to be performed in a business process.

 Forming, testing, and continually shaping the question are essential in producing high-quality decision logic.

Guidelines for Expressing the Question Addressed by Some Decision Logic

Avoid the word *how*. The interrogative *how* often suggests process or procedure. For example, a question worded as *How should an order be filled?* might be taken to mean "What steps are appropriate in actually filling orders?" Steering clear of any potential confusion with process or procedure is always best for decision analysis.

 This convention does not apply to *how much* or *how many*, both of which refer to some quantity rather than some action.

Avoid the word *must* in favor of *should*. For example: *What sales tax should be charged on an order? When should an appointment be scheduled?* The answers provided by decision logic simply indicate appropriate outcomes for given cases. How strictly these outcomes are to be applied or followed in actual business activity is a separate concern.

Avoid discourse shortcuts (e.g., I, we, you, here, now, etc.). For example: Instead of *How should we price this order?* write *How should this order be priced?*

Avoid *and's* and *but's*. Decisions with conjunctions are unlikely to be atomic. For example avoid: *What is wrong with this machine and what approach should be used for fixing it?*. The *and* indicates separate decisions, each of which should be analyzed in its own right.

Avoid words that are ambiguous or undefined. The phrasing of questions should be based directly on the structured business vocabulary (**fact model**).

Defining the Scope of Decision Analysis

The scope of an operational business decision (*decision scope*) is always ultimately based on cases. The decision logic produced from decision analysis must be able to give a definite outcome for every case demonstrably in decision scope. A case that is not in decision scope must be handed off (to some expert, manager, business process, or other decision logic).

Decision scope is based on three essential elements: (1) The question the decision logic answers. (2) Limitations about the kinds of cases covered. (3) Exceptions.

The first two elements are highly intertwined. For example, the question for some decision logic might be expressed in either of the following two ways.

> *(a) Is an applicant eligible for <u>auto</u> insurance?*

> *(b) Is an applicant eligible for insurance?*

> > Cases in decision scope: *<u>auto</u> insurance*

The resulting decision scope is the same for either form of specification.

Refinements to decision scope mean adding additional limitations that narrow the range of cases the decision logic handles (i.e., should give definite outcomes for). For example, the decision scope of the decision logic above might be further refined in either of the following ways:

> *(a) Is an applicant eligible for auto insurance <u>for USA</u> <u>under $1 million</u>?*

> *(b) Is an applicant eligible for insurance?*

> > Cases in decision scope:
> > - *auto insurance*
> > - *<u>USA</u>*
> > - *<u>under $1 million</u>*

Two more limitations, *USA* and *under $1 million,* have been added to each of the expressions above. As before, both forms of specification result in exactly the same decision scope.

An implicit AND is understood to exist among all three decision scope items in each expression. If there is any doubt about the intended ANDing, the ANDing should be given explicitly.

As decision scope is increasingly refined, listing limitations on decision scope separately (as in *b*) usually proves more effective. For example:

Question: *Is an applicant eligible?*

Cases in decision scope: *Any application submitted by an applicant that:*
- *is for the product 'auto insurance'*
- *is for a policy covering the 'USA'*
- *requests a coverage amount less than $1 million*

The vocabulary used to phrase cases in decision scope should be based on the structured business vocabulary (fact model).

Considerations and Exceptions

The outcome for a case in decision scope is usually determined by a standard or typical set of *considerations*. If not, then the case is an *exceptional case*.

A *consideration* is a factor for making an operational business decision. Considerations will provide the basis for organizing decision tables when decision analysis gets to that stage. For auto insurance, considerations might include *driving history, evidence of insurance, insurance risk score, credit rating,* and *state/province.*

Business Analysts experienced with developing decision tables generally recommend limiting the number of considerations to 7+/-2.

An *exceptional case* (or simply *exception*) is a case that is based on *none* of the standard or typical considerations. Suppose, as before, that for auto insurance the standard considerations are: *driving history, evidence of insurance, insurance risk score, credit rating,* and *state/province.* Then suppose there are business rules denying auto insurance for any *felon* or *person under age 16.* Since *criminal status* and *age* respectively are not among the standard or typical considerations for the decision logic, these cases are deemed *exceptions*.

It is important to note that exceptions *are* in decision scope. Definite outcomes are always given for exceptions, even if simply to deny (or accept) some result out-of-hand.

 Typically at most 20% of all possible cases are exceptional. If the percentage of exceptional cases exceeds 20% for some decision logic, the standard or typical considerations should be re-examined.

Cases that are not exceptional are considered *standard*. A *standard case* is a *case in decision scope* that is:

- Regular or common.
- Based on some or all the usual considerations.
- Subject to normal treatment and cannot be denied (or accepted) out-of-hand.

To complete specification of decision scope for some decision logic, the business rules for handling exceptions must be given. For example:

Business Rule: *An applicant that has been convicted of a felony involving a motor vehicle must be considered ineligible for auto insurance.*

Business Rule: *An applicant younger than 16 years of age must be considered ineligible for auto insurance.*

Divide and Conquer

A key to simplifying the analysis of decision logic for standard cases is to *divide and conquer.* That way the decision analysis can be conducted in separate streams and, if resources permit, in parallel.

Example: Suppose the considerations used to determine eligibility for auto insurance in the USA for *well-heeled applicants* are different from those for *ordinary applicants* in terms of income, employment, and experience. The decision logic for the two kinds (subsets) of cases can be developed separately if both the following are true:

1. The two subsets of cases are non-overlapping. (Otherwise, some cases could be decided by either decision logic, resulting in potentially inconsistent results.)

2. The two sets of considerations are not exactly the same. (If the same, there is no particular advantage in treating the cases separately.)

Often, the divide-and-conquer strategy leads to *independent subdecisions*. An **independent subdecision** is one of a collection of two or more operational business decisions on which another operational business decision is dependent. Each subdecision has a distinct outcome and a different set of considerations (usually non-overlapping) from its peers in the collection.

A good example of independent subdecisions is the launching of a space shuttle or manned rocket. Before the ultimate decision *Should the craft be launched?* is addressed, an entire checklist of subdecisions is addressed, each with its own set of considerations. These subdecisions pertain to weather, fuel systems, communications, down-field recovery, etc.

The decision logic for the operational business decision *Is an applicant eligible for auto insurance for USA under $1 million?* might be analyzed as independent subdecisions:

■ *Is the applicant's driving history acceptable?*

■ *Has the applicant given acceptable evidence of insurance?*

■ *Is the applicant's Insurance Risk Score O.K.?*

■ etc.

Each of these subdecisions would have a distinct outcome and probably a non-overlapping set of considerations.

An overall blueprint for the decision logic can be portrayed as a *Question Chart* (*Q-Chart* for short) as in Figure 12-2. A Q-Chart, as discussed in the next Chapter, provides a visualization of a **decision structure**; that is, how some interrelated operational business decisions are formally organized.

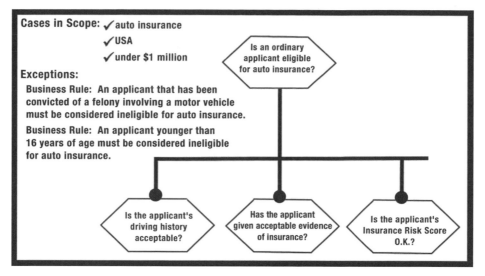

Figure 12-2. Q-Chart for the Operational Business decision *Is an applicant eligible for auto insurance for USA under $1 million?*

How Far is Too Far with Decision Analysis

When law-makers write laws, they're not thinking about decisions. When regulators write regulations, they're not thinking about decisions. When lawyers write contracts, they're not thinking about decisions. When insurance people create insurance products, they're not thinking about decisions. When outsourcers create agreements with companies to handle work, they're not thinking about decisions. When managers create business policies they're not thinking about decisions.

We could go on. Business rules that govern business activity, **behavioral rules**, exist in great abundance. (Refer to Chapter 14 for discussion.) In many respects they are more fundamental than decision rules. *Decision analysis and decision tables don't begin to do it all with respect to business rules, much less engineer robust* **business capabilities**! Business Analysts need the entire suite of techniques described in this book to create **business models** effectively. *Don't let anyone tell you otherwise!*

Summary

Decision analysis, a key part of business analysis, involves identifying and analyzing key questions (operational business decisions) in day-to-day business activity and capturing the decision logic used to answer those questions.

The end-product of decision analysis is decision logic in the form of decision structures, decision tables, and business rules statements. This decision logic is rendered in a form that is practicable (ready to **deploy** whether to staff or ultimately to machines), enterprise-robust, and business-friendly. **Single-sourcing** decision logic is essential in achieving **business agility**.

Externalizing decision logic from business process models reduces the complexity of those models dramatically. It also results in decision logic that is far more accessible, adaptable (easier to change), and re-usable (e.g., in other business processes). The problem seems complex only because we've never stood back and taken a good look at the whole. **See the elephant!**

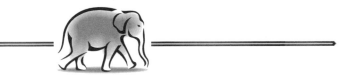

CHAPTER 13

Modeling Decisions

Q-Charts

Question Charts (Q-Charts™ for short) are a technique used to analyze, diagram, and visualize the structure of **operational business decisions**. In a Q-Chart, an elongated hexagon stands for a decision. The question representing the decision is indicated inside the hexagon.

We use the hexagon shape in facilitated sessions and other analysis work for brainstorming key elements of an operational business decision. As illustrated in Figure 13-1, a **Q-COE**™ is a graphic representation indicating what question ("Q") is being asked, and usually one or more of the following: considerations ("C"), outcomes ("O"), and exceptions ("E").

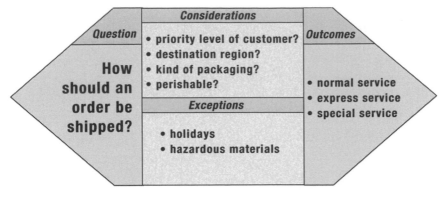

**Figure 13-1. A Q-COE for Brainstorming the Operational
Business Decision** *How should an order be shipped?*

Decision analysis should begin in 'sketch' mode, where the four key elements of an operational business decision are captured, named, analyzed, and organized in a Q-COE. Too much structure and detail early-on work against effective collaboration and dialog.

Later, as decision analysis moves into detail mode, Q-Charts become more rigorous. For example, specification of decision scope and **exceptional cases** should be refined and carefully coordinated with the **fact model**. Then **decision tables** can take center stage.

Decision Dependency

In a Q-Chart, connections between Q-COEs always pertain to **dependencies** between the operational business decisions. Such a dependency occurs when one operational business decision is prerequisite for another. Table 13-1 identifies the three kinds of decision dependency relevant for Q-Charts. Each kind of decision dependency is discussed individually below.

Table 13-1. The Three Kinds of Decision Dependency in Q-Charts

	Basis of Decision Dependency	Kind of Decision Dependency
1.	**Q**uestion	*relevance dependency*
2.	**C**onsideration	*consideration dependency*
3.	**O**utcome	*outcome dependency*

Decision dependencies are always oriented vertically in Q-Charts, rather than horizontally, to avoid any suggestion of flow or sequence. A Q-Chart always portrays only *logical* dependencies.

What about Mathematical Dependencies?

Not among the decision dependencies in Table 13-1 are *mathematical* dependencies — for example the mathematical dependence of $(C - D = E)$ on $(A + B = C)$. (The first equation depends on computation of "C" as prescribed by the second equation.) Business rules for computation are best given by formulas featuring appropriate re-use of terms (e.g., "C" in the two equations above).

 Hierarchical visualization of mathematical dependencies often proves useful, but to avoid confusion, Q-Charts should not be used for that purpose.

Relevance Dependency

In **relevance dependency**, one operational business decision depends on the outcome of another decision such that the outcome of this other decision may completely eliminate the need for any outcome from the dependent one. In auto insurance, for example, if an *applicant* is not *eligible* for coverage, there is no need to determine what to charge the applicant as a *premium*. In other words, the dependent decision is *preempted* — indeed, meaningless. The appropriate relevance dependency is illustrated in Figure 13-2 using a dashed connector.

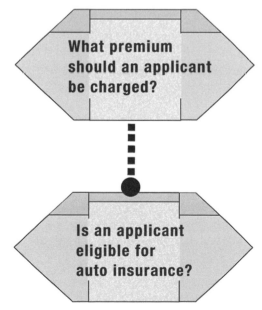

Figure 13-2. Relevance Dependency Between Q-COEs

As shown in Figure 13-2, a dependency connection always includes a *hitch point* (a solid circle) at the bottom. The hitch point always goes with the operational business decision most able to stand on its own — i.e., with the bottom, more independent one.

Mandatory Sequence?

Do **business processes** always have to ask the questions involved in a relevance dependency in bottom-to-top sequence? *No.* For the questions in Figure 13-2, for example, a customer-friendly, web-based interface might permit price-conscious consumers to ask about the premium *before* asking about eligibility.

Caution should be exercised, though. If such ability were supported, it would probably be a good idea to include a disclaimer indicating that securing coverage at the given price is subject to eligibility. In other words, a business rule should be specified to ensure a disclaimer is given by any business process or **ad hoc business activity** that supports a price-before-eligibility sequence.

Consideration Dependency

In **consideration dependency**, one operational business decision depends on the outcome of another such that the outcome of this other provides or supports a consideration for the dependent one. In shipping an order, for example, it might not be possible to decide what *shipping service* to use unless you decide the *priority level* of the customer. Deciding on the *priority level* of a customer might have considerations all its own. This consideration dependency is illustrated in Figure 13-3 using a solid-line connector.

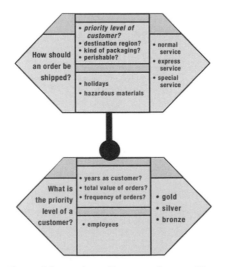

Figure 13-3. Consideration Dependency Between Q-COEs

Outcome Dependency

In **outcome dependency**, one operational business decision is dependent on the outcome of another decision such that the outcome of this other decision dictates some outcome(s) of the dependent decision. Both decisions must have the same *kind* of outcome. In addition, the set of considerations of the less dependent ("lower") decision must be the same as, or a subset of, the set of considerations of the more dependent ("upper") decision. Figure 13-4 illustrates.

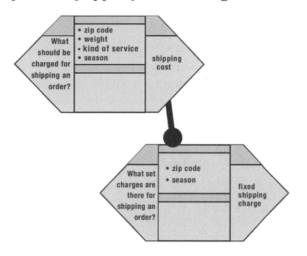

Figure 13-4. Outcome Dependency Between Q-COEs

Figure 13-4 illustrates an outcome dependency.

■ The lower (independent) Q-COE represents the question *What set charges are there for shipping an order?* and has the outcome *fixed shipping charge*.

■ The upper (dependent) Q-COE represents the question *What should be charged for shipping an order?* and has the outcome *shipping cost*.

■ The structured business vocabulary (**fact model**) should indicate *fixed shipping charge* and *shipping cost* to be the same kind of thing.

■ The lower Q-COE uses the considerations *zip code* and *season,* a proper subset of the four considerations for the upper (dependent) Q-COE.

■ The net effect is that the lower Q-COE will dictate some (but not all) outcomes for the upper (dependent) Q-COE. For example, if the *zip code* is in Alaska, and the *season* is winter, all *shipping costs* might be $250, regardless of *weight* or *kind of package*. This business rule might be just one of many that dictate shipping cost for multiple cases.

As Figure 13-4 illustrates, an outcome dependency is represented using the same kind of non-dashed thick line and hitch point that are used to represent consideration dependencies. For an outcome dependency, however, the thick line should extend from the outcome area of the Q-COE for the dependent ("upper") decision.

Q-Charts vs. Business Process Models

The **decision structure** represented by a Q-Chart serves a fundamentally different purpose than a **business process** model.

- A Q-Chart and the **decision logic** developed from it provide the best or optimal answers to business questions. Decision logic does not flow. It should not be viewed as actually *doing* (transforming) anything.

- A business process model indicates how business tasks should be performed in some meaningful sequence. Business process models always flow. They always actually *do* (transform) something.

Best Practices for Decision Tables

To ensure that decision logic always remains declarative, we recommend the following best practices for **decision tables** (the next step in developing decision logic). These best practices not only produce the most business-friendly decision tables, but also ensure that decision logic remains distinct from models serving other purposes, especially business process models.

- **Never use a decision table simply to indicate what to do next.** Representations of decision logic should never include any actions, whether explicit or implicit. All outcomes should simply be answers to some business question.

- **Reading or interpreting a decision table should never require following any particular sequence.** The order in which rows or columns are evaluated should never matter. Sequence should simply not be a factor.

 Don't fall into the trap of using decision tables for software development(!).

In short, decision logic should be **declarative**; business process models (by definition) are **procedural**. Maintaining this hard-and-fast distinction is important because decision logic represented in purely declarative form is:

- Best for addressing the inherent complexity of operational business decisions.

- Completely independent of choices made by IT in designing systems or using particular hardware/software platforms for implementation.

- Most re-usable, most manageable, and most conducive for achieving **business agility**.

Figure 13-5 presents a more complete decision structure in the form of a Q-Chart.

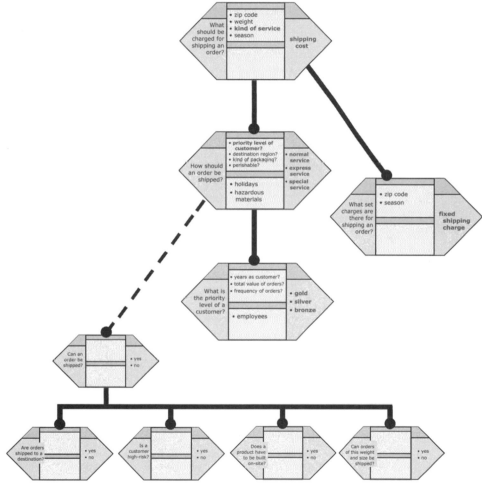

**Figure 13-5. Q-Chart for Deciding How Much
to Charge for Shipping an Order**

Observations:

- The highest Q-COE, representing the most dependent decision, represents the question *What should be charged for shipping an order?* Four considerations are used in determining the outcome *shipping cost.*

- The consideration dependency presented earlier connects the top Q-COE with the Q-COE beneath it *How should an order be shipped?* The outcome of the lower Q-COE provides the consideration *kind of service* for the upper (more dependent) Q-COE.

- The Q-COE *How should an order be shipped?* is connected via another consideration dependency to the Q-COE beneath it *What is the priority level of a customer?* The outcome of the lower Q-COE provides the consideration *priority level of customer* for the upper (more dependent) Q-COE.

- The Q-COE *How should an order be shipped?* is also connected via a relevance dependency to the Q-COE (lower left) *Can an order be shipped?* If an order cannot be shipped, it is meaningless to ask *How should an order be shipped?*

- The Q-COE *Can an order be shipped?* has four independent subdecisions beneath it, each presumably based on its own considerations.

- Finally, the consideration dependency presented earlier connects the top Q-COE with the Q-COE beneath it (middle right) *What set charges are there for shipping an order?* This lower Q-COE will dictate certain outcomes for the upper (dependent) Q-COE.

Summary

Q-Charts are a diagramming technique for capturing, visualizing, and analyzing decision structures in declarative form. Q-Charts serve a very different purpose than business process models. Q-Charts comprise:

- Q-COEs, used to capture the basic elements of operational business decisions.

- Decision dependencies, used to show how Q-COEs relate logically.

Operational business decisions often prove much more complex than they first seem. Develop Q-Charts before plunging into decision tables. **See the elephant!**

CHAPTER 14

Modeling Know-How

True-to-Life Business Models

Business analysis with business rules focuses on capturing, encoding, and managing a specific kind of knowledge — operational business know-how. (We call it **know-how** for short.) Know-how is represented in the form of **business rules** based on a structured business vocabulary (**fact model**). In many respects, the fact model is the most fundamental know-how of all.

The previous two Chapters focused on decision analysis, the gateway to developing **decision rules.** Your organization undoubtedly has a great many decision rules, but it also has a great many *behavioral rules,* which predominated in Chapters 5, 7, 9, and 11.

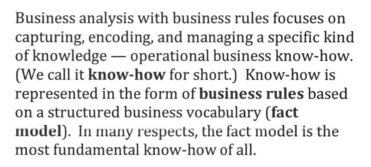

Behavioral rules govern the conduct of on-going business activity by 'watching' for violations. Understanding how these business rules work is essential in creating *true-to-life* business models.

Behavioral Rules vs. Decision Rules

Table 14-1 identifies fundamental differences between behavioral rules and decision rules.

Example of a behavioral rule: A student with a failing grade must not be an active member of a sports team.

Discussion: This business rule is not about selecting the most appropriate sports team for a student, nor does it apply only at a single point of determination (e.g., when a case of a student wanting to join a team comes up). Instead, the business rule is meant to be enforced continuously — for example, if a student who is already active on some sports team should let his or her grades fall. In other words, the business rule is about shaping (governing) the conduct of on-going business activity.

 Identify and document the original source of behavioral rules whenever possible. If unavailable or unknown (which should raise some concerns!), document that too.

Flash Points

As indicated above, behavioral rules generally need to be applied at *various* points in time. What are these points in time? How can you find them? Why are they important for Business Analysts?

Each of the various points in time when a behavioral rule needs to be evaluated represents an **operational business event**. Such events can arise in either **business processes** or **ad hoc business activity**.

How do you find these operational business events? Consider the behavioral rule: *A customer must be assigned to an agent if the customer has placed an order.* Figure 14-1 shows the relevant terms and wordings for this business rule.

Figure 14-1. Terms and Wordings for the Agent-Assignment Business Rule

Table 14-1. Behavioral Rules vs. Decision Rules

	Behavioral Rules	**Decision Rules**
Focus	Operational business governance	**Operational business decisions**
Purpose	Shaping (governing) the conduct of on-going business activity	Providing answers for repetitive questions arising in day-to-day business activity
Featured Kind of Business Rule	Business rules that can be violated	Business rules that indicate the correct or best outcome for some case
Most Common Original Source	Interpretation of some law, act, statute, regulation, contract, agreement, business deal, **business policy**, license, certification, service level agreement, etc.	Judgments or evaluations made by subject matter experts
Special Analysis Techniques	**Pattern Questions**	**Q-Charts**
Role in the Business Model	Prevent situations (**states**) the business deems undesirable	Ensure consistency of operational business decisions
Point(s) of Evaluation	Each **operational business event** where the business rule could be violated	The single point of determination in day-to-day business activity at which an operational business decision is made for a **case**
Most Frequent Representation	Generally fit no pattern, so usually must be expressed as individual statements (e.g., using **RuleSpeak**)	Generally fall into patterns, so often can be expressed in **decision tables**
Drill-Down to Additional Business Rules	Yes, significant drill-down to underlying **definitional rules**	Yes, significant drill-down to underlying **definitional rules**
Quantity in a Typical **Business Capability**	A great many	Each decision table has multiple — overall, a great many

The business rule has been expressed in **declarative** manner. This means, in part, that it does not indicate any particular process, procedure, or other means to enforce or apply it. It is simply a business rule — nothing more, nothing less.

The business rule makes no reference to any event where it potentially could be violated or needs to be evaluated. The business rule does not say, for example, "*When* a customer places an order, then ...."

This observation is extremely important for the following reason. "*When* a customer places an order" *is not the only event when the business rule could potentially be violated and therefore needs to be evaluated.*

Actually, there is another event when this business rule could be violated: "*When* an agent leaves our company...." The business rule needs to be evaluated when this event occurs too since the event could pose a violation under the following circumstances: (a) The agent is assigned to a customer, and (b) that customer has placed at least one order.

In other words, the business rule could potentially be violated during *two* quite distinct kinds of operational business event. The first — "*When* a customer places an order ..." — is rather obvious. The second — "*When* an agent leaves our company ..." — might be much less so. Both events are nonetheless important because either could produce a violation of the business rule.

This example is not atypical or unusual in any way. In general, *every* business rule produces two or more kinds of operational business events where it could potentially be violated or needs to be evaluated. (We mean *produces* here in the sense of *can be analyzed to discover.*)

These operational business events are called the business rule's **flash points**. Business rules do exist that are specific to an individual event, but they represent a small minority.

Expressing each business rule in **declarative** form helps ensure none of its flash points is exempted *inadvertently*.

Discovering and analyzing flash points for business rules can also prove useful in validating business rules with business people. Important (and sometimes surprising) business policy questions often crop up. Automated support for identifying flash points is something a **general rulebook system** (GRBS) should offer.

Your Current IT Requirements Approach: *The Big Question*

Each business rule usually produces multiple flash points. Why is this insight so important? *The two or more* events *where any given business rule needs to be evaluated are almost certain to occur within at least two, and possibly many, different processes, procedures, or use cases.* Yet for all these different processes, procedures, and use cases there is only a *single* business rule.

Now ask yourself this: *What in your current IT requirements methodology ensures you will* get consistent results for each business rule across all these *processes, procedures, and use cases?*

Unfortunately, the answer today is almost always *nothing*. In the past, business rules have seldom been treated as a first-class citizen. No wonder legacy systems often act in such unexpected and inconsistent ways(!). Organizations today need **business operation systems** where business governance, not simply information, is the central concern.

Business rules should be seen as one of the starting points for creating system models — not something designers eventually work *down to* in use cases. That's the tail wagging the dog.

By unifying each business rule (**single-sourcing**), and faithfully supporting all its flash points wherever they occur, Business Analysts can ensure consistent results across all processes, procedures, and use cases. *Is there really any other way?!*

How to Assemble Know-How: Case Study

Let's walk through a case study to understand how behavioral rules, flash points, and operational business decisions should relate in a **business model**.

Scenario: A customer places an order.

Flash point: The operational business event *"when a customer places an order"* is a flash point for some behavioral rule(s).

Behavioral rule: A customer must be assigned to an agent if the customer has placed an order.

Motivation: The business thinking behind the business rule is briefly:

> *The company's products are complex, expensive, and available in a large variety of configurations. Customization is often warranted. Assigning an agent helps customers identify the best solution for their particular circumstances. Assisted acquisition also ensures the highest chance of customer success and reduces returns and replacements.*

This business thinking is the motivation for the business rule — its pedigree. The motivation should be recorded (as part of **rulebook management**) and accessible to everyone properly authorized.

 Never assume the original motivation for a business rule will be remembered and properly understood by all. Document it! See Chapter 20 on rulebook management.

Violation event: The particular customer placing the order does not have an assigned agent.

Detection of the violation: Some staff person, business rules engine (BRE), or other platform recognizes that an agent needs to be assigned. That staff person, BRE, or other platform did not 'decide' the customer needed an agent. No operational business decision or choice among alternatives is needed to recognize the violation. An order being placed by a customer without an agent simply results in a violation of the business rule.

Response to the violation: Something must be done to assign an agent to the customer. When the business rule was created, the company decided the best *violation response* would be to hand the case over to a line manager and let her handle the situation. Presumably, she's in the best position to know which agent is optimal to assign to any given customer.

Operational business decision: The need to pick and assign a particular agent from among alternatives for the given customer at the given point in time *does* represent an operational business decision. The business is trying to answer the question *Which is the best agent to assign to a customer?* The manager decides and assigns an agent for the given case. Business activity moves on from there.

Potential decision analysis: The operational business decision has been identified and included in a list of possible targets for future decision analysis.

As illustrated by this case study, the dynamics of behavioral rules are fundamentally different from those of decision rules. The differences are summarized in Table 14-2.

Table 14-2. Differences in the Dynamics of Behavioral Rules vs. Decision Rules

	Behavioral Rules	Decision Rules
Key Concern	Shaping (governing) on-going business behavior	What business question is being asked
Central Issue for Analysis	Detection of violations and the appropriate response to such violations	What is the correct or optimal answer for each case at a given point in time
Is Choice Involved?	A violation of a behavioral rule just happens. No choice is involved in the detection of a violation.	Choice is center stage. A choice among alternatives (outcomes) is always involved.

 As discussed in the next Chapter, enforcement of behavioral rules involves three things: *enforcement level*, *guidance message*, and *violation response*. Each behavioral rule should be examined along those three lines in completing the business model.

Business Rules in Real Life

Several factors can conspire to make situations involving behavioral rules seem complicated. Sometimes you really have to dig. Consider the real-world case of a posted speed limit and radar speed trap.

1. *What the Real Business Rules Are*

- The *real* business rule is probably not the published business rule (the posted speed limit). It's probably something more like: *A vehicle must not exceed the posted speed limit by more than 9 miles per hour.*

- Notable exceptions probably apply — for example, the *permission statement*: *A government vehicle with siren and lights flashing may exceed the posted speed limit.*

2. *Response to Violations*

The policeperson operating the speed trap (being only flesh and blood) has discretion about how to respond when the radar gun indicates a violation of the speed-limit rule. Some possible factors:

- *"I'm eating my doughnut and drinking my coffee, and I'm not going to spoil the moment by chasing someone down the street."*
- *"I'm behind on my quota and the sergeant is really cranky today, so I'm going to chase down everybody without mercy."*

In other words, choice does come to play in how the policeperson *responds* to a violation. The choices might be: *Let the speeder go, chase the speeder, hand the speeder off to another unit down the street.* Real-time choice among alternatives does represent a decision.

How to respond to a violation, however, is not at all the same thing as the business rule itself. A vehicle going down the street either violates the speed-limit rule or it doesn't. A violation either happens or it doesn't happen.

 'Condition-action' and 'event-condition action' syntax for expressing rules (e.g., in the form of **production rules**) badly conflates the distinctions among behavioral rule, violation, and violation response. For business analysis, stick with **RuleSpeak**.

Responding to Non-Violations

The real-world event that corresponds to a flash point is actually an event that could *present* a violation, not a violation per se. Sometimes you might want to respond to a *non*-violation. For motorists *not* speeding, for example, a message could be posted on a street-side electronic sign, "Thank *you* for not speeding today!" (Not very likely where I live.)

---

3. The Decision to Create a Business Rule

Sometime in the past the city government, concerned about public safety, decided a speed limit was needed. What speed limit should it post? There were choices, of course — a range of possible speed limits — and it had to choose a speed limit considering a variety of factors. The speed limit posted (deployed) is the one that got selected. That posted speed limit is the business rule (at least officially).

So the *creation* of a business rule does represent a decision because it involves choice (selection from among alternatives). Business rules don't simply spring forth immaculately (good ones anyway).

That kind of decision, however, is not real-time with respect to day-to-day business activity (i.e., motorists driving down streets). Rather than an operational business decision, the creation of a business rule represents a **governance decision**.

A governance decision is part of the organization's *governance process*, not part of its operational (real-time) business processes (i.e., policing day-to-day traffic). The governance process is *higher-level*. Don't confuse the two levels.

Back to Decision Analysis

Returning to the agent-assignment rule, let's say the company recently decided to automate the operational business decision: *Which is the best agent to assign to a customer?* The Business Analysts will have:

- Undertaken decision analysis and created a Q-Chart.

- Developed decision tables, spending time with business leads to get the decision logic right.

Then the decision logic was deployed under a business rule engine (BRE). Now, instead of the line manager performing the decision task 'manually' as each case arises, the BRE does it automatically by evaluating the decision tables. No matter, it's still an operational business decision — a selection or choice among alternatives to be made in real time.

 The decision logic can be evaluated as a violation response for the original behavioral rule: *A customer must be assigned to an agent if the customer has placed an order.*

From a business perspective, automation of the operational business decision changed only two things, both for the better:

(1) The line manager has been freed up to do other (perhaps more challenging) work.

(2) Her know-how has been encoded so the company won't lose it should she leave. Decision logic, like all business rules, is inherently about **know-how retention**.

When Operational Business Decisions Should Be Made

Like behavioral rules, decision rules also generally have multiple flash points. The implicit assumption in decision analysis, however, is that evaluation of decision rules need *not* be based on flash points. Instead, the default point of determination is *case-based*. In other words, an operational business decision is made for a case simply because either the particular case is ready for the decision or the related circumstances demand it.

Example: An order has been filled and packaged and is ready to be shipped to the customer. All behavioral rules have been satisfied. Now the correct or optimal delivery method for shipping the package needs to be selected (an operational business decision). The correct or optimal answer is determined by evaluating the decision rules. Afterwards, things move along as per the business process (e.g., the package is shipped).

Sometimes, as in this example, once a decision is made for a case there is no practical way of turning back. In other words, barring some unforeseen scenario, the operational business decision is final (irreversible).

Not all operational business decisions have that degree of finality. In essence some decisions can be reversed or improved, at least for a period of time. Indeed, *not* revisiting such decisions can prove counter-productive, wasteful, or even dangerous.

Example: An agent needs to be assigned to a customer. Unfortunately, all the agents most highly qualified for that customer are currently unavailable or overloaded with work. The best approach might be to assign an *interim* agent, then revisit the case later. You never know, a highly qualified agent might suddenly shake loose in the next little while.

As this example suggests, a reversible decision can be revisited by introducing time-based criteria (some business rule(s)) to re-evaluate selected cases after a certain period of time, perhaps repeatedly. The possibility of significant over-time improvement in reversible decisions is always worth exploring.

 Adding business task(s) downstream in a business process model for the purpose of improving earlier decisions is usually not recommended (too complex). A better approach, especially for last-chance improvement opportunities, is to include some appropriate business milestone(s) in a business milestone model.

Available Resources in Short Supply?

Some operational business decisions are characterized by a potential shortfall in resources relative to demand. For example, a car rental agency at an airport might not have enough rental cars of the right models to satisfy all outstanding reservations.

The best approach in such circumstances is generally to wait as long as you can to make *any* decision. During the delay, you save up a 'batch' of incoming cases, then make decisions for the whole batch at once. This approach ensures the best possible match-ups for higher-priority cases.

Example: Reservations from high-status customers might come in at the beginning of the delay period, but rental cars of the requested models might become available only toward the very end. Had you assigned rental cars in real-time (i.e., as each reservation is received), your aggregate solution would be suboptimal for the time period. In plain English, *suboptimal* means your best customers are needlessly unhappy.

The trick, of course, is determining how long a delay in making the decisions is *too* long. Answering that question involves analyzing trade-offs among your **business goals**. Remember, we're not modeling know-how for the sake of the know-how. We're modeling it for the sake of deploying the best-possible business solution!

Summary

Operational business know-how is complex, involving both behavioral rules and decision rules. Understanding their intertwined roles is key to creating high-quality, *true-to-life* business models and, from them, effective **business operation systems**. Treating business rules as a first-class citizen also shifts your focus toward operational business events, especially *flash points*.

Business Analysts should not work *down* to business rules in use cases or other system models; business rules should be a primary focus in creating a business model. The resulting business solution will be unbeatable in its support for **business agility** and **know-how retention**.

CHAPTER **15**

More on Business Rules and Their Enforcement

Final Areas of Analysis

In rounding out your **business model**, two additional areas of analysis for business rules are needed. First, business organization and business geography should be examined for business rules. Second, business questions regarding appropriate enforcement of each **behavioral rule** should be answered. These two areas of analysis are the last ones specifically related to business rules in creating the business model.

Business organization and business geography represent the two final basic engineering questions in the **Zachman Architecture Framework** — *who* and *where*, respectively.

Business Rules about Business Organization

The key word in understanding business rules for business organization is *interaction*. By *interaction*, we mean person-to-person or role-to-role *business* interactions in the real world (even if separated by time and distance). Often such interactions are supported by special *work products* and take place over *active channels* (e.g., connections via the internet).

Business roles generally may be filled only by people properly qualified.

Pattern Question for Business Role Qualifications

Pattern Question BO1:
Qualifications for Business Roles
  What qualifications or experience should a person have
  to fill a business role?

Sample business rule specifying a business role qualification:
  An operational manager must have at least 3 years experience in a
  field office.

Sample business rule specifying a business role qualification:
  An inspector must attend a course covering new technical
  developments at least once a year.

Business roles are often charged with certain business responsibilities.

Pattern Question for Business Role Responsibilities

Pattern Question BO2:
Responsibilities of Business Roles
What <u>business responsibilities</u> should a business role have?

Sample business rule specifying business role responsibilities:
An order of a given amount must be approved by the following.

Amount of Order:	Approval Required By:
$1,000,000 or above	vice president
$500,000 up to (but not including) $1,000,000	regional manager
$100,000 up to (but not including) $500,000	store manager
less than $100,000	none

Interactions between business roles are often restricted in certain ways.

Pattern Question for Business Interactions

Pattern Question BO3:
Business Interactions
What restrictions are placed on how different roles should or should not <u>interact</u> in their business activity?

Sample business rule restricting a business interaction:
A union member may meet face-to-face with a company official only if a union representative is present.

Sample business rule restricting a business interaction:
A trainee may send a memo to a manager only with the permission of his supervisor.

Business interactions are not limited to just people or roles. An organizational unit (e.g., the eMarketing Department) or another company (e.g., a partner in a supply chain) can also be involved in business interactions.

A business model often identifies work products in certain forms (e.g., notifications, requests, sign-offs, analyses, position papers, legal agreements, etc.) to support business interactions properly.

Pattern Question for Work Products

Pattern Question BO4:
Work Products
What restrictions are placed on the form that <u>work products</u> should or should not take based on their business purpose?

Sample business rule restricting a work product:
A contract over $100,000 for construction of a new vessel may be signed only if all the following are true:
- A feasibility study has been performed for the new vessel.
- The feasibility study includes all stress tests appropriate for that kind of vessel.
- Each stress test is completed and certified by a qualified engineer.

These days, interactions between people take place over an ever-growing number of active channels. Business rules are often needed to coordinate the business (not technical) aspects of interacting via such channels.

Pattern Question for Business Channels

Pattern Question BO5:
Business Channels
What restrictions are placed on the business aspect of interacting through <u>specific channels</u>?

Sample business rule involving a business channel:
An opt-in choice covering promotional offers must be made available to every registered member of the company's web-site.

Sample business rule involving a business channel:
A promotional offer may be sent only to registered members of the company's web-site who opt-in.

Interactions over-time or at-a-distance require infrastructure (e.g., the internet). Designing how such infrastructure is best used (e.g., based on GUIs and use cases), should be addressed as part of the **system model**, *not* the business model.

Business Rules about Business Geography

The key word in understanding business rules for business geography is *linkage*. By *linkage*, we mean *site-to-site* or *location-to-location* business linkage in the real world (not networks and nodes). Here, issues of transport and logistics play a central role.

Business sites of various kinds (e.g., bank branches, factories, warehouses, distribution centers, etc.) must be located correctly or optimally for their purpose.

Pattern Question for Business Location

Pattern Question BG1:
Business Location
What restrictions are placed on where business sites should or should not be <u>located</u>?

Sample business rule restricting business location:
A franchise must not be located within 5 miles of another franchise.

Appropriate transport and logistics must be established among the business sites.

Pattern Question for Business Transport

Pattern Question BG2:
Business Transport
What restrictions are placed on the <u>routing</u> of business-related travel or on the <u>physical movement</u> of business goods?

Sample business rule restricting business transport:
A truck carrying hazardous material must not be routed through a downtown street.

Business sites must be able to communicate effectively for business purposes at a distance.

Pattern Question for Business Communications

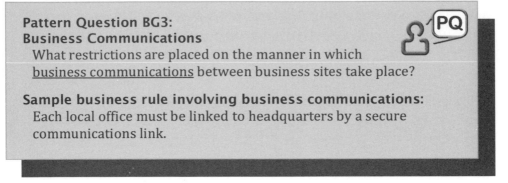

Pattern Question BG3:
Business Communications
   What restrictions are placed on the manner in which
   <u>business communications</u> between business sites take place?

Sample business rule involving business communications:
   Each local office must be linked to headquarters by a secure
   communications link.

Sometimes physical products or their movement require constraints on spatial configurations.

Pattern Question for Spatial Configurations

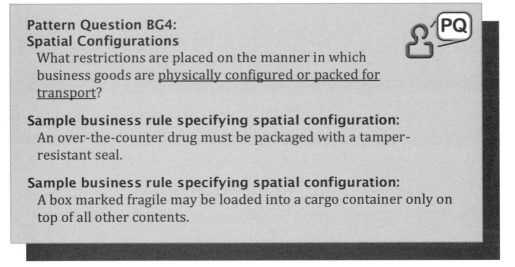

Pattern Question BG4:
Spatial Configurations
   What restrictions are placed on the manner in which
   business goods are <u>physically configured or packed for
   transport</u>?

Sample business rule specifying spatial configuration:
   An over-the-counter drug must be packaged with a tamper-
   resistant seal.

Sample business rule specifying spatial configuration:
   A box marked fragile may be loaded into a cargo container only on
   top of all other contents.

Enforcement Specifications for Behavioral Rules

Once you have created a working set of business rules for the business model, business questions regarding appropriate *enforcement* of each **behavioral rule** must be examined. *How strictly should each business rule be enforced? What message is appropriate when a violation occurs? What business response is needed?*

Addressing these enforcement questions intelligently is key to creating a highly agile business solution, one that can evolve rapidly in day-to-day operation.

As discussed in the previous Chapter, fundamental to business analysis with business rules is the assumption that violations of business rules can be detected so the business can react to the violations appropriately. If you can't detect violations, how can you run the business?!

 To say it differently, if you can't detect violations of a business rule, but you can still run the business, perhaps you don't need the business rule at all(!).

Three key questions about potential violations of each behavioral rule should be answered.

1. Enforcement Level

How strictly should the behavioral rule be enforced?

Example:

Business Rule: *A service representative must not be assigned to good customers in more than 3 states or provinces.*

Ask: *How strictly should this business rule be enforced?*

Enforcement Level: *Override by pre-authorized actor*

 Strictly enforced is assumed as the default enforcement level.

Enforcement Levels

The most obvious enforcement levels for behavioral rules are listed in Table 15-1. Don't overlook the last one in the table. A business rule that is actively evaluated, but not enforced, is (literally) a guideline. Guidelines are business rules too!

 Table 12-1 of *Business Rule Concepts*, 3rd Ed. (Chapter 12) discusses additional enforcement levels. It also provides tips for designing procedures where behavioral rules are involved (which is just about all of them!).

Table 15-1. Common Enforcement Levels for Behavioral Rules

Enforcement Level	Description
strictly enforced	*Violations are disallowed in all cases — achieving some new* **state** *successfully is always prevented.*
override by pre-authorized actor	*The behavioral rule is enforced, but an actor with proper before-the-fact authorization may override it.*
override with explanation	*The behavioral rule may be overridden simply by providing an explanation.*
guideline	*Suggested, but not enforced.*

2. Guidance Message

What message should be returned when a violation of the behavioral rule occurs?

When a behavioral rule is violated, somebody, often a business actor directly engaged in a business process, usually needs to know about it. The violation means the work being conducted has strayed outside the boundaries of what the business deems acceptable or desirable. From the business perspective some error has been made, so some error message should go to someone. What should that error message say?

As a default, we like to say that the business rule statement *is* the error message. From a business point of view, that equivalence must *always* be true — what else are business rules about?! For the *service-representative* business rule earlier, the appropriate message might therefore simply be *"A service representative must not be assigned to good customers in more than 3 states or provinces."*

 Rather than 'error message' (which sounds technical) or 'violation message' (which sounds harsh, especially for guidelines), we prefer *guidance message*.

Every guidance message should be as friendly and as helpful as possible. More explanation or suggestions can be appended or substituted as desired. Perhaps a link to other media (e.g., a how-to video) can be provided. Sometimes the best guidance message takes the form of some icon or signal (e.g., a warning light turning to yellow or red). In all cases, guidance messages should be made available *only* to people who are qualified and capable.

3. Violation Response

Does the appropriate violation response for the behavioral rule need to be more selective, rigorous, or comprehensive than simply a message?

Example:

Business Rule: *A cursory review of a received engineering design must be conducted within 5 business days from the date received.*

Ask: *What violation response is appropriate for this business rule?*

Violation Response: *The received engineering design must be brought to the attention of the manager of the department by the morning of the next business day.*

In general, a violation response can be one or more of some business processes, sanctions, operational business decisions, special notifications, etc.

 Some appropriate real-time violation response is critical in cases of potential fraud or malicious business behavior.

Table 15-2. Summary of Default Enforcement Specifications for Behavioral Rules

Enforcement Item	Default
enforcement level	*strictly enforced*
guidance message	*the business rule statement itself*
violation response	*none*

When Is Your Working Set of Business Rules 'Done'?

Assuming you have been diligent about creating the business model, your working set of business rules should now be well on its way to completion. At this stage in harvesting business rules you should have:

- Applied all pattern questions presented in previous Chapters.

- Analyzed each targeted operational business decision to develop appropriate decision logic.

- Examined business organization and business geography for required business rules (as discussed in this Chapter).

- Determined the appropriate enforcement level, guidance message, and violation response for each behavioral rule.

Still to be developed for the business solution are metrics and business requirements. As discussed in the next two Chapters, both will result in yet more business rules.

Summary

In finalizing a business model, several areas of completeness for your working set of business rules should be addressed. First, business rules relating to business organization (interactions), and business geography (linkages) should be captured. Second, three issues concerning the enforcement of each behavioral rule should be addressed: enforcement level, guidance message, and violation response. Addressing these enforcement concerns intelligently is central to achieving true **business agility**.

CHAPTER 16

Metrics

Measuring Business Performance

The final stage in creating a business model is identifying metrics, specifically **key performance indicators**. What things should you monitor and what's the best way to do so? What things are truly make-or-break in the day-to-day business operation of the future-form business capability? How can you tell whether the business solution is really successful once in operation?

Developing the right key performance indicators requires a solid understanding of what things are crucial for the on-going success of the future-form **business capability**. Such understanding comes straight from the **strategy** for the business solution (**Policy Charter**), in particular from **business goals** and **business policies**. Basing metrics on business goals and business policies permits you to demonstrate true **business alignment** *quantitatively*.

Potential metrics generally do not materialize out of thin air. Ideas for high-value key performance indicators will have inevitably surfaced during development of the business model.

Now is the time to collect those ideas, refine them, and pass them by the business leads for feedback, refinement, and sign-off. In the process, you are likely to harvest a substantial number of additional **business rules**.

Strategy-Based Performance Metrics

The most critical metrics for the future-form business capability focus on the strategy for the business solution (Policy Charter). They aim toward assessing the success (performance) of the strategy on a continuing basis. Strategy-based metrics fall into two categories: *goal-based* and *policy-based*.

Goal-Based Strategy Monitors

Goal monitors are metrics for determining whether business goals are being satisfied. At first glance, goal monitors often seem relatively straightforward. The devil is in the details. Capturing and specifying **practicable** business rules that support goal monitors often requires significant analysis. An example:

Business Goal: *To keep customers satisfied*

Ask: *How can we determine whether this business goal is being met?*

Table 16-1. Potential Goal Monitors and Related Business Questions for Developing Practicable Business Rules

Potential Goal Monitor	Related Business Questions for Developing Practicable Business Rules
No more than 10% attrition rate of customers per year.	*The manner in which the attrition rate is determined.*
At least 50% of customers placing more than one order in a six-month period.	*The manner in which the number of orders placed in a given period by a given customer is determined. Are rejected orders counted? Are cancelled orders counted? Are customers who haven't paid counted?*
At least 33% of customers providing at least one referral per year.	*The manner in which referrals are associated with customers. What constitutes a referral?*

Policy-Based Strategy Monitors

Policy monitors are metrics for determining whether the true business intent of a business policy is being satisfied. Here are some facts of life about actors in the everyday drama of business activity:

- Actors *will* modify their behavior to adjust to your business rules.

- Actors *will* come to know some of your business rules – including some you probably didn't want them to.

- Actors *will* see that some of your business rules could be exploited or subverted – and some actors will attempt to do so.

If the exploited or subverted business rules are based directly on business policies, *that can't be good!* Table 16-2 presents an example.

Table 16-2. Example of a Policy Monitor for the Business Capability
Order Fulfillment

Unacceptable Business Risk	*Orders $1,000 or over on credit without a credit check.*
Business Policy	*Orders on credit over $1000 should be credit checked.*
Potential Pattern of Subversion	*Instead of one order for $5,000, the bad guys might start putting in five orders for $999 each.*
Policy Monitor	*Number of defaults in the last 2 months on orders whose total amount is between $850 and $999.*
Related Business Questions for Developing Practicable Business Rules	*The manner in which the total number of defaults is determined based on time frame and order total amounts. What constitutes a default on an order?*

The policy monitor in this example keeps tabs on actor activity right at the threshold of business risk ($1,000). Other policy monitors might address changes in rates of compliance and changes in related patterns of actor behavior.

Unintended Effects Will Happen

A colleague of mine on the **BMM** standards team, John Hall, relates a humorous but telling example of thwarted business intent. (He tells the story much better.)

The buses in London *always* ran late. To improve on-time performance, someone had a bright idea for a new business policy. Why not give drivers a monetary incentive for on-time end-of-route arrivals? So that's exactly what they did.

In due course they conducted a survey to determine how well the new business policy was performing. What did they find? Not at all what they expected. To their dismay many bus drivers had simply stopped picking up passengers when running late! But on-time end-of-route arrivals? *You betcha!*

 Start off with a relatively modest set of well-focused key performance indicators. You want the business leads to gain a hands-on feel for 'driving' the new business capability. Upfront prototypes using existing data often prove quite useful for this purpose and cause little or no disruption in designing systems. Always remember though, the *right* metrics are more important than showy tools.

Performance Metrics for Business Processes

Discussion of metrics often focuses on **business processes**, rather than on strategy for the business solution (Policy Charter). Although metrics for the former can be important, we think metrics for the latter are generally much more so.

Nonetheless, you should consider carefully what key performance indicators you need for business processes. Your business model is not complete until you have done so. Aspects of business process models you might consider (factored as appropriate by time, location, role, worker, product variation, etc.):

- Throughput
- Average, maximum, and minimum elapsed time between completion of business tasks
- Queue volumes, bottlenecks, and resource load comparisons
- Percent of work following exception paths or requiring manual intervention
- Delays, wastage, and rate of product defects

When Are Metrics 'Done'?

Key performance indicators are really *never* done. Perception of business risks changes with time; modifications of business policies produce new patterns of business activity; customers become smarter (faster and faster) ... the list goes on. Inevitably, initial specifications for key performance indicators will evolve and new key performance indicators will emerge.

Basing deployment of key performance indicators on business rules enables rapid, continuing adaptation. And *meaningful* adaptation. As business rules, the key performance indicators will remain grounded in the structured business vocabulary (**fact model**). Without such grounding, metrics can quickly come to have literally *no* meaning whatsoever.

Summary

To finalize a business model, you need to develop appropriate metrics, called *key performance indicators*. These metrics can be based on the strategy for the business solution (Policy Charter) or on business process models. You'll probably want metrics based on both, but we believe the former are ultimately more important.

Business capabilities are complex. Once the business solution is deployed, key performance indicators allow managers to **see the elephant** going forward in day-to-day business operation.

CHAPTER 17

Understanding Business Requirements

Business Model vs. System Model

The **business model** you have created to express your business solution can be evaluated to produce many **business requirements**. These business requirements form the basis for designing a well-aligned system, one that best handles **business rules**.

The key word in understanding business requirements is
interpretation. You will interpret the business model to identify key
features for a **system model**. Work on developing business
requirements should not commence until the business model is
complete.

What Business Requirements Are About

Merriam-Webster Unabridged Dictionary [MWUD] defines
requirement as *something called for or demanded*. In the context of
business analysis, the business model you've created will *call for* or
demand certain abilities from the system model. Any such demand is
a *business requirement*.

Use of the term "business requirement" in this book is
always taken to mean "business requirement *for a system
model.*" We don't mean "requirements for doing business."
Be sure to clarify this point with business leads should any confusion
arise.

In our approach a business requirement is expressed in the form of an
ability statement. An ability statement identifies how some
aspect(s) of the business model should be supported within the yet-
to-be-designed system. In general, an ability statement serves as a
first-cut interpretation of some selected business model item(s) into
appropriate system features.

Ability statements are more or less equivalent to *functional
requirements* except that ability statements are *always*
interpreted from a business model.

Working directly from the business model to identify system features
dramatically reduces not only the number of design choices that
designers must make, but the time required to make the remaining
choices as well. *Asking the right questions in the right ways of the right
people at the right times doesn't slow you down; it speeds you up!*

Ability statements apply only to the automatable parts of a
business model. Non-automatable portions (including any
business rules) must be assessed and allocated as job
responsibilities and non-automated procedures.

What Business Requirements and Ability Statements Should Cover

Following the **Zachman Architecture Framework**, a complete system model should address the six areas *(basic engineering questions)* in Table 17-1. Table 17-1 also presents six *general ability statements* (GAS), which serve as guiding principles for developing business requirements. In addition, a system model should address *integration relationships*. In business analysis with business rules, integration relationships for the business model have been captured and expressed as business rules.

Table 17-1. The Six Basic Engineering Questions and Related General Ability Statements (GAS)

Basic Engineering Question	Key Descriptive Word	General Ability Statements (GAS)
what	structure	*Ability to record data and use that data to guide system behavior by evaluating the then-current business rules.*
how	transform	*Ability to execute processes and use those processes to create value-add according to the then-current business rules.*
where	geography	*Ability to address geographical or spatial distribution, and organize transport, logistics, and business communications, all according to the then-current business rules.*
who	interaction	*Ability to interact with users and support those users in achieving desired behavior, as permitted and guided by the then-current business rules.*
when	time	*Ability to orchestrate business milestones and schedule execution of processes, all according to the then-current business rules.*
why	motivation	*Ability to demonstrate that business goals are being met, that business risks are being mitigated, and that the then-current business rules are achieving the desired business ends.*

Note the all-important modifier *the then current* before 'business rules' in the description for each of the six general ability statements in Table 17-1. A key goal in business analysis with business rules is support for continuous change to business rules, the key to **business agility**.

What vs. How

In Table 17-1, the basic engineering questions *what* and *how* are indicated as peers, each addressing a distinct area of the system model. Many IT professionals, however, characterize 'requirements' as the *what,* and the design for a system as the *how*. Contradiction? *No, just a bit of confusion over perspective.*

- From the perspective of designing a system, both *what* (data) and *how* (processes) must be addressed. Both question words (as well as the other four) are essential for engineering a complete, robust solution.

- From the perspective of IT methodologies, requirements are always incomplete, so *what* the requirements say must be transformed into a system model that indicates *how* the requirements will be supported.

In other words, the former use of *what* and *how* is based on an engineering point of view; the latter use is based on an IT-methodology point of view. Don't confuse business people or IT professionals — *or yourself* — by failing to make the distinction.

 If you follow the approach described in this book, your business requirements will inherently satisfy *both* uses of *what* and *how*.

The vocabulary of system models naturally diverges from the vocabulary of business models, as indicated at a high level in Table 17-2. We also start talking about *system rules* rather than business rules.

Always remember that the representation of something in a system model is *not* the same as the something in the real world. For example, what you know about an employee represented as data is not the same as the flesh-and-blood person in the real world. Don't confuse business people or IT professionals — *or yourself* — by failing to make this important distinction. **Business people talk about real-world things!**

Table 17-2. Vocabulary for Business Models vs. System Models

Basic Engineering Question	Business Model *Instead of ...*	System Model *We talk about ...*
what	business vocabulary (**fact model**)	data model and/or class diagram
how	**business processes**	system processes
where	business geography	system nodes and links
who	business organization	use cases and GUIs
when	business events (**business milestones**)	system events and states
why	business strategy (**Policy Charter**)	optimization-of-business models

 By '*system* process' we mean a process that is computationally viable but still platform-independent.

Requirements are Rules: *True or False?*

"Requirements are rules." Perhaps you've heard the argument. Maybe you've even made it yourself. Are they? *No!* Basic reasons why requirements are not rules:

Business people don't naturally think of a 'requirement' as a 'rule'. To ensure the best possible communication with business people, use of 'rule' should remain consistent with the real-world understanding of 'rule'. Say 'rule' to business people and they will naturally think "guide for conduct or action" or "criteria for making judgments or business decisions." If a business person says 'rule' he/she almost certainly means a rule for the business (e.g., no shirt, no service), *not* 'requirement for a software system'.

Many 'requirements' never become rules. The "no shirt, no service" rule doesn't happen to be automatable (at least easily). Many other rules of the business are — e.g., *no credit card, no sale.* When interpreted into an implementation form, the business rules ideally should still be recognizable as a form of rule. The same cannot be said, however, for other aspects of a business model — say, processes. In designing a business process for implementation, why would you ever say, "Now it represents rules."?!

Rules are rules, processes are processes, locations are locations, people are people. Each can be cast into some design-level counterpart (e.g., GUIs can substitute for face-to-face communication between people.) Nonetheless, each retains some sense or reflection of what it was originally (or should anyway). Looking at operational business design any other way inevitably leads to a break-down in communication and needless complexity.

Avoid confusing business people or IT professionals — *or yourself* — by calling requirements 'rules'. *Requirements are not rules!*

But Are Business Rules 'Requirements'??

Clearly, requirements are not rules. What about the reverse question? Can it be helpful to think of business rules *as requirements*?

To answer it's essential to keep in mind what business rules are about. In plain English, business rules are about guiding and shaping day-to-day operations *of the business*. Business people would need business rules to operate the business even if there were no systems. The business rules just are what they are. And if well-specified, they essentially *speak for themselves*.

All the following, though, are certainly true about business rules:

- They should arise from, or at least be approved by, business people.

- They should be considered very carefully in designing a system.

- They should be automated whenever possible.

All said and done, whether business rules are a form of requirement is really a judgment call. The best answer is whichever is likely to prove most productive in your work.

When Are Business Requirements 'Done'?

Your work on business requirements is done when ability statements have addressed all parts of the business model to be automated. The level of detail for different sets of ability statements, however, can vary. Much depends on good lines of communication among business leads, Business Analysts, and IT staff. Familiarity of the IT staff with business rules can also make a big difference.

We think of ability statements as a contract between Business Analysts and system designers. In writing contracts you generally hope for the best, but prepare for the worst.

Worst case. Communication between Business Analysts and system designers is tenuous. Poor communication frequently results from geographical separation, language barriers, or business disconnects (e.g., as often is the case in outsourcing). It can also result from IT developers not being given clear direction (or decent requirements). Not infrequently the business leads themselves seem to want the IT staff to do their business thinking for them. (So the IT staff does, *in code.*) Sometimes everybody just seems to want a miracle happen — a perfect running system before the business problem is fully understood and a business solution worked out. To top it all out is the issue of learning curves.

Best case. Communication between Business Analysts and system designers is excellent. Both are dedicated to achieving the best results for the business. Effective project management is in place. There's no significant learning curve. Ample patience and trust is evident on all sides.

You know your circumstances best. In the worst case, your ability statements may need to cross every 't' and dot every 'i'. In the best case, you can probably just let much of the business model and many or all of the business rules 'speak for themselves'. *You* need to determine the best answer in your own situation.

Summary

Business requirements arise directly from review and analysis of a business model. Indeed, 'business requirements' merit the modifier 'business' *only* in such case. Why would requirements for designing a system of any other origin deserve to be characterized that way?!

We express business requirements as ability statements. How extensive and detailed these statements become depends as much on the relationship among Business Analysts and system developers as on technical concerns. Ability statements are simply about letting system designers **see the elephant** too. Then the designers are good to go for use cases.

CHAPTER 18

Developing Business Requirements

Ability Statements

To recap: After establishing a **ballpark view** of architectural scope, the first step in creating a **business model** is the strategy for the business solution (**Policy Charter**). The Policy Charter provides a fundamental answer to the business engineering question *why*. Then the other five **business engineering questions** are addressed: *what, how, where, who,* and *when.* Appropriate **business rules** are developed along the way.

205

This Chapter explains how to interpret **ability statements** from these last five business engineering questions and from related business rules. In discussing the five questions we'll follow a sequence convenient for the discussion, starting with *how*.

 Manage your ability statements within a unified list so as to avoid duplication and overlap. Try never to write an ability statement more than once!

 For clarity and consistency we deliberately start every ability statement with the phrase *"Ability to ...."*

Ability Statements from the Basic Engineering Question *How*

Business process models should include documentation for each **business task**. As illustrated in Table 18-1, this documentation can often be analyzed to produce ability statements.

Table 18-1. Documentation for the Business Task *Enter Hours Worked*

Task No. & Name	310 - Enter Hours Worked	Ability Statement
BUSINESS ROLE	Employee	—
INPUTS	Hours Worked Project Name	—
OUTPUT	Hours Worked Allocated by Project	—
DESCRIPTION	An employee can: 1. Clock-in and clock-out. 2. Enter hours through a website offsite. 3. Enter hours through a smart phone. 4. Manually record hours on a timesheet.	 *1. Ability to collect time from clock-in, clock-out.* *2. Ability to enter hours through a website. (Note: Security must be provided for any employee using a client computer.)* *3. Ability to enter hours using any smart phone.* —

Scenario #4 in the description of the business task is manual, so that scenario requires no ability statement.

Discussion of business tasks to create ability statements often results in additional business rules. For example:

Business Rule: *The total number of hours worked by an employee during a 24-hour period must not exceed 18 consecutive hours.*

Business Rule: *The total number of hours worked by a salaried employee in Salt Lake City must not exceed 40 hours a week.*

Business Rule: *The total number of hours worked by a salaried employee in Minneapolis must not exceed 50 hours a week.*

Additional ability statements in turn might be interpreted from these new business rules. Examples:

Ability Statement: *Ability to accumulate hours worked during a continuous period, even if the hours are entered in different 'chunks' at different locations at different times.* (Note: The system needs the ability to determine that the hours are nonetheless continuous.)

Ability Statement: *Ability to accumulate hours worked in a week and in a city.*

Ability Statements from the Basic Engineering Question *Who*

A business model often addresses interactions among people playing various roles in day-to-day business operations. Restrictions may be placed on which people can play what roles, how different roles should or should not interact, and how business interactions should or should not take place over active channels (e.g., connections via the internet).

In addition, the business model often identifies work products needed to support business interactions (e.g., notifications, requests, sign-offs, analyses, position papers, legal agreements, licenses, certifications, service level agreements, etc.). Restrictions may be placed on what form these work products should or should not take.

If some part of your business model addresses any of these concerns, you should identify and review related business rules, then create appropriate ability statements from them. An example:

Business Rule: *A supervisor must complete and sign a standard evaluation checklist within 3 business days for each applicant interviewed for a job position.*

Ability Statement: *Ability to support the completion of standard evaluation checklists.*

Ability Statement: *Ability to capture electronic signatures for completed evaluation checklists.*

Ability Statement: *Ability to identify applicants interviewed but not evaluated for more than three business days.*

This last ability statement detects violations of the business rule. The appropriate business reaction for violations should not be specified as an ability statement, but rather as a **violation response**. Example:

Violation Response: *A reminder must be sent to the supervisor.*

The violation response might in turn produce:

Ability Statement: *The ability to insert a to-do entry in a work queue visible on the supervisor's home page.*

Ability statements also should be developed covering use of system features based on business roles and related skill levels. Such ability statements provide a business basis for setting up 'users' with appropriate authorizations, creating GUIs (graphical user interfaces), and more.

 In creating a business model, we **never say user**. There are users only once a *system* is being developed. (Anyway, these days everybody is a user of *some* system!)

To illustrate let's revisit the description of the business task *Enter hours worked* specified for the business role *employee* (presented earlier in Table 18-1). How will workers filling this role use the system? Aspects to explore:

Level of Technical Ability. Each human interface should be based on the level or range of technical skill and experience anticipated for the business role. For example, Table 18-1 includes multiple ability statements probably based in part on the range of technical abilities evident across employees.

Suitable Work Products. Interactions between business roles require appropriate work products. For example, a manager should be able to track the hours worked for each person in his/her area in various ways. For example:

> Ability Statement: *Ability to display total hours worked by employee or by project for any suitable timeframe including the current week and the current month.*

Request Criteria. What are the relevant request and/or search criteria for each work product? For example:

> Ability Statement: *Ability to support requests for hours worked by project, by timeframe, by worker, or by any combination thereof.*

Authorization. Delineate who is permitted to access or do what, and identify appropriate measures to ensure security. For example:

> Ability Statement: *Ability to support creation and replacement of passwords and to require passwords for all access.*

As always, development of ability statements may lead to new business rules, and in turn to additional ability statements. An example:

> Business Rule: *An employee must change his/her password every 3 months.*

> Ability Statement: *Ability to determine when an employee has not changed a password for 3 months and remind him/her.*

Presentation. Specify required or optimal display formats. For example:

> Business Rule: *Service providers must be listed in order of preference for a service request.*

 Restrictions on work products to ensure correct or optimal support of *business* interactions qualify as business rules rather than system rules.

> Ability Statement: *Ability to capture order of preference and apply it in listing service providers.*

Presentation issues include:

- Consistent placement or appearance of the company's logo, letterhead, etc.

- Deference to cultural sensitivities (e.g., use of certain colors).

- Personal or group preferences. For example:

    Business Rule: *The project name and client's logo must be displayed on the top right corner of every engineering work product.*

 If a 'formatting' rule has direct business motivation, it qualifies as a business rule rather than a system rule. The motivation of this business rule, for example, may pertain to professionalism and customer-orientation.

    Ability Statement: *Ability to associate a project with the client's logo.*

    Ability Statement: *Ability to display the project name and client's logo as currently directed.*

Usability. The usability of a system entails both convenience for the person fulfilling a business role (user friendliness) and adequacy for business purpose. For example, when employees are at a client's site, reporting hours worked should be fast and easy. They shouldn't have to spend time on work-arounds or toggling between systems.

Discussion of usability often leads to additional business rules. For example, sometimes it might not be practical to report time on an as-you-go or daily basis:

    Business Rule: *An employee's time reporting for a work week must be completed by the end of the next business day after the end of the work week.*

The business milestone *completed* might involve satisfying other business rules about gaps, overlaps, or how the numbers add up. To ensure usability, the application of such business rules should be *deferred* according to the timing criteria specified by the business rule above:

    Ability Statement: *The ability to defer the application of certain business rules until a specified point in time.*

Deferred application of **behavioral rules** is an **enforcement level**. A suitable violation response might be a reminder to the employee to fix problems found during the delayed application of the business rules.

Ability Statements from Analysis of Business Rule Enforcement

Fundamental to business analysis with business rules is the assumption that violations of business rules can be detected so that you can react to them appropriately. As discussed in Chapter 15, an important step in finalizing a business model and interpreting business rules into business requirements is elaborating three key items concerning violations of each **behavioral rule**.

Enforcement Level. How strictly should a behavioral rule be enforced? An example:

> Behavioral Rule: *A service representative must not be assigned to good customers in more than 3 states or provinces.*

> Ask: *How strictly should this behavioral rule be enforced?*

> Enforcement Level: *Strictly enforced. No exceptions or overrides permitted.*

An appropriate ability statement for the behavioral rule at this enforcement level:

> Ability Statement: *Ability to strictly enforce this behavioral rule.*

Guidance Message. What violation or error message should be returned to the business person (or somebody else) when a violation of the behavioral rule occurs?

> Ability Statement: *Ability to provide the business rule statement and/or other text or material as an error message when the behavioral rule is violated.*

Violation Response. Besides enforcing a behavioral rule and providing a guidance message (if appropriate), some additional response is often useful or advisable. For the behavioral rule above, for example, perhaps a manager should receive notice of violations as an indication that staff is stretched thin:

Violation Response: *Notify the department manager by urgent email of each violation and the related circumstances (requestor, service representative, states or provinces, date/time, company, etc.).*

A violation response can mention use of infrastructure (e.g., email) so long as it doesn't get into the design of that infrastructure.

This company clearly considers service representation important. Often the department manager wants to follow up immediately by reviewing the customer's profile and history. The violation response might consequently lead to:

Ability Statement: *Ability to quick-link to the customer's profile and history with automatic sign-on.*

This example highlights the importance of having tool support for readily associating business rules and ability statements.

Let's examine a violation response for another behavioral rule:

Behavioral Rule: *A cursory review of a received engineering design must be conducted within 5 business days from the date received.*

Ask: *What violation response is appropriate for this behavioral rule?*

Violation Response: *The received engineering design must be brought to the attention of the manager of the department by the morning of the next business day.*

In developing business requirements, this violation response might lead to:

Ability Statement: *Ability to automatically identify engineering designs for which no cursory review has been performed within 5 days and report on them to the appropriate manager each morning of the next business day.*

This ability statement merely echoes the business rule statement and violation response. As you become more experienced with business rules, you'll find you can often just let a business rule specification 'speak for itself' — no additional ability statement needed.

Ability Statements from the Basic Engineering Question *Where*

A business model often addresses the geography of day-to-day business operations and the linkages between business sites of activity. Sometimes it addresses spatial configurations for business products (e.g., business rules for packing boxes or crates).

Business sites of various kinds (e.g., bank branches, factories, warehouses, distribution centers, etc.) must be located in the correct or optimal location for their purpose. Appropriate transport and logistics must be established among the business sites. The business sites must also be able to communicate at a distance.

If any part of your business model addresses these concerns, you should identify and review related business rules, then create appropriate ability statements from them. An example:

> Business Rule: *A truck carrying hazardous material must not be routed through a downtown street.*

> Ability Statement: *Ability to provide routing for trucks.*

> Ability Statement: *Ability to identify the type of material a truck carries.*

> Ability Statement: *Ability to identify downtown areas.*

> Ability Statement: *Ability to provide special routing for trucks carrying hazardous materials.*

 Inspect the strategy for the business solution (Policy Charter) for any **business risks** or **business policies** involving the reliability, security or availability of inter-site communications. Such business risks and business policies can provide a starting point for system designers in developing 'non-functional requirements'.

Ability Statements from the Basic Engineering Question *When*

Figure 18-1 presents an informal model of **business milestones**. Each model of business milestones for some business thing should be inspected to determine what **states** need to be represented in the **system model**.

Since business milestones are represented by unary facts in models of business milestones, the issue really concerns how the system model handles unary fact types. Alternatives include Booleans and type codes. If the latter is chosen, valid type code values should be specified. In either case, coordination with the data model is required.

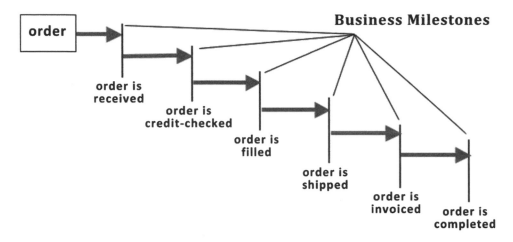

Figure 18-1. Informal Business Milestone Model for Orders

In system models, achievement of states can occur in either of two ways:

1. ***Automatically.*** Sometimes, if all the criteria a state must satisfy are met (as specified by some business rule(s)), the system can be tasked with asserting the state automatically. An example:

   Business Rule: *An order must be considered completed if invoiced and paid in full.*

   Ability Statement: *Ability to calculate how much has been paid for an order.*

   Ability Statement: *Ability to automatically indicate an order as completed if invoiced and paid in full.*

2. ***Manually.*** Often, the assertion of a state will be manual rather than automatic. In such case, the system model must provide the ability for users to assert the state themselves. In addition the system model should *prevent* users from asserting the state successfully unless all business rules relevant for that state have been satisfied. (The system must be designed to 'know' which business rules these are.) An example:

> Business Rule: *A rejected order must not be credit-checked.*
>
> Ability Statement: *Ability to support users indicating that an order has been rejected.*
>
> Ability Statement: *Ability to identify and evaluate all business rules relevant to indicating an order is rejected.*
>
> Ability Statement: *Ability to exclude rejected orders when a batch of orders is sent to the credit bureau for credit check.*

Whether automatic or manual, any system model resulting from business analysis with business rules must provide coordination for all states with respect to business rules.

 At issue is not what can be automated. A system can automate just about anything you can specify. The real issue is about the *quality* of what you specify.

Ability Statements from the Basic Engineering Question *What*

The structured business vocabulary (**fact model**) should be inspected to determine what data or class structures are required. In general, any system model resulting from business analysis with business rules must support all elements of a fact model:

- Each **term** designating a general concept.

- Each **term** designating an instance.

- Each **category**.

- Each **categorization scheme**.

- Each **fact type**.

- Each **property**.

- Each **whole-part (partitive) structure**.

Remember that details of the fact model are never created arbitrarily. The fact model is a carefully-crafted structural blueprint of basic operational business **know-how**. Deviations from the fact model by the system model can haunt the business for many years to come.

Many ability statements can be based on business rules harvested by **pattern questions** using the fact model. (Refer to Chapter 9.) Examples are given in Table 18-2. Refer to Figure 18-2 for the underlying fact model.

Table 18-2. Examples of Ability Statements Interpreted from Business Rules Captured Using Pattern Questions Based on a Fact Model

Business Rule	Ability Statement
1. A book must not be both fiction and non-fiction.	1. Ability to restrict categories of a concept. (Note: Allow entering only one category for each book.) 2. Ability to default to 'fiction'.
2. A borrower must not hold more than three active library cards simultaneously.	3. Ability to determine if a library card is active on a given date. 4. Ability to detect the number of active library cards per borrower. 5. Ability to disallow more than 3 active library cards per borrower.
3. A library card may be used to check-out a book only if the book is owned by a library for which the card is authorized. Guidance Message: *We're sorry, you can't check out this book because your library card is not authorized for the library that owns this book. Please get your library card authorized by that library, then try again.*	6. Ability to determine which library owns a book, to determine which library authorizes a library card, and to record which library card is used to check-out a book. 7. Ability to disallow using a library card to check out a book owned by a library for which the library card is not authorized. 8. Ability to display the more friendly guidance message (given at left).

 The second business rule in Table 18-2 mentions *active* library cards. Additional business rules probably specify whether a library card can be considered active. Ability statement #3 could easily arise for those other business rules too. Avoid redundancy. Remember to maintain a consolidated list of ability statements.

 As discussed in Chapter 15, the default 'error message' when a behavioral rule is violated is the business rule statement itself. The guidance message for the third business rule illustrates an alternative, friendlier message.

Underlying the individual ability statements in Table 18-2 is the assumption that a system can 'remember' things that happen. That's what databases do after all. Ability statement #6 in Table 18-2 could therefore simply be assumed (i.e., does not really need to be expressed).

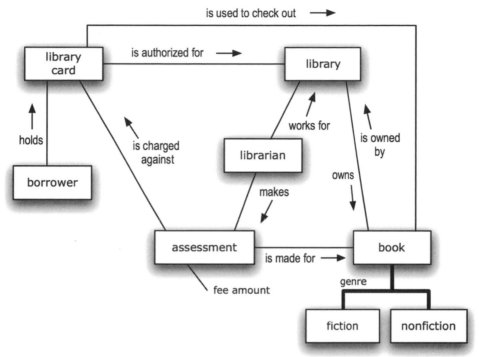

Figure 18-2. Fact Model for a Library

A fact model developed as part of a business model sometimes proves deficient with respect to 'remembering' (i.e., retaining history). Often a more complete history for business things within scope is needed in the system model (data model) to support all business rules and business processes. Special care should be taken to scrutinize the completeness of the fact model carefully in this regard.

 Inspect the strategy for the business solution (Policy Charter) for any business risks or business policies involving the availability or recoverability of retained history (data). Such business risks and business policies can provide a starting point for system designers in developing 'non-functional requirements'.

Business Rule vs. System Rule: *Data Rules*

Business rules are always independent of whatever system model is created. System rules are not. Many system rules, for example, depend on the form in which data about the real world is received. System rules like these are *data rules*.

Data rules can be quite numerous, so distinguish them carefully from business rules.

For example, when we give lectures we often raffle off free copies of our books. We list some business rules for the purpose, one of which (for fairness) is the following.

> Business Rule: *An attendee of a presentation may enter the book raffle for the presentation only once*.

Simple enough. But consider our 'data-receiving system'. We simply pass around the hat for business cards. If an attendee doesn't have a business card (seems many people don't these days), the attendee can write his/her name, company affiliation, and email address on a slip of paper. As a result we receive data that varies widely in format, completeness and legibility. To manage this variability we need data rules, for example:

> Data Rule: *Two or more entries must be considered as being from the same presentation attendee if all the following are true:*
> - *The entries have the same last name.*
> - *One or more entries have a full first name.*
> - *One or more entries have an initialized first name, but the initializing letter is the same as the first letter of the full first name.*
> - *One or more email addresses for any entry is/are illegible or missing.*

> Data Rule: *Two or more entries must be considered as being from the same presentation attendee if all the following are true:*
> - *The company affiliations are the same.*
> - *The first names are the same.*
> - *The first three letters of the last name are the same.*
> - *One or more letters of the last name for any entry is/are illegible.*
> - *One or more email addresses for any entry is/are illegible or missing.*

Data rules like these often arise simply because complete data is not always available as needed. The number of such data rules, even for a single business rule (as above), can sometimes prove quite large.

In eCommerce we essentially become ePersons. For companies in the eCommerce space, establishing consistent identity for ePersons is definitely a *business* concern, not a system ('data receiving') concern.

Summary

Business requirements for a system model are expressed in the form of ability statements. Ability statements are interpreted directly from analysis of each of the five business engineering questions *what, how, where, who,* and *when*, and from related business rules.

Often the process is iterative. An ability statement suggests some additional business rule(s), then these business rules suggest more ability statements. What's important is that every ability statement traces back to specific aspect(s) of the business model. This traceability ensures the system model aligns faithfully with the business solution. It also accelerates development of the system model itself — the tough business questions have already been answered(!).

CHAPTER 19

Smart Systems

Ability Statements
for Know-How

Smart systems arise from smart business analysis, *not* smart platforms. Business Analysts need breakthrough techniques for organizing business **know-how** from top to bottom.

This Chapter explains the basis for designing **business operation systems** that can support continuous change to business rules *after* deployment. Development of new decision logic can take place in manageable, non-disruptive increments. Armed with these potent techniques, Business Analysts can now take the lead in the quest for **business agility**.

Ability Statements from Decision Analysis

A **decision task** can be performed either manually (i.e., by humans) or by automatic evaluation of encoded **decision logic**. Decision tasks based on encoded decision logic need an ability statement with three simple parts:

1. What **cases** are covered.

2. What kind of **outcome** is no longer manual for these cases.

3. What decision logic should be applied in determining these outcomes.

For example, Chapter 12 discussed decision logic for the decision task *Determine eligibility for insurance.* Consequently, the following ability statement is needed:

> Ability Statement: *Ability to (1) Select cases for auto insurance in the USA under $1 million; (2) Assert yes/no for the output 'eligibility decision'; and (3) Evaluate the decision logic "Is an applicant eligible for insurance?".*

Incremental Design

With business rules, support for **incremental design** is straightforward. A decision task might start off manual (performed by humans). The system simply provides a field in the GUI for a worker to enter an outcome for the given operational business decision. For applicants for auto insurance, the outcome might be codes for 'eligible' or 'ineligible'. For other operational business decisions, it might be the name or id of the service representative assigned to a customer, the dollar amount of a discount, etc.

As time and resources permit, **decision rules** for handling the simplest cases can be captured and encoded. The system can evaluate the decision logic and automatically decide the applicant's eligibility (or make the assignment, or decide the discount, etc.). For these cases, the worker no longer provides the outcome — the system asserts it automatically.

As new decision rules are identified, more and more cases can be handled automatically. Perhaps you start with a modest 20% of all cases, the easiest ones. As time goes by you ramp up to 50%, then perhaps 80%. At each step along the way, the operational business decision becomes less and less manual (i.e., fewer cases decided by humans) and more and more automated (i.e., more cases decided by the system). Also at each step along the way, workers can devote more time to 'problem' cases.

You may never actually get to a full 100%. *Nobody is talking about taking humans out of the loop for every operational business decision.* You simply want to use your human resources where best suited, the especially hard or rare cases.

Ability Statements from Analysis of Flash Points

Chapter 14 discussed **flash points** for the following business rule statement. Relevant terms and wordings are given in Figure 19-1.

Business Rule: *A customer must be assigned to an agent if the customer has placed an order.*

Figure 19-1. Terms and Wordings for the Agent-Assignment Business Rule

The flash points identified for this business rule:

- "*When* a customer places an order ...."
- "*When* an agent leaves our company ...."

For each **behavioral rule**, you need an ability statement (a *flash-point ability statement*) for each associated flash point. For the agent-assignment business rule above:

Ability Statement: *The ability to detect when a customer places an order.*

Ability Statement: *The ability to detect when an agent leaves the company.*

The same flash point is often associated with multiple business rules. For example, a great many business rules could pertain to a customer placing an order. In general, the relationship of flash points and business rules is many-to-many.

Flash Points and Use Cases

Each flash point for a behavioral rule is an **event** that also potentially initiates a use case. It's essential that the designer of that use case know all the behavioral rules with that event as a flash point. Any given use case is very likely to touch on other flash points as well. The designer of the use case needs to know about those too.

Overall, organizing work on use cases can be greatly facilitated by creating and maintaining a consolidated list of flash points. Each flash point in the list should be related to all the behavioral rules it involves (and vice versa). This is an area where a **general rulebook system (GRBS)** could be of great assistance.

The resolution of flash points can become quite fine-grained. For the agent-assignment business rule above:

Ability Statement: *The ability to detect when a customer places an order, but does not have an assigned agent.*

Ability Statement: *The ability to detect when an agent leaves the company, and that agent is assigned to a customer, and that customer has placed at least one order.*

How fine-grained you take the resolution of flash points is a judgment call based on level of experience, tool support, and most importantly, what works best for the approach being used to create the system model.

Since (presumably) assigning agents is currently manual, an additional ability statement is probably needed:

Ability Statement: *The ability to manually assign an agent to a customer.*

For clarity you might instead prefer two ability statements, each specific to a flash point.

Two ability statements are recommended if best business practices differ substantially when first assigning an agent vs. when replacing an existing agent.

Usability should be a consideration (as always) in developing ability statements. In this example, you might want ability statements to assign a *group* of companies to an agent or to *reassign* agents to different companies. You might also want an ability statement to reassign agents *automatically,* based on who currently has the lightest workloads.

Decision analysis could be useful here. There are two apparent **operational business decisions**: (1) *Is the current workload for agents unbalanced?* (2) *Which agent should a customer be reassigned to?* The second question is relevance-dependent on the first. Refer to Chapters 12 and 13.

Decision Logic Based on Flash Points

Sooner or later the business probably *will* want agents selected and assigned to customers automatically when the agent-assignment business rule is violated. The appropriate **decision rules** might be based on the customer's volume of business, typical purchase profile, product expertise of the agent, geographical location, etc.

What new is required? Besides the new decision rules, *not much at all*. The system model should already provide support for the two flash-point ability statements from earlier. The only two changes required:

- The new decision logic is specified as the violation response for the agent-assignment business rule.

- The assigned-agent field or link is changed from manual to automatic.

Business rules support really smart systems!

Summary

Smart system models feature incremental design for business operation systems in a very straightforward way. Decision logic can be developed and deployed stage-by-stage, working comfortably but deliberately as time and resources permit.

Flash-point analysis is business-rule-centric. It's just common sense. Yet it is not featured in *any* traditional IT methodology. Once you really get that point, you can begin to see why legacy systems so often produce such inconsistent results. **See the elephant!**

CHAPTER 20

Rulebook Management

Now the Life Cycle of Business Rules Begins

At this point business rules and **business requirements** (ability statements) move off in very different directions. The **ability statements** bridge you into designing a system, then implementing, testing and deploying it. The usefulness of ability statements essentially ends with deployment (if not well before).

For business rules, deployment is just the beginning of life. A central goal of business analysis with business rules is to establish a

rulebook for the **business capability**. This rulebook is the touchstone for true **business agility**. It will play a central role in enabling continuous change in business practices once the business capability is operational.

 You also need **rulebook management** for business analysis. Organizing significant numbers of **business rules**, and coordinating them with a structured business vocabulary (**fact model**), is not trivial. Don't waste time you should be spending on other matters.

Why Rulebook Management

Every Business Analyst should fully understand the need for rulebook management. The basic rationale is explained in the following set of questions and answers. We've asked these questions of a great many audiences and clients worldwide, so we're fairly confident about the answers. Ask yourself these questions about *your* business.

How many business rules does your organization have?

After a bit of reflection, the answers inevitably come into the 1000s, and frequently (and probably more accurately) into the 10,000s. If you think your company has only dozens or 100s of business rules, read no further. We're almost certain you're wrong, but you need not go on. The problem we're talking about is one of *scale*.

Do you know where your business rules are today?

Almost everyone says *no* to this question. Or given a little more time to ponder it, they say their business rules are actually *everywhere* (i.e., not **single-sourced**). The business rules are buried in legacy code, in documentation, in help screens, in procedure manuals, in agreements, just in people's heads (scary) — *everywhere in general and nowhere in particular.* How can you effectively make changes in business operations like that?!

What percentage of your business rules change relatively fast?

The good news is that not all your business rules actually do. Across many industries, we've consistently found the answer to be 30-45%.

Some of those business rules, though, change *really* fast. And almost all of them change faster than two or three official software releases per year(!).

How long does it take you to change a business rule the first time?

The time needed for business managers and Business Analysts to adequately assess the business impact of changing a business rule (or a set of business rules) can range anywhere from mere seconds to days or weeks. Typically the answer is hours or days. *If only assessing business impact was all there was to it!*

Remember that your business rules today are everywhere in general and nowhere in particular (not single-sourced). So that means you first have to track down the existing business rule(s), which can often take weeks or sometimes months. For any given business rule, there are probably multiple versions currently 'out there', some likely deep in legacy code. That means taking time to reverse-engineer the business rules and trying to discern their original intent. That's hard! Then after that you need to reconcile the multiple versions.

All that work has to be done *before* you can even begin to assess business impact. Companies today are paying a huge price in lowered productivity (and elevated drudgery) all the time, day in and day out. It's so big a price that many organizations don't even recognize they're paying it. (But service providers sure know!) First you have to **see the elephant**.

How long does it take you to change a business rule each time after the first time?

Here the news gets worse. Once you've gone through all that work the first time, what then happens to the understanding you've gained about where the business rules are and what they mean? *It evaporates into thin air.* And what happens to what you know about who made the call to change the business rule and why they did it? *Ditto.*

So the *next* time the same business rule changes, back you go, starting at square one to track-down all the particulars yet again. And so on, *each time the business rule changes.* We're letting this **corporate memory** disappear right in front of our very eyes.

Best Practices for Rulebook Management

Some basic best practices for rulebook management:

Best Practice for Rulebook Management #1: *Express Business Rules for Business People*

> Write your business rules in structured English (**RuleSpeak**) and organize the ones you can into **decision tables** so business people can understand them.

Best Practice for Rulebook Management #2: *It All Starts with Business Vocabulary*

> Base your representations of business rules on a structured business vocabulary (**fact model**) rather than on IT artifacts such as business object models (BOMs), class diagrams, or data models.

Best Practice for Rulebook Management #3: *It's Not about Software Requirements*

> Put your rulebook and related business vocabulary at the fingertips of business people and Business Analysts; don't bury them in repositories for software requirements. For business-oriented rulebook management you need a **general rulebook system** (GRBS). Repositories for software requirements and GRBS are *not the same!*

Best Practice for Rulebook Management #4: *The Pay-Off is Traceability*

> Provide meaningful traceability for business rules. Where do business rules originally come from? Contracts, agreements, deals, business policies, regulations, laws, licenses, certifications, service level agreements, etc. Traceability for business rules and traceability for software requirements are also simply *not the same!* Rulebook management is about corporate memory, not IT memory.

Best Practice for Rulebook Management #5: *Retaining Know-How is a No-Cost Extra*

> Understand that **rulebook management** and **know-how retention** *are* the same thing.

Best Practice for Rulebook Management #6: *Avoid Attempting the Enterprise Thing*

> Don't start with rulebook management at the enterprise level. There's no need to. Start with one business capability (or one project or one business process or one operational business decision) at a time. Show success. Get the feel of it. Show what can be done. Then go from there. The initial results might not be perfect (i.e., completely re-usable on an enterprise scale), but simple credibility ultimately counts for much more.

When Is Rulebook Management 'Done'?

Never.

Summary

When you express business rules, you are in the realm of **semantics**. When you express things *about* business rules, you are in the realm of rulebook management. A rulebook supports traceability for business rules, not software requirements, and provides a means to retain the related corporate memory.

Is there any alternative to rulebook management? We don't see one. Our world is fast-changing, highly-regulated, and know-how-intensive. It's rapidly becoming more and more so. Business rules need to be managed directly as a business proposition — *of, by, and for* business people and Business Analysts.

Once you see this big picture, things become clear. You realize the problem is actually a relatively simple one. The same is true for its solution, a general rulebook system (GRBS). Only the scale of the problem makes it seem hard. So stand back and take a long, hard look. **See the elephant!**

Annotated Glossary

Reference Sources	
[BMM]	*The Business Motivation Model (BMM) ~ Business Governance in a Volatile World.* [May 2010]. Originally published Nov. 2000. Now an adopted standard of the Object Management Group (OMG).
[MWUD]	*Merriam-Webster Unabridged Dictionary* (Version 2.5). [2000]. Merriam-Webster Inc.
[SBVR]	*Semantics of Business Vocabulary and Business Rules (SBVR)* (Version 1.0). [January 2008]. Object Management Group.
[Wikipedia]	http://en.wikipedia.org

ability statement: *an expression of a* **business requirement** *in business analysis with* **business rules**

action: *that which someone or something does;* [MWUD 3]: *the process of doing : exertion of energy : PERFORMANCE*

actor: *some person or organization taking part in day-to-day business activity*

actor event: *an* **event** *in which some person or organization does something*

ad hoc business activity: *some activity in day-to-day business operations that either: (a) is for some* **scenario** *not modeled for any* **business process**, *or (b) does not follow the* **scenario** *that has been prescribed by some* **business process** *model*

>   ***Notes:*** Like all business activity, *ad hoc business activity* must conform to all relevant **business rules**.

advice: [SBVR]: *an* **element of guidance** *that something is permissible or possible, that there is no* **rule** *against it*

>   ***Notes:*** A real-world **rule** always tends to remove a degree of freedom. If some guidance is given but does not tend to remove some degree of freedom, it still might be useful, but it

is not a **rule** per se. Consider the statement: *A bank account may be held by a person of any age.* Although the statement certainly gives business guidance, it does not directly place any obligation or prohibition on business conduct. Therefore it does not express a **behavioral rule**. Nor does it establish any necessity or impossibility for **know-how** about business operations. Therefore it does not express a **definitional rule**. Because the statement removes no degree of freedom, it does not express a **business rule** at all. Rather, it expresses something that is a non-**rule** — a.k.a. an *advice.* A statement of advice that specifically refutes obligation and prohibition (as does the one above) is called a **permission statement**.

Is it important then to write the advice down (i.e., capture and manage it)? *Maybe.* Suppose the statement reflects the final resolution of a long-standing debate in the company about how old a person must be to hold a bank account. Some say 21, others 18, some 12, and some say there should be no age restriction at all. Finally the issue is resolved in favor of no age restriction. It's definitely worth writing that down!

Now consider this statement: *An order $1,000 or less may be accepted on credit without a credit check.* This advice is different. It suggests a **business rule** that possibly hasn't been captured yet: *An order over $1,000 must not be accepted on credit without a credit check.* Let's assume the business does need this **business rule** and considers it valid. In that case you should write the **business rule** down — *not* the advice — because only the **business rule** actually removes any degree of freedom. Just because the advice says an order $1,000 or less may be accepted on credit without a credit check, that does not necessarily mean an order over $1,000 *must not.* A statement of advice only says just what it says.

agile: *see* **business agility**

anomaly: [MWUD 3]: *something irregular or abnormal*

> *Notes:* The prevention, detection, and elimination of *anomalies* among **business rules**, including but by no means limited to **conflicts**, are extremely important for high-quality **business models** and **business operation systems**. If undetected, anomalies can lead directly to inconsistent actions or **decisions**. *Anomalies* among **business rules** generally fall into

well-known categories. Certain anomalies can be detected among **business rules** by software available today; **SBVR** envisions expanded detection of anomalies by an order of magnitude or more. It is important to note that **declarative** representation of **business rules** does not somehow *cause* anomalies. Just the opposite, it makes them far easier to detect (and to detect very *early*) compared to **procedural** representations.

architectural scope: *what is included in a* **business model**

> *Notes:* A **business capability** has *architectural scope* whose boundaries are established by what business items are deemed to fall within scope (**scope items**) and what business items are not. **Scope items** fall into six categories *(scope lists)* based on the **Zachman Architecture Framework**: **core business concepts**, **central business processes**, **business locations**, **principal business actors**, **operational business events**, and **business goals**. Creating these six lists establishes an initial or **ballpark view** of architectural scope. A complete **business model** is self-defining with respect to architectural scope.

ballpark view [of architectural scope]: *first-cut* **architectural scope** *based on* **scope lists**

basic engineering question: *see* **primitive**

behavioral rule: [SBVR]: *a* **business rule** *that there is an obligation concerning conduct, action, practice, or procedure; a* **business rule** *whose purpose is to shape (govern) day-to-day business activity and prevent undesirable situations* (**states**) *that could occur at any of various points in time*

> *Notes:* Consider the **business rule**: *A gold customer must be allowed access to the warehouse.* Clearly this **business rule** can be violated. If a gold customer is denied access to the warehouse, then a violation has occurred. Presumably, some sanction is associated with such violation — for example, the security guard might be called on the carpet. (Such reaction is called a **violation response**.) Any **business rule** that can be violated *directly* is a *behavioral rule.* It doesn't matter whether the **behavioral rule** is automatable or not, although a great many are.

> Contrast with **definitional rule**. **Definitional rules** and behavioral rules are fundamentally different. **Definitional**

rules are about how the business organizes (i.e., *structures*) the operational business **concepts** basic to its **know-how**. In **SBVR**, definitional rules always carry the sense of *necessity* or *impossibility*; behavioral rules always carry the sense of *obligation* or *prohibition*. In contrast to **definitional rules**, behavioral rules (also called *operative rules* in SBVR) are really *people* rules. Behavioral rules enable the business to run (i.e., to *operate*) its day-to-day activity in a manner deemed suitable, optimal, or best aligned with **business goals**. Behavioral rules deliberately preclude specific **states** that are deemed undesirable, less effective, or potentially harmful. Behavioral rules remove those degrees of freedom. Often, sanction is real and immediate if a behavioral rule is broken. Day-to-day business activity typically involves a great many behavioral rules.

Also, contrast with **decision rule**. Unlike decision rules, behavioral rules do not pertain directly to determining the best or optimal answer (**outcome**) for an **operational business decision**, nor are they applied at only at a single point of determination for individual **cases**. Behavioral rules generally arise as interpretations of some law, act, statute, regulation, contract, agreement, business deal, **business policy**, license, certification, service level agreement, etc. Since behavioral rules generally fit no particular pattern, they cannot be effectively managed in **decision tables**. Instead, they usually need to be expressed as individual statements (e.g., using **RuleSpeak**). A **business capability** of any size usually has hundreds of behavioral rules, sometimes a great many more.

binary fact type: *a* **fact type** *that involves exactly two* **noun concepts**

business action: *an* **action** *taken in day-to-day business activity*

business agility: *being able to deploy change in* **business policies** *and* **business rules** *into day-to-day business activity as fast as business people and Business Analysts can determine the full business impact of the change and assess whether the change makes good business sense*

> ***Notes:*** *Business agility* results when the IT aspect of change in **business policies** and **business rules** disappears into the plumbing. All artificial (IT-based) production-freeze dates for deployment disappear and the software release cycle becomes irrelevant. The only constraint is how long it takes **business**

leads and Business Analysts to think through the change as thoroughly as they feel they need to.

Agile in software development is an IT development method featuring rapid iteration and prototyping. Agile methods and business agility have *nothing* to do with each other. *Agile* in software development leaves off *exactly* where business agility picks up — *at deployment*.

In working with clients we frequently come across systems that feature a very 'open' environment with few enterprise controls. Typically, this 'flexibility' resulted from diligent efforts by IT to satisfy many stakeholders individually. But the 'flexibility' is just an illusion. The failure of business-side stakeholders to come together and develop a collective business solution before 'agile' software development commences can plague the company for years to come. It reduces overall productivity, lowers customer satisfaction, and diminishes the capacity to make sound **operational business decisions**. It makes apple-to-apple financial comparisons virtually impossible. And it always costs *a lot* in 'maintenance'. There are simply *no magic bullets* for building business solutions.

business alignment: *alignment of* **business capabilities** *with* **business strategy**

> ***Notes:*** *Business alignment* is like motherhood and apple pie, no one will argue much against it. But for all the hand waving, questions remain. *What* are you aligning? *How* do you align? Answers generally center on aligning IT with the business. But shouldn't that be a given?! Methodologies recommend a great many touch points with individual users and good interpersonal relationships. But do those things ensure good business practices — or just good *GUIs?* And why just IT? Aren't there other kinds of projects in the business too?
>
> True business alignment results from engineering real business solutions for real business problems based on deliberate strategy (a **Policy Charter**). The approach should be exactly the same whether the business solution involves comprehensive automation, just partial automation — or none at all. True business alignment is also something you can demonstrate *quantitatively*. How fully are **business goals** being achieved? What is the failure rate of **business policies**? How quickly can emerging **risks** and opportunities be spotted?

Only metrics (**key performance indicators**) based on the strategy for the business solution (a **Policy Charter**) can reliably answer make-or-break business questions like these.

business capability: *what the business must know and be able to do to execute* **business strategy**

> *Notes:* When you create a business solution to an operational business problem business you're not simply creating an application or system or database or GUIs or even a **rulebook**, although any or all of those things might ultimately emerge. Instead, we say you are creating a *business capability* based on a **business model**. A business capability should have a well-defined **architectural scope** and produce operational business results that satisfy **business goals**.
>
> As defined by MWUD, *capability* means *ability*, and *ability* means *being able*. *Able* in turn means *having the power to perform a task or achieve an end*. That definition neatly implies two basic ways by which a business can prepare itself to get things done: (1) To perform **business tasks**, the business can develop **business process** models. A business process model will almost always include **operational business decisions**. (2) To achieve an **end**, the business can develop a strategy for the business solution (**Policy Charter**). A Policy Charter inevitably leads to **business policies**, **business rules**, and **know-how**.

business communication: *one or more written statements concerning day-to-day business activity*

> *Notes:* Operational *business communications* include agreements, contracts, deals, licenses, certifications, service level agreements, **procedure** manuals, schedules, training materials, instructions, and so on. Requirements for IT systems, non-technical documentation, 'help' in operational IT systems, and **guidance messages** are additional forms of business communication. So are **business policies** and **business rules**. All operational business communications should be based on a structured business vocabulary (**fact model**) since in one way or another they're all about **know-how**.

business goal: *an effect a* **business capability** *is tasked with achieving on an on-going basis in day-to-day activity*

business governance: *a process, organizational function, set of techniques, and systematic approach for creating and deploying* **business policies** *and* **business rules** *into day-to-day business activity*

> **Notes:** *Business governance* and **business rules** are *directly* linked. Note the high-profile roles of **business policies** and **business rules** in the definition above, which is based on MWUD definitions for *governance* 1, 2a, 4a, and 5. And have a look at the MWUD definition of *govern* [1a]: *to exercise arbitrarily or by established rules continuous sovereign authority over; especially: to control and direct the making and administration of policy in.* So 'governing' a business involves coordinating how **business policies** and **business rules** are created (*the making ... of*) and deployed (managed, distributed and monitored) within day-to-day business operations (*administration*). Why haven't more people recognized the direct link between business governance and business rules? It's simply hard to **see the elephant**.

> The original **decision** to create a **business policy** or **business rule** is an example of a **governance decision**. **Governance decisions** should be part of a special **business process**, the **governance process**, which also coordinates deployment and retirement of **business rules**. To support business governance you need a systematic approach, which is provided by a **rulebook** and **general rulebook system** (**GRBS**). These tools also provide the traceability needed to support compliance.

business lead: *an operational business manager or subject matter expert who participates directly and actively in creation of a* **business model**

business location: *a physical or logical place where some* **principal business actor** *is located, some* **operational business event** *occurs, or some* **central business process** *takes place*

business milestone: *a* **milestone** *representing the initial or beginning point of a recognized* **state** *in the* **life** *of some operational business thing*

> **Notes:** A *business milestone* implies a **business action** that completed successfully (e.g., an order has been *shipped*). The important thing about the **business action** completing successfully is that all **business rules** applicable to the **state** must be satisfied at that given point in time. So a business

milestone also generally implies a **flash point** for one or more **business rules**, often many.

business mission: *what a* **business capability** *is responsible for doing in day-to-day operation*

business model: *a blueprint for a* **business capability** *based directly on real-world things and ideas strictly named and represented using words natural to business people*

> ***Notes:*** *Contrast with* **system model**. Even the words used for the building blocks of business models (e.g., the vocabulary used to develop **structured business vocabularies**) must be natural for business people — again, *real-world*. **Business people talk about real-world things!** A *business model* enables business people and Business Analysts to engage in discussion about what needs to be created, managed, operated, changed, and discontinued in the business in business terms. Developing a business solution using a **future-form business model** does not necessarily imply software development, but if software development does ensue (as it usually does) the business model provides a solid grounding. Examples of business models include strategies for business solutions (**Policy Charters**), **business process** models, structured business vocabulary (**fact models**), **business milestone** models, and **Q-Charts** (for **decision analysis**). The term *business model* is also used collectively to designate all the business models for a particular **business capability**. A business model is always subject both individually and collectively to the **business rules** specified for it.

Business Motivation Model (BMM): *the standard for organizing* **business strategy** *first released in 2000 by the Business Rules Group (BRG) and subsequently by the Object Management Group (OMG) for UML in 2007*

> ***Notes:*** The BMM was created in the form of a structured business vocabulary (**fact model**). For a readable (free) copy see www.BusinessRulesGroup.org. The OMG's version for UML is available at:
> www.omg.org/technology/documents/br_pm_spec_catalog.htm.

business operation system (BOS): *a business system for a* **business capability** *that supports full* **business agility** *and built-in* **business governance**

Notes: See also **know-how economy.** Table AG1 outlines three generations of business application systems. This book is about building *third-generation* application systems. Information systems alone, even highly interactive ones, are no longer adequate.

Table AG1. Generations of Business Application Systems

characteristic	*1st Generation* Data Processing Systems	*2nd Generation* Information Systems	*3rd Generation* Business Operation Systems
fundamental purpose	automate clerical processes	put business processes online and make them interactive	create **smart business processes**
focal point of design	master file	database	**rulebook**
level of traceability / logging	batch of updates	individual transaction	**business rules** used to make individual judgments and **operational business decisions**
key operational feature	transaction files	queries	**flash points**
source language	COBOL	SQL, HTML	structured natural language (e.g., **RuleSpeak**)

Distinctive features of *Business Operation Systems* (BOS):

- No special computer languages required
- Structured business vocabularies (**fact models**)
- **Externalized semantics**
- Business-level **rulebooks**
- **Know-how** and **know-how retention**
- Manageable customization on a massive scale

business people talk about real world things: *the natural language of business people being about things in the real world, not* **surrogates** *for those things as represented in a* **system model**

Notes: Business Analysts should always encourage business people to talk directly about real-world things. That's what the business people know, that's what they do. So when business people say "employee" they should mean employee in the real world, not employee as a bundle of data *about* the employee in the real world. When they say "process" they should mean **business process** in the real world, not process as managed within a machine. When they say "interaction" they should mean business interaction in the real world, not a use case. When they say **rule** they should mean **business rule**, not **production rule** or other representation for machine purposes.

Unfortunately, some business people are so indoctrinated by years and years of IT-oriented requirements development that they themselves have a hard time talking directly about real-world things. They fall back on *ITspeak* instead. This distortion of language is neither productive nor necessary; it's a case of the cart leading the horse. The purpose of a **business model** is to get business people back in touch with the real world so they can deal with business complexity in its *own* terms.

business policy: *a* **means** *that limits or establishes a degree of freedom for day-to-day business activity*

Notes: Business managers create *business policies* to control, guide, and shape day-to-day business activity. Business policies are an important element of **business strategy** (e.g., **Policy Charters**) and the source of **core business rules**. A business policy is not a **business rule** per se. To become some business rule(s) first the business policy must be interpreted into a **practicable** form. The **Business Motivation Model** [BMM] contrasts business policies and business rules this way: *"Compared to a business rule, a business policy tends to be less structured, less discrete, less atomic, less compliant with standard business vocabulary, and less formally articulated."* In general, **business policies** can address any of the concerns in Table AG2, often in combinations (e.g., how many *people* are needed to produce a desired *yield* in the desired *cycle time*). Business policies can also address **exceptions** (**rules**).

Table AG2. Concerns that Business Policies Can Address

Question Word	General Focus of Concern	More Selective Examples
What	what things should (or should not) be available	required kinds, quantities, states, or configurations
How	how things should (or should not) be done	required outputs or yields
Where	where things that should (or should not) be done	required facilities, locations, or transfer rates
Who	who should (or should not) do things	required responsibilities, interactions, or **work products**
When	when things should (or should not) be done	required scheduling or cycle times
Why	why certain choices should (or should not) be made	required priorities

business process: *the* **business tasks** *required for an enterprise to satisfy a planned response to an* **operational business event** *from beginning to end with a focus on the* **roles** *of actors, rather than the actors' day-to-day job*

> ***Notes:*** This definition for *business process* was presented by Janey Conkey Frazier at the very first *Business Rule Forum* conference in 1997. We haven't found one better. A business process takes operational business things as inputs and *transforms* them into outputs. These outputs might be the same operational business things in some new **state**, or altogether new operational business thing(s). For example, a business process might take raw materials and transform them into finished goods. A successful transform creates or adds value, though not always in a direct way. Collectively, the boxes and arrows in a business process model represent management's blueprint for understanding, coordinating and revising how operational work in the organization gets done.

business requirement: *something called for or demanded by a* **business model** *that a* **system model** *must support*

> ***Notes:*** Contrast with **functional requirement**. A business can have many kinds of business requirements (e.g., about staffing, working capital, insurance, communications, marketing, etc.).

Use of the term "business requirement" in this book is always taken to mean "business requirement *for a system model.*"

business risk: *an exposure arising in day-to-day business activity that can preclude or complicate satisfaction of some* **business goal(s)** *or imperil or subvert some* **business tactic(s)** *or some* **business policy(ies)**

> ***Notes:*** Noted strategy expert Richard Rumelt [Rumelt 2011, p. 42] says the following about business risks: *"If you fail to identify and analyze the obstacles, you don't have a strategy. Instead, you have either a stretch goal, a budget, or a list of things you wish would happen."*

business rule: [SBVR]: *a* **rule** *that is* **under business jurisdiction**

> ***Notes:*** A *business rule* is a criterion used to guide day-to-day business activity, shape operational business judgments, or make **operational business decisions.** Some people think of business rules as loosely formed, very general requirements. *Wrong.* Business rules have definite form, and are very specific. Here are a few simple examples expressed in **RuleSpeak**: *A customer that has ordered a product must have an assigned agent. The sales tax for a purchase must be 6.25% if the purchase is made in Texas. A customer may be considered preferred only if the customer has placed more than $10,000 worth of orders during the most recent calendar year.*
>
> Each business rule gives well-formed, **practicable** guidance. Each uses **terms** and **wordings** about operational business things that should based on a structured business vocabulary (**fact model**). Each expression is **declarative**, rather than **procedural**. Your company's business rules need to be managed and **single-sourced**, so we strongly recommend **rulebook management**.
>
> A number of years ago, a colleague of ours, Mark Myers, came up with a highly pragmatic test to determine whether some statement represents a business rule or a **system rule**. Except for eCommerce, it almost always works. Imagine you threw out all the systems running your business and did it all by hand (somehow). If you still need the statement, it's a business rule. If you don't, it's not. A colleague on the SBVR standardization team, Don Baisley, puts it another way: *"Business people don't set variables and they don't call functions."*

Business rules represent a form of **business communication** and must make sense (communicate) to business people. If some statement doesn't communicate, it's not a business rule. Consider this example: *If ACT-BL LT 0 then set OD-Flag to 'yes'. Not* a business rule. Consider another example: *An account must be considered overdrawn if the account balance is less than $0.* This statement communicates and therefore *is* a business rule. Business rules can be technical, but only in terms of the company's **know-how** or specialized product/service, not in terms of IT designs or platforms.

SBVR provides the semantics for business rules. In SBVR a business rule can be either a **behavioral** rule or a **definitional rule**. Incidentally, SBVR does not standardize notation. We use **RuleSpeak** to express business rules (including 'exceptions') in structured natural language. In SBVR, a real-world rule always tends to remove some degree of freedom. If it does not, it's not a rule, but rather an **advice**. A business rule is always **under business jurisdiction** of your organization. The point with respect to external regulation and law is that your organization has a choice about how to interpret the regulations and laws for deployment into its day-to-day business activity — and even whether to follow them at all.

Business rules are not about mimicking intelligent behavior, they are about *running a business*. Mimicking intelligent behavior in a generalized way is far harder (an order of magnitude or more) than capturing the business rules of an organization. Unfortunately, **expert systems** have generally focused on the former problem, causing considerable confusion among business practitioners.

Business Rules Manifesto: *the 2003 work product of the Business Rules Group (BRG) laying out the basic principles of the* **business rules** *paradigm*

> **Notes:** The *Manifesto* (free) is only two pages and has been translated into more than a dozen languages. See www.BusinessRulesGroup.org.

business strategy: *the* **ends** *a business seeks to achieve and the* **means** *it elects to achieve them*

> **Notes:** How do you distinguish between good business strategy and bad business strategy? Noted strategy expert Richard Rumelt [Rumelt 2011, p. 20] says *"good strategy requires*

leaders who are willing and able to say no to a wide variety of actions and interests. Strategy is at least as much about what an organization does not do as it is about what it does." He also explains [Rumelt 2011, p. 243] that *"good strategy is, in the end, a hypothesis about what will work. Not a wild theory, but an educated judgment. And there isn't anyone more educated about your [business] than the group in [the] room."* Bad strategy [Rumelt 2011, p. 32] *"... is not simply the absence of good strategy. It grows out of specific misconceptions and leadership dysfunctions. To detect a bad strategy, look for ... Failure to face the challenge. ... When you cannot define the challenge, you cannot evaluate a strategy or improve it. Mistaking goals for strategy. Many bad strategies are just statements of desire rather than plans for overcoming obstacles."* Bad strategy *"... is long on goals and short on policy or action. ... It uses high-sounding words and phrases to hide [its] failings."* He means (and says) **fluff**.

What do you need to be successful with strategy? Rumelt [Rumelt 2011, p. 268] says, *"you must cultivate three essential skills or habits. First, you must have a variety of tools for fighting your own myopia and for guiding you own attention. Second, you must develop the ability to question your own judgment. If your reasoning cannot withstand a vigorous attack, your strategy cannot be expected to stand in the face of real competition. Third, you must cultivate the habit of making and recording judgments so that you can improve."*

A **Policy Charter** is the deliverable in our approach that lays out the elements of strategy and their **motivation (know-why)**. The standard for organizing business strategy is provided by the **Business Motivation Model (BMM)**.

business tactic: *a* **means** *that identifies some needed characteristic(s), feature(s) or use(s) for some* **scope item(s)**

business task: [MWUD 1b]: *something that has to be done or needs to be done and usually involves some difficulty or problem*

business vocabulary: *see* **structured business vocabulary**

case: *a particular situation;* [MWUD] 1b: *a set of circumstances constituting a problem: a matter for consideration or decision: as (1): a circumstance or situation*

Notes: Example of a *case*: *John Smith*, an ordinary applicant in terms of income, employment, and experience, applies for auto insurance. For **operational business decisions**, the relation of **consideration** to case is generally *class to instance*. A **consideration** is a *kind* of circumstance that some **decision logic** addresses. A case is some *particular* circumstance(s) the **decision logic** addresses. For example, suppose *state/province* is a **consideration** for an **operational business decision**. Then the particular instances *Texas* and *British Columbia* are cases of that **consideration** for that **operational business decision**.

case in scope (decision analysis): *any* **case** *that satisfies the* **considerations** *used to establish* **decision scope** *for an* **operational business decision**

Notes: **Decision logic** should be able to give **outcomes** for all cases provably within the specified scope of an **operational business decision**. Any case not in scope must be handed off (to some expert, manager, **business process**, or other **decision logic**). **Cases in scope** include both **standard cases** and **exceptional cases** (if any). They may also include **general** cases and **specific** cases.

categorization: *a special kind of fact that indicates one class of things to be a* **category** *of some other class of things*

categorization scheme: *a scheme used to categorize things into two or more* **categories**

Notes: For example, 'gender' is the *categorization scheme* for categorizing people as 'male' and 'female'.

category: *a class of things whose meaning is more restrictive, but otherwise compliant with, some other class of things*

Notes: For example, person and organization are *categories* of party.

central business process: *a* **business process** *that produces results of foremost importance, complexity, or value*

classification: *a special kind of fact that indicates a thing to be an instance of a class of things*

concept: [MWUD]: *something conceived in the mind : THOUGHT, IDEA, NOTION*

concept system: *a set of* **concepts** *structured according to the relations among them*

> *Notes:* **SBVR** was based in part on the existing terminology standards from the International Standards Organization (ISO), specifically 1087-1 and 704 (quite good). These standards are the source for the term *concept system* and its definition above. Although the ISO notion of a *concept system* did have structural elements representing certain kinds of connections (relations) between **noun concepts**, it does not include the fundamental notion of **fact types** (verb concepts) as do **fact models**. At the risk of greatly oversimplifying, SBVR added **fact types** (verb concepts) such that the full **semantics** of **business rules** and **business communications** can be captured, encoded, and transferred between machines.

conditional event: *see* **spontaneous event**

conflict: [MWUD 1a]: *clash, competition, or mutual interference of opposing or incompatible forces or qualities*

conflict (business rules): *an* **anomaly** *within or among some* **business rule(s)** *such that multiple* **states** *or* **outcomes** *are required that cannot all be satisfied simultaneously*

> *Notes:* A *conflict* arises for one or more **business rules** (usually two or more) if the same circumstances or **cases** require mutually-exclusive **states** or **outcomes**. Consider the **operational business decision**, *What is the right delivery method for an order?* The **potential outcome** *picked up by customer* is mutually exclusive with the **potential outcome** *shipped by normal service.* (If an order is picked up it can't be shipped, and if it's shipped it can't be picked up.) If some **business rule(s)** require(s) both **outcomes** for the very same circumstances or **case**, a conflict arises. In general, only business people or Business Analysts can resolve conflicts.

conflict (business strategy): *a clash between* **business goals** *such that the likelihood of full or consistent achievement of one* **business goal** *is diminished or pre-empted by* **business tactics** *and* **business policies** *that intentionally or necessarily favor or provide support for the achievement of some other* **business goal(s)**

Notes: Based on **conflict** [MWUD 1a]. At some level of drill-down in **business strategy**, **business goals** *always* conflict. Finding optimal trade-offs is key to the art.

connection cycle (fact model): *a circular series of facts for a* **recursive structure**, *one fact per* **fact type**

consideration: *a factor in making an* **operational business decision**; *something that can be resolved into two or more* **cases**

Notes: Consideration is to **case** as *class* is to *instance.* A consideration, sometimes called a *condition*, can always be posed as a question to be answered.

consideration dependency: *one* **operational business decision** *being dependent on the* **outcome** *of another* **operational business decision** *such that the* **outcome** *of the latter* **decision** *provides or supports one of the* **considerations** *for the former (dependent)* **decision**

Notes: For example, for the **decision** *What should be worn today?* the appropriate **outcome** depends on the **consideration** *Is it cold?* That **consideration** can be resolved only by evaluating the **decision logic** for another **decision** *What is the weather?* Deciding whether the weather is cold (based on appropriate **considerations**) is prerequisite for determining what to wear.

core business concept: *a* **concept** *representing a base thing, resource, or construct in a* **future-form business capability** *that is relevant to satisfying* **business goals**, *coordinating day-to-day business activity, or expressing necessary* **know-how**

core business rule: *a* **business rule** *that is a* **practicable** *interpretation of a* **business policy**

corporate memory: *the ability to recall* **governance decisions** *made in the past, understand their* **motivation (know-why)**, *and trace their impacts*

data rule: *a* **system rule** *that depends on the form in which data about the real world is received*

decision: *a determination requiring* **know-how**; *the resolving of a question by reasoning*

Notes: *Decisions* may either be ones an individual makes pertaining to that person's own activity or ones the organization makes pertaining to the day-to-day business activity in which the organization engages. Only the latter kind, **operational business decisions**, is of interest to **business rules** and **decision analysis**. The clear distinction between individual and organizational decisions has not generally been recognized by **expert systems**.

decision analysis: *identifying and analyzing key questions arising in day-to-day business activity* (**operational business decisions**) *and capturing the* **decision logic** *used to answer the questions*

> *Notes:* Does *decision analysis* enable you to capture every relevant **business rule**? *No.* Does every **business rule** fit into some **decision table**? *No.* A great many **business rules** cannot be captured effectively using decision analysis or **decision tables**. Many other techniques are needed.

decision dependency: *one* **operational business decision** *being dependent on another*

> *Notes:* Three kinds of *decision dependency* are recognized for **Q-Charts** in **decision analysis**: **relevance dependency**, **consideration dependency**, and **outcome dependency**.

decision logic: *the set of all* **decision rules** *for* **cases** *in* **decision scope**

> *Notes:* *Decision logic* is captured and expressed in the form of **decision structures**, **decision tables**, and **business rule** statements. **Decision analysis** might also be suitable where the end-products are statistical models, neural nets, or similar forms of non-verbal representation, but these other forms are outside the scope of this book. We assume decision logic is always to be encoded in a verbal form that can be understood, managed, and traced-back by business people and Business Analysts.
>
> Decision logic includes **decision rules** for both **standard cases** and **exceptional cases** (if any), as well as **general rules** and **specific rules** (as appropriate). Decision logic should be rendered in a form that is **practicable**, enterprise-robust, and business-friendly. Externalizing decision logic from **business processes** (a form of **rule independence**) can reduce the complexity of **business process** models dramatically. It also

results in decision logic that is highly accessible, adaptable (easy to change), and re-usable (e.g., in other **business processes**). Overall, externalizing and **single-sourcing** decision logic is essential in achieving **business agility**.

decision rule: *a* **definitional rule** *that links a* **case** *to some appropriate* **outcome**

> **Notes:** Contrast with **behavioral rule**. *Decision rules* are the target of **decision analysis**. Groups of decision rules, usually represented as **decision tables**, provide the correct or optimal answer to some business question (**operational business decision**) that arises at a particular point of determination for individual **cases** in day-to-day business activity. Decision rules are always **definitional rules**. By no means all definitional rules, however, are decision rules.

decision scope: *see* **case in scope (decision analysis)**

decision structure: *how one or more* **operational business decisions** *are formally organized*

> **Notes:** **Operational business decisions** often have natural **dependencies** that can be formally organized and diagrammed. These **dependencies** are always logical rather than sequential, distinguishing *decision structures* clearly and cleanly from **business process** models. **Q-Charts** serve to visualize and analyze decision structures and provide a starting point for developing **decision logic**.

decision table: *a structured means of visualizing* **decision rules** *in rows and columns*

> **Notes:** A *decision table* is a representation technique used to organize and visualize **decision rules** for an **operational business decision** in rows and columns without having to write a **business rule** statement for each **decision rule** individually. A decision table identifies the appropriate **outcome** from among all **potential outcomes** for each **case** it covers based on the specified **considerations**. Decision tables are an important means to develop and deploy **decision logic**.

decision task: *a* **business task** *centered on making an* **operational business decision** — *that is, on deciding something rather than on doing something*

declarative (statement): [MWUD 2]: *constituting a statement that can be either true or false*

> *Notes:* Contrast with **procedural (statement)**. *Declarative* expression of **business rules** is based on **logical dependencies**. In graduate school in the early 1970s, I learned the following highly pragmatic test for determining whether specifications are declarative: (1) Take each statement of the specification and type it on an individual punch card. (It's really hard to find punch cards these days, but for the sake of discussion, let's ignore that.) (2) Assemble the deck. (3) Test it to make sure it works. (4) Throw the whole deck up in the air. (5) Pick up all the cards in random order. (6) Re-test it. If the logic still works, the statements are *declarative*. If not, they are **procedural**. The point is that in declarative specifications no logic is lost 'between the lines' — i.e., none is intrinsic to the sequence of presentation. There is no *hidden meaning* (**semantics**). Declarative expression is a key idea for **business rules**. It provides the best guarantee that they remain platform-independent, highly re-usable, and most easily understood by business people.

definition: [MWUD 2]: *a word or phrase expressing the essential nature of a person or thing or class of persons or of things : an answer to the question "what is x?" or "what is an x?"*

> *Notes:* Good business *definitions* are front-and-center for **business models**, structured business vocabularies (**fact models**), and **business rules**. A great many things in today's business world and its **know-how** are intangible (e.g., insurance coverages, financial products, reservations, assignments, etc.). Often there's nothing in the real world you can point to (like a bird or a tree or a building) and say, "There, *that's* what I mean!" You have only the definitions to go by.
>
> We say definitions are for *people* and for *human* communication (not **semantic** *computation*). We focus on the core meaning of a **concept** to the business, its very essence. Why? That core essence will remain relatively constant. Stability is crucial in facilitating over-time and at-a-distance communication, maintaining continuity of **know-how**, training newcomers, and talking with outsiders. To take a highly publicized example, consider the celestial body Pluto. Why should our ability to talk about planets be impacted because a majority of astronomers no longer considers Pluto a planet?! If definitions are a bit fuzzy

around the edges, so be it. *(But read on!* There's more to a **concept** than just its definition.)

Compare to **definitional rule**. To define a **concept** *fully* at any given point in time you also need **definitional rules**. They indicate exact lines of demarcation — that is, the precise 'edges' of the **concept**. Consider this 'essence' definition of 'gold customer': *a customer that does a significant amount of business over a sustained period of time.* Informative and stable, but fuzzy around the edges. Compare that with the associated **definitional rule**: *A customer is always considered a gold customer if the customer places more than 12 orders during a calendar year.* The **definitional rule** makes up for what the definition lacks — precise criteria at the given point in time for determining whether a customer is or is not *gold*.

In summary, three key points: (1) Definitions are for people, not computation. (2) Conveying the full meaning of a **concept** sometimes (but not always) requires both a definition and some **definitional rule(s)**. (3) Any aspect of business practices subject to change should be treated as some **business rule(s)**, not embedded in definitions.

definitional rule: [SBVR]: *a **rule** that is intended as a definitional criterion*

Notes: Compare to **definition**. Evaluation of a *definitional rule* (also called *structural rule* in **SBVR**) always classifies or computes something using known facts, shaping what the business knows about itself and the world. Consider the example: *A customer must be considered a gold customer if the customer places more than 12 orders during a calendar year.* Evaluation of this definitional rule for any given customer indicates whether the customer is or is not *gold* given known facts. Consider another example: *The total price of an order item must be computed as the product unit price times its quantity.* Given any order item, evaluation of this definitional rule indicates the one result for *total price* that the known facts justify.

Although **SBVR** does not require it, we prefer to treat definitional rules separately from **definitions**. During day-to-day business activity, definitional rules are used to evaluate 'where you are' — that is, the current state of affairs — as the need arises. The result reached in each evaluation is only as good as the definitional rules themselves. Poor or misapplied definitional rules yield poor or inconsistent results. In that case, some aspect of the **know-how** 'breaks down' — it simply does not 'work' properly.

Contrast with **behavioral rule**. Definitional rules and **behavioral rules** are fundamentally different. Definitional rules are about how the business organizes (i.e., *structures*) the operational business **concepts** basic to its **know-how**. They give shape — i.e., *structure* — to core operational **concepts** of the business. In **SBVR**, definitional rules always carry the sense of *necessity* or *impossibility*; **behavioral rules** always carry the sense of *obligation* or *prohibition*. Disregard for **behavioral rules** leads to violations and possible sanctions; misapplication of definitional rules leads to miscalculations and off-base conclusions — but only indirectly, if at all, to violations.

deployed business rule: *a* **business rule** *currently being applied in day-to-day business activity*

> ***Notes:*** A **business rule** might have been *deployed* by one or both of the following means: (1) Publishing it to workers and others with a need to know. Enforcing the **business rule** might have been given to some workers(s) as a job responsibility. (2) Automating it in a suitable platform — e.g., a business rule engine (BRE).

element of guidance: [SBVR]: *a* **business policy**, **business rule**, *or an* **advice**

elementary fact type: *a* **fact type** *that cannot be broken down into two or more other* **fact types**, *each with fewer* **noun concepts**, *without losing knowledge*

end: [MWUD 4a]: *an outcome worked toward especially with forethought, deliberate planning, and organized effort : PURPOSE;* [BMM]: *something that is to be accomplished*

> ***Notes:*** In a **Policy Charter** the *ends* are **business goals**.

enforcement level: *how strictly a* **behavioral rule** *is to be enforced*

enterprise goal: *an effect an organization as a whole is tasked with achieving on an on-going basis in day-to-day activity*

enterprise mission: *what the organization as a whole is responsible for doing in day-to-day operation*

error message: *see* **guidance message**

event: [MWUD — event 1a(1)]: *something that happens*

> *Notes:* At the risk of stating the obvious, *events* and **business rules** are not the same thing. A **flash point** for a **business rule**, on the other hand, *is* an event.

exception: [MWUD 2]: *one that is excepted or taken out from others *almost every general rule has its exceptions**

exception (business rule): *a* **business rule** *that addresses some set of circumstances viewed as an* **exception** *or* **exceptional case** *in day-to-day business activity*

> *Notes:* Are there *really* any such things as *exceptions* to **business rules**? Consider the following two warehouse **business rules**: (1) *A gold customer must be allowed access to the warehouse.* (2) *A customer may have access to the warehouse only during regular business hours.* Suppose some *gold* customer seeks access *after* regular business hours. In those circumstances we have a **conflict**.
>
> A basic **SBVR** principle is that any **guidance statement** whose meaning conflicts with some other **guidance statement(s)** (or even some other part of the same statement) must be taken that way. In other words, if by taking some expression(s) literally you find that a potential **conflict** could arise, you are right — it can. You need to fix it. The principle is really about being able to fully trust what you read in front of you. If **guidance statements** don't mean *literally* what they say, then can you really ever be sure what they *do* say!? Remember, **guidance statements** are often read out of context, separated in time and distance from the author(s). So **guidance statements** should always be taken to mean exactly what they actually say — no more, no less. Potential **conflicts** such as the above must be resolved explicitly, within the actual statement(s).
>
> Several approaches that *don't* work in that regard: (1) Setting up some priority scheme to determine which 'wins'. (2) Expressing some separate **guidance statement(s)** to determine which 'wins'. (3) Deferring to some level of **categorization** to determine which 'wins'. (Example: a gold customer is a **category** of customer; therefore 'customer' **rules** 'win' over 'gold customer' **rules**.) To apply each **business rule**

correctly under any of these approaches, sometimes you need to know more than just what a statement says. In other words, sometimes **semantics** are hidden or absent. *Never good.* The only viable solution is that once a potential **conflict** is discovered, the **guidance statement(s)** that produce(s) that **conflict** need to be restated to avoid it. In other words, the statement(s) must *accommodate* the problematic circumstances. This guiding **SBVR** principle — the correct one for **business communications** — is called *Accommodation*.

So one of the warehouse **business rules** needs to be re-written. *Which one?* The answer depends entirely on business practice. Which of the following reworded versions might represent the correct or desired business practice? (1) *A customer must be given access to the warehouse if the customer is a gold customer and the access is during business hours.* (2) *A customer that is not a gold customer may have access to the warehouse only during business hours.* Let's say the desired business practice is given by the second statement. So the two **business rules** jointly representing the *correct* business practices for warehouse access are: (1) *A gold customer must be allowed access to the warehouse.* (2) *A customer that is not a gold customer may have access to the warehouse only during business hours.* Looking at the two resulting warehouse-access **business rules** ask yourself: *Which is an* **exception***?! Both? Neither?* The formal answer is, once you *accommodate*, there really are *no* **exceptions**(!). There are just well-stated, *fully-trustworthy* **guidance statements**.

In conversation and other informal business communication, we often do talk about "exceptions" to **business rules**. For example we might say: *A customer may have access to the warehouse only during regular business hours.* Then later in the same conversation or message we might add: *By the way, none of what I've said applies to gold customers.* **Guidance statements**, however, should not be informal in that sense. You can never be sure when or where a statement might be read or what the context might be. So a **guidance statement** needs to express its full meaning. David Crystal, a noted world authority on language, explains things this way [Crystal 2005, p. 465]:

> *"When someone consults a reference book ... [in which] information is stored for future use, it is impossible to predict who is likely to use it ... There is no 'dialogue' element in the communication. The information has to be as self-contained*

as possible, for it is impossible to predict the demands which may one day be made on it, and in most cases there is no way in which the user can respond so as to influence the writer. Accordingly, when language is used for [such] purposes ... it is very different from that used in everyday conversation — in particular, it displays a much greater degree of organization, impersonality, and explicitness."

Now I've never met or talked to David Crystal, but I'm confident I get his meaning. This **SBVR** principle of expressing the full meaning of each **guidance statement** is called *Wholeness*. Suppose your **rulebook** is deemed free of **conflicts** and you understand the **business vocabulary** correctly (two big *if's* of course). If your **guidance statements** are all expressed *wholly* then: (a) *Every statement is always self-explanatory. No need to appeal to any other statement should ever arise in understanding the full meaning.* (b) *Every statement can always be taken at face value. Take it out of conversational context and you can still trust exactly what it says.* By the way, there's a great deal a **general rulebook system** (GRBS) could do to simplify and condense *whole* statements for easier consumption — *if* it knew each worker's preferred conversational context. Such support would give you friendly *and* formal **business communication**.

exceptional case: *a* **case in scope** of an **operational business decision** *that does not use the* **considerations** *of a* **standard case**; *i.e., a* **case in scope** *that is based on some* **consideration(s)** *that is/are not among the* **considerations** *for a* **standard case**

Notes: The **decision logic** for an *exceptional case* might be as simple as a single **decision rule** (e.g., *The boss's daughter must be accepted for auto insurance.*), or decidedly more complex.

expert system: [Wikipedia]: *software that uses a knowledge base of human expertise for problem solving, or to clarify uncertainties where normally one or more human experts would need to be consulted ... a traditional application and/or subfield of artificial intelligence (AI)*

Notes: Bob Whyte, a practitioner for a major insurance company, makes the following observation about the difference between **business rules** and *expert systems* (which are usually based on **production rules**):

"What makes the real-world challenge of managing business rules so much more tractable than it appeared to academics and researchers in the1980s, the heyday of knowledge engineering and expert systems, is that in the day-to-day business world the institution plays role of 'god'. In other words, the business has the often unrecognized advantage that it gets to invent and define the rules for how it operates. So for business rules the problem is not one of having to discover and define hidden, unknown or unexpressed rules, which takes you into byzantine solution spaces, but rather one of documenting known rules invented overtly and explicitly by actual historical person(s). With business rules you are generally not discovering rules no one has ever consciously considered, but rather uncovering rules that some manager, lawyer or other expert decided on one day, but probably did not record simply for lack of an appropriate infrastructure for rulebook management."

externalizing semantics: *developing and managing a structured business vocabulary* **(fact model)** *and* **definitional business rules** *apart from* **business processes** *(and other* **procedural** *models or specifications)*

> ***Notes:*** *Externalizing* **semantics** in **declarative** form allows them to be understood and evolved directly by business people and Business Analysts. **Procedural** approaches, in contrast, are **token**-based and are essentially black-box with respect to **semantics**.

fact model: *a semantic blueprint for the operational business concepts basic to* **know-how** *as expressed by a* **structured business vocabulary**

fact type: *something specific that can be known about one or more* **noun concepts(s)** *important to day-to-day business activity*

> ***Notes:*** The fact type worded "customer places order" indicates that some customer placing some order probably happens repetitively in day-to-day business activity. The fact type therefore represents something that can be known about that activity *(e.g., that a customer can place an order).*

fall-back position: *see* **remedy**

flash point: *an* **event** *when a* **business rule** *needs to be evaluated*

Notes: In general most business rules, even simple ones, have two or more *flash points*. All flash points for a well-specified **declarative** business rule can be identified by analyzing it against the structured business vocabulary (**fact model**). Such identification, particularly important for **behavioral rules** and those **definitional rules** that are not **decision rules**, is automatable.

fluff: [MWUD 2b]: *something essentially trivial and lacking importance or solid worth*

Notes: As described by strategy expert Richard Rumelt [Rumelt 2011, p. 32], *"fluff is a form of gibberish masquerading as strategic concepts or arguments. It uses 'Sunday' words (words that are inflated and unnecessarily abstruse) and apparently esoteric concepts to create the illusion of high-level thinking." Fluff* is one of Gladys' favorite words. She is very good at detecting it.

functional requirement: [Wikipedia]: *a requirement that defines a function of a software system ... what a system is supposed to accomplish*

Notes: Contrast with **business requirement**.

future form [business model]: *a **business model** delineating the form a **business capability** is to operate in the future*

Notes: Also called a *to-be* **business model**.

GAS: *see* **general ability statement**

general ability statement: *an **ability statement** that holds for every **system model** resulting from business analysis with **business rules**; a guiding principle for developing **business requirements***

general case: *a **case** that could be treated as more than one **case** if some additional instance(s) were specified for the **considerations***

Notes: A **case** considered by an **operational business decision** can be as simple as a single instance for just one of multiple **considerations**. Such a **case** is very *general*. For example, suppose *state/province* is one of several **considerations** for an **operational business decision** that also involves the **considerations** *driving history, evidence of insurance, insurance risk score,* and *credit rating*. The instance

Texas on its own represents a very general case. Contrast with **specific case**.

general rulebook system (GRBS): *an automated, specialized, business-level platform for* **rulebook management**

> *Notes:* Key features of a *general rulebook system (GRBS)* include rich, interactive support for **structured business vocabularies** (fact models) and comprehensive traceability for **business rules** (not software requirements). Unlike a business rule engine (BRE) a GRBS is not run-time. *Think of a GRBS as more or less like a general ledger system, except for Business Analysts.* Because of the potential of GRBS to support compliance and accountability, a GRBS is indispensable for improved **business governance**.

goal monitor: *a* **key performance indicator** *(metric) for determining whether* **business goals** *are being satisfied*

governance: *see* **business governance**

governance decision: *a* **decision** *in* **business governance**

> *Notes:* The original **decision** to create a **business policy** or **business rule** is an example of a *governance decision*. A governance decision is *not* an **operational business decision** because it is not real-time with respect to day-to-day business activity.

governance process: *a series of* **business actions** *and checkpoints indicating who should be doing what (business* **roles***), and when, with respect to deploying* **business policy** *and* **business rules**

GRBS: *see* **general rulebook system**

guidance message: *a message given to someone at a* **flash point** *for a* **behavioral business rule** *when a violation is detected*

> *Notes:* What should happen when someone violates a **behavioral rule**? Assuming the person is authorized and knowledgeable, some explanation should be provided about what caused the problem. You might call that explanation an error message or violation message, but we prefer *guidance message*. The intent should be to inform and to shape appropriate business behavior, rather than simply reprimand or inhibit it. After all, **business rules** represent encoded **know-how**. What should the guidance message say? *As a*

default, the guidance message should say exactly what the business rule says. In other words, the **business rule** statement *is* the guidance/error message. Obviously, additional or customized text can be provided to explain the relevance of the **business rule** for the particular **flash point**, to suggest corrective measures, to give examples, and so on. The main point is this: The guidance messages that business workers see once a **business operation system** is deployed should be the very same **business rules** developed during business analysis for the **business model**. Guidance messages (error messages about business things being done incorrectly) and **business rule** statements — *literally one and the same.*

guidance statement: a statement of a **business rule** or an **advice**

guideline: *a* **behavioral rule** *that is active but not enforced*

> ***Notes:*** Consider the **behavioral rule**: *An order over $1,000 must not be accepted on credit without a credit check.* Suppose this **behavioral rule** is restated with a *should* instead of a *must* (not recommended in **RuleSpeak**): *An order over $1,000 should not be accepted on credit without a credit check.* Is it still a **business rule**? *Yes,* still a **business rule**, only with a lighter sense of prohibition. What actually changed was the business rule's **enforcement level**. Rather than strictly enforced, now the **business rule** has the sense: *It's a good thing to try to do this, but if you can't there's no sanction.* In other words, now it's simply a *guideline* (or *suggestion,* if you prefer).

happy life: *a* **life** *for an operational business thing (e.g., order) consisting of the* **states** *(e.g., received, credit-checked, filled, etc.) through which instances progress that complete successfully from the business's point of view*

happy path: *a* **scenario** *that works out in the easiest and best way possible for the business*

> ***Notes:*** A *happy path* is generally free of exceptions and features a normal progression of **events**, high-frequency infrastructure, and the 'usual cast' of actors.

implicit business rule: *a* **business rule** *not expressed anywhere*

> ***Notes:*** *There is no such thing as an implicit business rule!* A business rule must be *explicit,* otherwise it is assumed not to exist (**Business Rules Manifesto** 3.3). In other words there are no **business rules** until you say there are — i.e., until you

specify them explicitly. This assumption is key for **rule independence**. It's a common-sense view of the business world with important implications. One is that there are never 'buried' (assumed) **business rules** in any form of **business model**, including **business process** models.

incremental design: *developing a system through repeated cycles (iteratively) and in smaller portions at a time (incrementally)*

> *Notes:* **Business rules** are unsurpassed for step-by-step enhancement of deployed **know-how** in **business capabilities** over time (*incremental design*). The **Business Rules Manifesto** puts it this way: *"An effective system can be based on a small number of rules. Additional, more discriminating rules can be subsequently added, so that over time the system becomes smarter."* That's exactly what you need for **know-how retention** and to move pragmatically toward the **know-how economy**. Support for *incremental design* with **business rules** is quite straightforward. A **decision task** might start off manual (performed by humans). As time and resources permit, **decision rules** for handling the simplest **cases** can be captured and encoded, removing these **cases** from the manual workload. Perhaps you start with a modest 20% of all **cases**. The only required changes to the system are to specify:
> (1) What **cases** are covered (by providing selection criteria).
> (2) What **outcome** is no longer manual for the **cases** covered.
> (3) What **decision logic** should be used. At a subsequent time, you ramp up to 50%, then perhaps 80%. You may never get to 100% — nobody is talking about taking humans completely out of the loop for every **operational business decision**(!). The net result is simply applying human resources where best suited, the really hard **cases**.

independent subdecision: *an* **operational business decision** *in a collection of two or more* **operational business decisions** *such that another* **operational business decision** *has a* **consideration dependency** *on each* **decision** *in the collection*

> *Notes:* Important — *independent subdecisions* may be evaluated separately and either (a) in parallel or (b) in any sequence. Each subdecision has a distinct **outcome** and a different set of **considerations** (usually non-overlapping) from its peers in the collection.

initiating event: *an* **event** *that does not result from some other* **event(s)**

integration relationships: *how the* **primitives** *are tied together (configured) at any point in time to create a complete and workable solution for an engineering problem*

key performance indicator: *a metric for assessing the business performance of a* **business capability**

> ***Notes:*** The **BMM** (**Business Motivation Model**) describes *key performance indicators* as follows (pp. 40-41):
>
>> *"In almost all organizations there are 'things of interest' that are heavily measured and tracked. These metrics govern, control, and influence a wide range of important aspects of the organization. The very fact these 'things' are so heavily measured makes them important. Some of the most important metrics of an enterprise are established by its [business] goals. Each [business] goal can have one or more measures of performance. For example, a metric of the [business] goal "to be profitable" is the measure of performance 'annual net revenue.' Another measure of performance of this [business] goal might be 'monthly net revenue.' ... If a metric is particularly important, it may attain a special status and be called a key performance indicator (KPI) or a critical success factor (CSF) — or something else. The choice of signifier is unimportant."*

know-how: [MWUD]: *accumulated practical skill or expertness ... especially: technical knowledge, ability, skill, or expertness of this sort*

> ***Notes:*** *Know-how* that you can encode and retain is represented by **business rules** and the structured business vocabularies (**fact models**) on which the **business rules** are based. Know-how is a subset, a small one probably, of *knowledge*. Briefly, *knowledge* can range from practical to theoretical, from certain to probabilistic, and from frequently applicable to infrequently applicable. *At the risk of saying the obvious, you can't run the day-to-day operations of a business on knowledge that is theoretical, probabilistic, or infrequently applicable.* In short, **business rules** are about *know-how* management, not about *knowledge* management except in a strictly limited sense. Contrast with **know-why**.

know-how economy: *the use of techniques for creating and managing* **know-how** *to produce economic benefits as well as job creation*

> *Notes:* See also **business operation system (BOS)**. Ask yourself: *Why should every business define its own* **business vocabulary** *even though almost everybody operates in some larger community of practice? Why should every business invent its own* **business rules** *even though perhaps only 20% of its* **business rules** *directly impact competitive advantage? Why should regulatory bodies issue regulations without adequate* **definitions** *and provably correct (***anomaly***-free)* **business rules**? *Why should contracts, agreements, and deals be signed with terms of agreement and* **definitions** *already spelled out, only to have IT implement them essentially from the ground-up?* Welcome to the idea of a *know-how economy!* According to Wikipedia ['knowledge economy']:
>
> > *"Various observers describe today's global economy as one in transition to a 'knowledge economy,' as an extension of an 'information society.' The transition requires that the rules and practices that determined success in the industrial economy need rewriting in an interconnected, globalized economy where knowledge resources such as know-how and expertise are as critical as other economic resources."*

know-how retention: *expressing* **know-how** *explicitly in a form understandable by business people and Business Analysts, and managing the* **know-how**, *such that it is always available for future reference or use (by those capable and authorized)*

> *Notes:* Like knowledge, **know-how** can be either *tacit* (in people's heads) or *explicit*. The classic test for when knowledge is tacit is 'lose the person, lose the knowledge'. **Know-how** is made explicit via structured business vocabularies (**fact models**) and **business rules**. The over-time infrastructure needed to retain **know-how** is provided by a **general rulebook system**. As a senior manager recently put it, *"No organization should depend on absent brains."*

know-why: [MWUD]: *understanding of the reasons underlying something (as a course of action)*

> *Notes:* Contrast with **know-how**.

life: [MWUD 20]: *something resembling animate life: as continued active existence and development*

> ***Notes:*** The instances of many operational business things have a *life* in that they can change **state** in some manner important to the business. Remember that to business people and customers, even intangible business things (e.g., insurance policies, financial products, etc.) are quite real. They too can have a **life**.

life pattern: *a regulated sequence for how an operational business thing is permitted to move through two or more* **states** *during its* **life**

> ***Notes:*** A *life pattern* is established by specifying the right combination of **business rules**. *The Business Rule Book* (1997) introduced the convenient short hands in Table AG3.

Table AG3. Shorthand Specifications for Governing a Life Pattern

Specification	Effect on the Life of Each Instance of the Operational Business Thing	Note
initializing (IZ)	It must start off at the *first* **state**, not beyond it.	—
forward (FW)	It must not *retrograde* (return to any earlier **state**).	—
progressive (PRO)	It must not *skip* any **state** moving forward.	—
retrogressive (RET)	It must not skip any **state** in *retrograding* (returning to an earlier **state**).	Meaningless if *forward*.
re-initializing (RIZ)	It must return to the first **state** each time *any* retrograding occurs before it can ever move forward again.	Meaningless if *forward*.
cyclical (CYCL)	*Both* of the following must be true: • It must return to the first **state** each time any retrograding occurs before it can ever move forward again. • It must reach the last **state** any time any forward movement occurs before it can ever retrograde again.	Meaningless if *forward*. Stronger than *re-initializing*.
frozen (FIX)	It must not change from its current **state**.	Used to discontinue any more **life** changes.

logical dependency: one expression using some **term** or **wording** computed or derived by another expression

> *Notes:* **Declarative** expression of **business rules** precludes only sequential dependencies, not *logical dependencies*. In fact, **declarative** expression depends on logical dependencies. Use of logical dependencies is a highly effective means of **single-sourcing business rules** at an atomic level of granularity and ensuring reusability at that level.

means: [BMM]: *a device, capability, regime, technique, restriction, agency, instrument, or method that may be called upon, activated, or enforced to achieve* **ends**

> *Notes:* A **Policy Charter** features two kinds of means: **business tactics** and **business policies**.

milestone: [MWUD 2]: *a significant point in any progress or development*

milestone imperative: *a* **business rule** *that must be satisfied for an instance of an operational business thing to achieve a* **business milestone**

motivation: [MWUD 'motive' 1b]: *the consideration or object influencing a choice or prompting an action;*
[MWUD 'motivation' 2a]: *motivating force or influence*

n-ary fact type: *a* **fact type** *that involves more than two* **noun concepts**

never say user: *a* **business model** *being about real people filling real business roles in real* **business processes** *subject to real* **business rules** *with real business* **motivation**

> *Notes:* There are no 'users' until you start to develop a **system model** to support the business solution embodied by a **business model**. (Anyway, these days everybody is a user of *some* system, so calling someone a 'user' just doesn't really say very much.)

non-functional requirement: [Wikipedia]: *a constraint imposed on the design or implementation of a system (such as performance requirements, security, or reliability)*

noun concept: *the* **concept** *that a* **term** *represents*

objectification: *the* **noun concept** *that results from* **objectifying** *a* **fact type**

objectify: *to cause a* **fact type** *(verb concept) to become or to assume the character of a* **noun concept**

> ***Notes:*** For example, the fact type 'student enrolls in course offering' could be *objectified* as 'enrollment'.

operational business decision: *a* **decision** *arising in day-to-day business activity*

> ***Notes:*** **Decisions** appropriate for **decision analysis** share five essential characteristics in common, collectively called *'DOORS'* for short. Such **decisions** are: **D**eterministic, rather than intuitive or ad hoc; **O**perational, rather than tactical or strategic; **O**bjective (encodable as explicit **decision rules**), rather than subjective; **R**epetitive, rather than one-off or infrequent; and **S**ingle-point (of determination), rather than multi-point. Examples: *Should an insurance claim be accepted, rejected, or examined for fraud?, Which resource should be assigned to a task?, Which service should be used to ship this package?*
>
> Typical kinds or patterns of **operational business decisions** include classification, evaluation, selection, approval, assessment, assignment, allocation, diagnosis, and prediction. As these kinds or patterns suggest, **operational business decisions** involve some significant determination for individual **cases** at a particular point in a **business process**. Such determination always involves a question arising in day-to-day business activity whose answers need to be determined, inferred or concluded. The operational business decision seeks to identify the best or optimal answer (**outcome**) whose kind is known in advance for **cases in scope**.

operational business event: *an* **event** *produced or recognized as a result of day-to-day business activity*

> ***Notes:*** An *operational business event* is an **event** that requires the business to respond, usually in a non-trivial way and often following some pattern of activity developed in advance, for example, a **business process** model. If important to the business, an operational business event generally moves some operational business thing to a new **business milestone**. In

doing so, the operational business event should cause all relevant **business rules** to be tested.

operative rule: [SBVR]: *see* **behavioral rule**

outcome: *a* **potential outcome** *that is deemed appropriate for some* **case**

> *Notes:* Sometimes called a *conclusion.*

outcome dependency: *one* **operational business decision** *being dependent on the* **outcome** *of another* **operational business decision** *such that the* **outcome** *of the latter* **decision** *dictates some* **outcome(s)** *of the former (dependent)* **decision**

> *Notes:* In an *outcome dependency*, kinds of **outcome** for the respective **decisions** must align.

participle: [MWUD]: *a word having the characteristics of both verb and adjective*

> *Notes:* See also **past participle** and **present participle**. In English, *participles* are made from verbs by adding any of the endings: *-ing, -ed, -d, -t, -en,* or *-n, and* are frequently used to refer to **state**.

partitive structure: *see* **whole–part structure**

past participle: [MWUD]: *a* **participle** *that typically expresses completed action ... as arrived in: the ship, arrived at last, signals for a tug.*

> *Notes:* In English, *past participles* are formed with any of the **participle** endings except *-ing.*

pattern question: *a thinking tool that assists Business Analysts in developing* **business rules** *from* **business models**

> *Notes:* Over the past decade we have developed a series of well-structured *pattern questions* in **Proteus (Pro-BA)** to help Business Analysts with harvesting **business rules** from different kinds of **business model** (e.g., **business process models**, **fact models**, etc.). Each pattern question focuses on a particular topical concern and some particular construct (pattern) found frequently in models of a given kind. Each pattern question typically leads to many **business rules** for the same model. The questions are designed to assist Business

Analysts in learning how to ask the right kinds of questions in the right ways to capture **business rules**. The pattern questions also prove quite useful in validating and refining the underlying models. In applying the pattern questions reflect carefully on each response. Answers typically lead to more questions — and to more **business rules**.

permission statement: a statement of **advice** that specifically refutes obligation and prohibition

> *Notes:* Examples: *A person of any age may hold a bank account. A government vehicle with siren and lights flashing may exceed the posted speed limit.*

policy: *see* **business policy**

Policy Charter: *a deliverable in business analysis with* **business rules** *that lays-out the* **strategy** *for a business solution*

> *Notes:* A conversation about **strategy** for the business solution, which in **Proteus (Pro-BA)** is organized as a *Policy Charter*, is exactly the one **business leads** are looking to have. A Policy Charter addresses fundamental questions in shaping a business solution: *What are the best* **means (business tactics** *and* **business policies)** *to achieve the* **ends (business goals)** *desired for a* **future-form business capability***? How are the associated* **business risks** *addressed? What is the business* **motivation (know-why)** *for each of the* **business tactics** *and* **business policies***? Why are those* **means** *most appropriate?* Basing your approach to **business requirements** on a **strategy** for the business solution — i.e., a Policy Charter — is the surest way to achieve true **business alignment**. The Policy Charter is a form of **business model** and also an important source of **core business rules**.

policy monitor: *a* **key performance indicator** *(metric) for determining whether the business intent of a* **business policy** *is being satisfied*

potential outcome: *some result, conclusion, or answer that might be deemed appropriate for some* **case**

practicable: [MWUD 1]: *possible to practice or perform : capable of being put into practice, done, or accomplished* [MWUD 2a]: *capable of being used : USABLE*

practicable [element of guidance]: [SBVR]: *an* **element of guidance** *sufficiently detailed and precise that a person who knows the* **element of guidance** *can apply it effectively and consistently in relevant circumstances to know what behavior is acceptable or not, or how something is understood*

> *Notes:* A *practicable* **business rule** (or **advice**) is one ready to become a **deployed business rule** (applied in day-to-day business activity). Whether the guidance is to be deployed to staff or ultimately to machines is immaterial — *you should get the same results either way!* **Business policies** are generally not practicable; **business rules** and **advices** always are.

present participle: [MWUD]: *a* **participle** *that typically expresses present action*

> *Notes:* In English, *present participles* are formed with the ending *-ing*.

primitive: [MWUD — adjective 1a]: *not derived from or reducible to something else*

> *Notes:* In the **Zachman Architecture Framework**, the columns represent the *primitives* of engineering problems and correspond to the six interrogatives *what, how, where, when, who, when,* and *why*. If an artifact is not primitive, then it's a *composite* and inevitably more complex and resistant to change.

principal business actor: *a real-world person or organization of primary importance in achieving* **business goals**

procedure: [MWUD 1b3]: *a series of steps followed in a regular orderly definite way*

procedural (statement): *a statement included in a series of other statements to specify a* **procedure**

> *Notes:* Contrast with **declarative (statement)**.

production rule: *the form of* **rule** *used in* **production rule systems**

> *Notes: Production rules* (also called *productions*) can be used to *implement* **business rules**, but are *not* **business rules** per se. Production rules typically provide support for **action** selection, which results in non-**declarative** statements.

production rule system: [Wikipedia]: *a computer program typically used to provide some form of artificial intelligence, which consists primarily of a set of rules about behavior*

> ***Notes:*** *Production rule systems* are a class of platform whose **rule** format and operation are aimed toward developers. See also **expert system**. According to Wikipedia:
>
> > *"A production system provides the mechanism necessary to execute productions in order to achieve some goal for the system. Productions consist of two parts: a sensory precondition (or 'IF' statement) and an action (or 'THEN'). If a production's precondition matches the current state of the world, then the production is said to be <u>triggered</u>. If a production's action is executed, it is said to have <u>fired</u>."*

prohibited antecedent: *a* **state** *of an operational business thing that if achieved by an instance precludes some other* **state** *being achieved by that same instance*

> ***Notes:*** Consider the business rule *A cancelled order must not have been shipped.* The state *shipped* is a prohibited antecedent for the state *cancelled.*

project objective: *a specific, measurable target that a project is tasked with attaining, often but not always time-based, which disappears when the project terminates*

property: [MWUD1a]: *a quality or trait belonging to a person or thing*

Proteus®: *the top-down, step-by-step methodology for business analysis,* **business rules***, and* **decision analysis** *offered by Business Rule Solutions, LLC (BRS)*

> ***Notes:*** In Greek mythology *Proteus* was a god that could take many forms, hence the English word *protean* meaning *versatile, mutable, capable of assuming many forms.* Protean **business capabilities** are exactly what you need for **business agility**, a central goal of Proteus.
>
> *Proteus for Business Analysis (Pro-BA™)* provides a hands-on, intuitive approach to engage business people and subject matter experts (SMEs) most productively, with minimal demands on their time. Distinctive deliverables from Pro-BA include: (1) a strategy for the business solution (**Policy Charter)**, and (2) **behavioral rules**. A key Pro-BA technique is to **walk the walls** when building a **business model**.

Proteus for Decision Analysis (Pro-DA™) provides a business-based approach for undertaking **decision analysis**, capturing **decision rules**, and organizing **decision tables**. Distinctive deliverables of Pro-DA include **Q-COEs** and **Q-Charts**. Pro-DA can be applied in either of two ways: (1) *Stand-alone — i.e.,* undertaken on its own for some specific **operational business decision(s)**. (2) *Embedded* — undertaken as part of another initiative (e.g., **business process** re-engineering, web-based eCommerce, legacy system modernization, etc.).

Q-Chart™: *a visualization or diagramming technique for representing and analyzing* **decision structures**, *including* **Q-COEs** *and their* **logical dependencies**

    Notes: A **Question Chart** (*Q-Chart* for short) organizes **Q-COEs** based on logical (not sequential) dependencies. A Q-Chart is purely **declarative**, in contrast to **business process** models, which are always **procedural**.

Q-COE™: a graphic representation of a single **operational business decision** indicating what question ('Q') is being asked, and possibly one or more of the following: **considerations** ('C'), **outcomes** ('O'), and **exceptions** ('E')

    Notes: *Q-COEs* can be used on their own for brainstorming, or included with other Q-COEs in **Q-Charts**.

Question Chart: *see* **Q-Chart**

recursive structure: *a circular series of two or more* **fact types**, *each fact type connected to the next by some* **term** *in common, such the last* **fact type** *connects to the same* **term** *at which the first* **fact type** *began*

relevance dependency: *one* **operational business decision** *being dependent on the* **outcome** *of another* **operational business decision** *such that the* **outcome** *of the latter (less dependent)* **decision** *may eliminate the need for any* **outcome** *from the former (dependent)* **decision**

    Notes: For example, if a company decides not to ship to Alaska, then it doesn't need to determine the cost of shipping there. The former **decision** *Can an order be shipped to a location?* pre-empts the latter **decision** *How much does it cost to ship to a location?* The latter **decision** is simply meaningless in the **case** of Alaska.

remedy: [MWUD 2]: *something that corrects or counteracts an evil : CORRECTIVE, COUNTERACTIVE, REPARATION*

requirement: *see* **business requirement**

risk: *see* **business risk**

risk bracket: *a section of a continuously numbered or graded series in calibrating* **business risk**

> ***Notes:*** Based on [MWUD 6] 'bracket'.

role (business): [MWUD 'role' 1b1]: *a part played by an actor;* [MWUD 'role' 2]: *a function performed by someone or something in a particular situation, process, or operation*

role (fact type): *a* **noun concept** *that reflects how another* **noun concept** *is viewed in the context of a fact type*

> ***Notes:*** For example, 'owner' is how 'person' is viewed in the **fact type** worded 'person [owner] owns vehicle'.

rule: [MWUD 'rule' 1a]: *guide for conduct or action;* [MWUD 'rule' 1f]: *one of a set of usually official regulations by which an activity (as a sport) is governed [e.g.,] *the infield fly rule* *the rules of professional basketball* ;* [MWUD 'criteria' 2]: *a standard on which a decision or judgment may be based*

> ***Notes:*** When we say *rule* we always mean *real-world* rule.

rule independence: *the externalization, unification, and management of* **rules** *separately from processes*

> ***Notes:*** As expressed by the **Business Rules Manifesto,** basic ideas of *rule independence* include these: **Business rules** should be treated as a first-class citizen of the requirements world. They should never be embedded in process models. Instead, they should be expressed independently of process (or other) models in a **declarative** form that business people and Business Analysts can understand and validate. **Business rules** are key to **business agility** and therefore need to be managed as a business asset.

rulebook: *the collection of* **elements of guidance** *for a* **business capability,** *along with the* **terms, definitions,** *and* **wordings** *that support them*

Notes: The *rulebook* of a game enumerates all the do's and don'ts (**rules**) of that game along with the **terms** and **definitions** (vocabulary) needed to understand the **rules**. Each participant in the game, whether player, coach, referee or umpire, scout, spectator, or media person, is presumed to understand and adhere to the **rules** to the extent his or her **role** in the activity requires. The rulebook sometimes suggests how to play the game to maximum advantage, but never dictates playing strategy.

Similarly, a rulebook in business includes the **business rules** (and **advices**) needed to perform day-to-day operational business activity correctly or optimally, along with the structured business vocabulary (**fact model**) needed to understand the **business rules** correctly. Each participant in the business activity must adhere to the **business rules** to the extent his or her **role** requires. The rulebook never dictates **business strategy**, but should reflect, enforce, and measure it. Unlike the **rules** for a game, however, **business rules** change, often quite rapidly. Therefore knowing the original source of each **business rule**, its **know-why**, and its full history of modifications, as well as how and where the **business rule** is currently **deployed**, is essential in effective **rulebook management**.

rulebook management: *the skills, techniques and processes needed to express, analyze, trace, retain, and manage the* **business rules** *needed for day-to-day business activity*

RuleSpeak®: *a set of guidelines for expressing* **business rules** *in concise, business-friendly fashion using structured natural language*

Notes: Emily Springer, business architect at a major insurance company, says:

> *"Before we started using RuleSpeak to express business rules, business people had no idea what they were signing off on. Introducing RuleSpeak to express business rules was fundamental to getting business people really engaged up-front in truly understanding the business side of requirements."*

RuleSpeak (free on www.RuleSpeak.com) is not a formal language or syntax per se, but a set of best practices. Its purpose is to bring greater clarity and consistency in communicating **business rules** among business people, Business Analysts, and IT, especially **behavioral rules** and those many **definitional rules** that cannot be handled by **decision tables**. RuleSpeak was developed by BRS starting in 1996. Since that time RuleSpeak has been applied in many hundreds of projects. It is the premier approach for expressing **business rules** worldwide. It was one of three reference notations used in the creation of **SBVR** and is fully consistent with that standard. (**SBVR** does not standardize notation.) Originally for English, parallel versions for Dutch, Spanish, and German were released in 2009. Versions for other natural languages are under development. RuleSpeak and **SBVR** recognize that **business rules** need to be expressed **declaratively** as complete sentences. *If sentences aren't the best way to communicate many kinds of* **know-how**, *we sure do waste a lot of money on all those years of grade-school and university education!*

SBVR: *see* **Semantics of Business Vocabularies and Business Rules**

scenario: [MWUD]: *a sequence of events especially when imagined*

> ***Notes:*** In business analysis, *scenario* generally refers to the handling appropriate for a specific **case** (or kind of **case**) that arises when an **operational business event** occurs under specific circumstances. The *handling* can be modeled as **business tasks** and flows in a **business process** model, specified as one or more **business rules**, or more likely, combination of both.

scope item: *a* **core business concept**, *a* **central business process**, *a* **business location**, *a* **principal business actor**, *an* **operational business event**, *the* **business mission**, *or a* **business goal**

scope list: *a list of* **scope items** *falling into one of six categories based on the* **primitives** *what, how, where, who, when, and why*

see the elephant: *perceive the true shape of a large, pervasive problem as the essential first step in solving it*

> ***Notes:*** Some problems are simply so big you can't see them because they're all around you, everywhere you look. Up-close, like an ant crawling up a leg of the elephant, they're impossible to see. To understand the beast you have to stand

back. Often as not, once you finally see the problem for what it is, the solution isn't nearly as hard as you might have imagined. Refer to the Preface for the traditional sources of the metaphor.

semantic(s): [MWUD (noun) — semantics]: *a system or theory of meaning*
[MWUD (adjective) — semantic]: *of or relating to meaning in language*

> *Notes:* In general, when you say *semantic* you are referring simply to what words mean. A structured business vocabulary (**fact model**) provides a semantic blueprint for verbalizing operational business **know-how**. A goal in business analysis with **business rules** is **externalizing semantics** from **business process models** and other artifacts.

Semantics of Business Vocabularies and Business Rules (SBVR): t*he standard initially released in December, 2007 by the Object Management Group (OMG) whose central goal is to enable the full* **semantics** *of* **business rules** *and other forms of* **business communication** *to be captured, encoded, analyzed (for* **anomalies***), and transferred between machines (thereby achieving* **semantic** *interoperability)*

> *Notes:* SBVR seeks to enable machines to directly 'speak' the language of the business (e.g., as in **RuleSpeak**), thereby eliminating the need for interpretation of business meanings into *ITspeak* and special-purpose languages (e.g., C++, SQL, **production rules**, etc.). SBVR represents an exciting frontier that will revolutionize how **know-how** is managed. At its heart, SBVR is a literally a vocabulary for developing structured business vocabularies (**fact models**). Much of the SBVR, however, is arcane. It's for logicians, linguists, and software engineers. For more digestible background on SBVR, refer to the *SBVR Insider* section on www.BRCommunity.com.

single-sourcing: *specifying* **business rules** *for a* **business capability** *only once no matter how many places* **deployed**

> *Notes:* A central goal for **rulebook management** is *specify once, use everywhere*. Making change(s) to **business rules**, including **decision logic**, should always be intentional and traceable, not accidental or haphazard. To maintain consistency and avoid duplication every **business rule** should be officially specified in a single place (the **rulebook**) and sourced from there, even if **deployed** to many places (across

both IT infrastructures and non-automated **procedures** and **role** responsibilities). *Single-sourcing* makes individual **business rules** easier to find and to change quickly and reliably, which is essential for **business agility**. One important caveat: We mean single-sourcing *only within* **architectural scope**. Single-sourcing **business rules** at the enterprise level might be desirable, but for organizations of any size or complexity, smaller steps are usually prudent.

smart business process: a **business process** that externalizes (1) **semantics**, (2) **business rules**, including **decision logic**, and (3) **violation responses** for **behavioral rules**

specific case: *a* **case** *for which a specific instance is specified for every* **consideration**

> *Notes:* Contrast with **general case**. **Cases** addressed by an **operational business decision** often represent combined instances of all of its **considerations**. Such a case is *specific*. For example, the following instances might combine to represent *one specific case* addressed by an **operational business decision**:

Consideration	Instance	
driving history	*good*	
evidence of insurance	*acceptable*	
insurance risk score	*154*	*one specific case*
credit rating	*poor*	
state	*Texas*	

spontaneous event: *an* **event** *based on some condition(s) becoming true, but not based on any timing criterion*

stage: *a* **state** *in a* **happy life**

> *Notes:* Based on MWUD: 5a: *a period or step in a process, activity, or development.*

standard case: *a* **case** *in* **decision scope** *that is regular or common, and unlike an* **exceptional case**, *cannot be excluded from normal treatment or rejected out of hand*

> *Notes: Standard cases* generally make up the bulk of **cases in scope**.

state: [MWUD 1a]: *a mode or condition of being;*
[MWUD — mode 6]: *a condition or state of being : a manifestation, form, or manner of arrangement*

Notes: A *state* implies a **business action** that completed successfully (e.g., an order has been *shipped*). All **business rules** applicable to the **state** must be satisfied at the **business milestone** for the state and generally for so long as the state exists. Among MWUD examples for *state* are: *the unsanitary state of the building, the married state.* Note the use of an adjective ("unsanitary") in the former example, and a **past participle** ("married") in the latter example. In natural language, adjectives and **participles** are the principle means of communicating the states of things. Expressing states is this fashion is a **semantic** alternative to **tokens**.

Past participles (e.g., *married, shipped,* etc.) are almost always used to designate states in our approach since their use implies (a) that some business action completed successfully, and (b) that all relevant business rules have been satisfied from that point on. A state can also represent an on-going **business action** — e.g., an order is *shipping*. Note use of a **present participle**, rather than a **past participle**, to indicate the **business action** as on-going, not completed. On-going **states** of this kind are occasionally needed to constrain concurrent activity (e.g., *no smoking while filling a gas tank*), but by and large do not play a major role in **business operation systems**.

strategy: *see* **business strategy**

strategy diagram: *a diagram that depicts the elements of* **strategy** *for a business solution (***Policy Charter***) and how they relate*

> *Notes:* A **strategy diagram** depicts only connections having to do with **motivation**.

structural rule: [SBVR]: *see* **definitional rule**

structured business vocabulary: *the set of* **terms** *and their* **definitions***, along with all* **wordings***, that organizes operational business* **know-how** *for a* **business capability**

> *Notes:* A **fact model** is represented by a *structured business vocabulary* that includes both **terms** for **noun concepts** and **wordings** for **fact types** (verb concepts). Its role in a **business model** is to provide a standard, shared basis for expressing **know-how** including **business rules**. Although a **fact model** can (and should) serve as the basis for creating a data model or class diagram, its central business purpose is to support **business communications**.

Fact models have a long pedigree that extends back to the 1970s. Refer to Nijssen, Sjir [July 1981] and Halpin, Terry [2008]. Until the early 2000s fact modeling was usually associated with data modeling. The grounding of **fact models** in formal logic, however, is far deeper than for most such techniques. A watershed for **fact models** came with **SBVR**, which took them squarely into **semantics** and the modeling of real-world business **concepts** and **business rules**. Much of the **SBVR** is arcane to say the least. It's for logicians, linguists, and software engineers. One critical subset, however, is business-facing, the actual vocabulary that business people and Business Analysts should use in developing structured business vocabularies for their companies. Only that subset of **SBVR** is discussed in this book. Incidentally, **SBVR** does not standardize notation for **fact models**. The diagramming conventions used in this book, specially developed to be as business-friendly as possible, are those of **Proteus**.

There are theoretical reasons why *fact model* as used by some proponents doesn't convey quite the right sense for **business rules**. For example, in some schemes, **behavioral rules** are simply viewed themselves as facts (true propositions). That might make sense to logicians, but it makes no sense whatsoever in the real world (no knock on logicians intended). Better names for **fact models** might be **concept systems** or **verbalization models**.

surrogate: [MWUD 2a]: *something that replaces or serves as a substitute for another*

suspense criterion: *a timing threshold for how long an instance of an operational business thing may remain in a given* **state**

Notes: Consider the business rule *An order may be shipped but not invoiced for only a week.* 'A week' is a suspense criterion.

system model: *a model that provides a design for an automatable system that is computationally competent*

Notes: For many years John Zachman, creator of the **Zachman Architecture Framework**, has explained that a **business model** is always about real-world things. These real-world things are as the business leads see or define them. A *system model* in contrast comprises "... *surrogates for the real-world things so that the real-world things can be managed on a scale and at a distance that is not possible in the real world.*"

Surrogates include data entities in place of real-world things; GUIs and use cases in place of face-to-face, real-world communication; network nodes in place of real-world locations; system events rather than **operational business events**; and so on.

Does the separation between **business model** and system model blur in eCommerce? *No.* If business leads see or define ePersons (for example) as *real-world,* then real-world they are. To ensure you have a winning business solution, the ePersons should be defined and shaped within a **business model.** Afterwards comes design of a computationally-competent system model so you can conduct actual business with the ePersons. [John Zachman, informal communication, June 2011]

system rule: *a* **rule** *that is dependent on, or aimed at, the manner in which data is received, stored or displayed in a* **system model**

task: *see* **business task**

temporal event: *an* **event** *based exclusively on a timing criterion*

term: [MWUD 8a]: *a word or expression that has a precisely-limited meaning in some uses or is peculiar to a science, art, profession, trade, or special subject*

thin process: *a process from which* **business rules** *are externalized*

token: *a pointer for a thread in a process or computer program serving to indicate current position*

> ***Notes:*** Don Baisley, a colleague in the **SBVR** standards group, explains:
>
> *"A token in BPMN [OMG's Business Process Model and Notation standard] is what moves through a process. A token begins its existence at a start event and then flows through activities, one by one, until it arrives at an end event where it terminates. In computer programming terms, it is the current code pointer for a thread. It is a programming view, but not just for computer programming. It could be television programming for one channel, which goes sequentially along from one thing to the next.*
>
> *When business people are defining or describing business activity, the 'token' concept tends to be poorly suited. A better approach is to write business rules about what is obligatory,*

appropriate, permitted, or prohibited in response to events or in certain states. 'Process state' in business activity is best understood in terms of some operational business thing that business people know about and that is affected by the process (e.g., an application for insurance or a purchase order). It is easier for a business person to think of an operational business thing going through different states than to think of a token moving through a flow chart. Also, 'token' thinking tends toward overly linear processes with unnecessary inefficiencies."

unary fact type: *a* **fact type** *that involves exactly one* **noun concept**

> ***Notes:*** Example — 'account is inactive'. This fact type includes only one noun concept, *account*.

under business jurisdiction (rule): [SBVR] *a rule that the business can opt to change or discard*

> ***Notes:*** **SBVR** explains: *"The laws of physics may be relevant to a company ... ; legislation and regulations may be imposed on it; external standards and best practices may be adopted. These things are not business rules from the company's perspective, since it does not have the authority to change them. The company will decide how to react to laws and regulations, and will create business rules to ensure compliance with them. Similarly, it will create business rules to ensure that standards or best practices are implemented as intended."*

use case: [Wikipedia]: *a description of a system's behavior as it responds to a request from the outside ... [which is] used to capture a system's behavioral requirements*

verb concept: *see* **fact type**

verbalization model: *see* **structured business vocabulary**

> ***Notes:*** A structured business vocabulary (**fact model**) provides standard words (nouns and verbs, including **participles** to represent **states**) to verbalize **business rules** and other kinds of **business communications** with precision and consistency. Since verbalization is the ultimate purpose of a **fact model** as we use it, *verbalization model* would be a better name than **fact model**. Also, a **fact model** should be viewed as independent of natural languages, but that idea (native **concepts** without words) is a bit hard for anyone but a computer scientist or linguist. Nonetheless, since **fact model**

is the best known term for a vocabulary-oriented approach to **business rules** and **know-how**, we use it in this book.

violation message: *see* **guidance message**

violation response: *a response deemed appropriate when a* **behavioral rule** *is violated*

> ***Notes:*** A violation response might be a **behavioral rule**, **business process**, sanction, **business communication**, **business rule**, etc.

walk the walls: *managing complexity in developing a* **business model** *by figuratively, and as much as possible literally, addressing each* **primitive** *as a separate concern (i.e., on a different wall)*

> ***Notes:*** In running facilitated sessions, we like to create each kind of **business model** on a different wall. We find that the physical act of walking or shifting focus from one wall to another helps participants rapidly grasp and remember what each wall represents. It also helps **business leads** and Business Analysts identify disconnects and gaps in the business solution more readily.
>
> In physically walking the walks, we usually put **business process** models on the left wall and the structured business vocabulary (**fact model**) on the right wall. On the front wall we put reminders about the **strategy** for the business solution (**Policy Charter**) and on the back wall we capture **business rules**. (**Business rules** go on the back wall to help resist the temptation of wordsmithing, which is better done offline.) In an ideal world, there would be one surface for each of the six **primitives** of the **Zachman Architecture Framework**. (Alas the ceiling and floor are hard to use.) **Business rules**, serving as **integration relationships**, would occupy the 3D space between the six surfaces (even harder to use!). Our approach approximates the notions well enough in practice.

whole–part structure: *a special collection of one or more* **binary fact types** *that together describe how an instance of one class of things (the whole) is composed of instances of (typically) two or more other classes of things (the parts)*

wording: *an expression including one or more* **terms** *and a verb or verb phrase organized appropriately to represent a* **fact type**

> *Notes:* Example — 'customer places order'.

work product: *something created to support a particular interaction between people,* **roles***, or organizations in business activity*

> *Notes:* Examples — notifications, requests, sign-offs, analyses, position papers, legal agreements, licenses, certifications, service level agreements, etc.

Zachman Architecture Framework: *the classification scheme or ontology created by John Zachman for engineering anything of complexity*

> *Notes:* Widely misunderstood and misrepresented, the *Zachman Architecture Framework* ("Framework") is simply a thinking tool, *not* a methodology of any kind. Its being fundamentally neutral with respect to methodology, in fact, is the secret to its power and the reason it has proven so enduring. It can, of course, be *applied* to create a methodology (as we have done in **Proteus Pro-BA**), but that's a different matter. Zachman's basic premise is that whenever you engineer anything of complexity, no matter what — a complex machine, a skyscraper, a microchip, a spacecraft, a product, a *business* (an enterprise), or some part of a business (a **business capability**) — there are two basic aspects that need to be addressed. These two aspects correspond to the columns and rows of the Framework.

> The *columns* represent the **primitives** of engineering problems and correspond to the six interrogatives (*business engineering questions*) *what, how, where, when, who, when,* and *why.* (The order doesn't matter.) If an artifact is not **primitive**, then it's a *composite* and inevitably more complex and resistant to change.

> The *rows* represent *reifications* in the sense of MWUD [*reify*]: *convert mentally into something concrete or objective : give definite content and form to : MATERIALIZE.* In engineering, an object is created for a particular audience with a certain perspective, set of needs, and agenda. The Framework recognizes six such reifications or audiences. (Their order *does* matter.)

Six **primitives** times six reifications (audiences) equals 36 cells in the Framework. You can think of those 36 cells as covering the universe of discourse for engineering things of complexity, a fundamental scheme for understanding and assessing completeness. Tables AG4 and AG5 provide additional insights about the columns and rows of the Framework, respectively.

Graphic depictions of the Framework naturally focus on **primitives**. A key question, however, is how the **primitives** are 'tied together' (configured) at any point in time to create a complete and workable solution. Tying together (configuring) **primitives** is the purpose of **integration relationships**. The effectiveness of their configuration determines the degree of **business agility** you achieve. Two basic choices to support **integration relationships** are **procedural** (processes) and **declarative** (**business rules**). Traditional processes with their hidden **semantics** are a poor choice (think **business rules** being hard-coded into software). **Business rules**, in contrast, support direct, business-friendly configuration, as well as rapid, traceable, continuous *re*-configuration.

Common myths about the Framework:

- The Framework requires you to create an artifact for each and every cell. *Wrong.* It's not a methodology, it's a classification scheme. Different methodologies emphasize problems of different kinds, so *in practice* some cells are likely to play a less prominent role than others.

- The Framework can be applied only at the enterprise level. *Wrong.* It can be applied for an engineering problem of any size (scope) deemed meaningful (e.g., for a **business capability**).

- The rows in the Framework are about increasing level of detail. *Wrong.* Each successive row represents a *transform* of the previous reification into a new reification. The new reification serves a new purpose for a distinct audience. Any artifact in any row can be pursued to *excruciating level of detail* (as Zachman puts it) if deemed useful and productive. The idea is to make the *next* audience's job in creating the *next* reification that much easier.

- The Framework discourages or precludes prototyping. *Wrong.* Again, the Framework isn't a methodology. Much can be learned about the best solution for any given audience by prototyping alternative approaches.

- The Framework somehow produces complexity. *Wrong.* Engineering problems are inherently complex, with business engineering being perhaps the most complex of all (as Zachman contends.) In other words the complexity already exists, the trick is to engage with it most effectively.

- The Framework slows you down. *Wrong.* That's not our experience at all. *Asking the right questions of the right audiences at the right times in the right ways* doesn't slow you down, it speeds you up (or avoids costly dead ends). That's especially true for the **business model**, which most IT methodologies neglect almost entirely (even if they say otherwise). Remember, the cost and time needed for rework does not rise linearly for each subsequent reification, it balloons. *Overall* acceleration is what you want, and not just for the build activity. You also want it for the inevitable, myriad changes to **business rules** you can expect *after* the business rules are **deployed**. Such solutions don't happen by accident, they require deliberate engineering. Zachman simply points out, like it or not, what such 'deliberate engineering' necessarily involves.

Table AG4. About the Six Columns in the Zachman Architecture Framework

Question Word	Key Descriptive Word	Zachman's Generic Model	Topical Concern for Engineering	Examples of Artifacts
what	structure	thing-relationship-thing	Organizing the inventory, the things to be dealt with, and understanding how they relate	**fact model** data model database
how	transform	input-transform-output	Organizing the processes, how they work, what inputs they take, and what outputs they produce	**business process** computer program object code
where	geography	location-link-location	Organizing logistics, distribution or interconnection in three dimensional space	network
who	interaction	party-**work product**-party	Organizing interactions between roles and how **work products** and presentation forms enable them	GUI
when	time	cycle-**event**-cycle	Organizing the scheduling of **events** and inter-**event** periods of time (cycles or **states**)	**business milestones** schedule **state** transition diagram
why	**motivation**	**end-means-end**	Organizing what goals and objectives are to be achieved and identifying what **means** best achieve them	**business strategy** constraint model

Table AG5. About the Six Rows in the Zachman Architecture Framework

Reification	Target Audience	Common Name	OMG Term	Purpose
identifi-cation	planners	scope	—	Establish a **ballpark view** for the engineering effort and first-cut boundaries
definition	**business leads**	**business model**	computation-independent model (CIM)	Create a business solution
represen-tation	architects	design logic	platform-independent model (PIM)	Design a computationally-competent **system model** that supports the business solution
specifi-cation	engineers	technology model	platform-specific model (PSM)	Translate the design logic into technical designs that take into account the classes of platforms that will support it
configu-ration	technicians	tool specifi-cations	—	Create a ready-to-use solution (e.g., writing software code)
instantia-tion	workers	operational instances	—	Operate the actual functioning solution

References

Berry, Daniel M., Erik Kamsties, Michael M. Krieger, and Willenken Loh Stris Lee & Tran. [November 2003]. *From Contract Drafting to Software Specification: Linguistic Sources of Ambiguity: A Handbook*, (Version 1.0). ["Ambiguity Handbook"]. Available at: http://se.uwaterloo.ca/~dberry/

Burlton, Roger T. [2001]. *Business Process Management: Profiting from Success.* Indianapolis, IN: Sams Publishing.

Business Rules Group. [May 2010]. *The Business Motivation Model (BMM) ~ Business Governance in a Volatile World* (Version 1.4). Available at: http://www.BusinessRulesGroup.org
Note: Originally published as *Organizing Business Plans ~ The Standard Model for Business Rule Motivation* (Nov. 2000). Now an adopted standard of the Object Management Group (OMG).

Business Rules Group. [2003]. *Business Rules Manifesto ~ The Principles of Rule Independence* (Version 2). Available at: http://www.BusinessRulesGroup.org
Note: In English as well as more than a dozen other languages.

Business Rules Group. [July 2000]. *Defining Business Rules ~ What Are They Really?* (4th ed). Available at: http://www.BusinessRulesGroup.org
Note: Formerly known as the *GUIDE Business Rules Project Report*, (1995).

Crystal, David. [2005]. *How Languages Work.* Woodstock, NY: The Overlook Press, Peter Mayer Publishers, Inc.

Editors of BRCommunity.com. [November 2008]. "A Brief History of the Business Rule Approach," *Business Rules Journal*, Vol. 9, No. 11. Available at: http://www.BRCommunity.com/a2008/b448.html

Halpin, Terry (with Tony Morgan). [2008]. *Information Modeling and Relational Databases* (2nd ed.), San Francisco, CA: Morgan Kaufmann.

International Institute of Business Analysis (IIBA®). [2009]. *A Guide to the Business Analysis Body of Knowledge® (BABOK® Guide)* (Version 2.0). Toronto.

ISO 1087-1. [2000]. *Terminology Work — Vocabulary, Part 1: Theory and Application*. English Ed.: ISO (International Organization for Standardization).

ISO 704. [2000]. *Terminology Work — Principles and Methods*. English Ed.: ISO (International Organization for Standardization).

Lam, Gladys S. W. [May/June 1998]. "Business Knowledge — Packaged in a Policy Charter," *DataToKnowledge Newsletter*, Vol. 26, No. 3.
Available at: http://www.BRCommunity.com/a1998/a385.html

Merriam-Webster Unabridged Dictionary (Version 2.5). [2000]. Merriam-Webster Inc.

Nijssen, Sjir. [July 1981]. *An Architecture for Knowledge Base Software*. Presented at the Australian Computer Society conference. Available at: http://www.FBMf.eu

Pinker, Steven. [2007]. *The Stuff of Thought: Language as a Window into Human Nature*. New York, NY: Viking.

Ross, Ronald G. [1997]. *The Business Rule Book — Classifying, Defining and Modeling Rules* (2nd ed.), Business Rule Solutions, LLC.
Originally published as *The Business Rule Book* (1st ed.). [1994].

Ross, Ronald G. [2009]. *Business Rule Concepts: Getting to the Point of Knowledge* (3rd ed.). Business Rule Solutions, LLC.
Available at: http://www.brsolutions.com/b_concepts.php

Ross, Ronald G. [2010]. *Decision Analysis Using Decision Tables and Business Rules*. Business Rule Solutions, LLC.
Available at: http://www.brsolutions.com/b_decision.php

Ross, Ronald G. [2003]. *Principles of the Business Rule Approach*. Boston, MA: Addison-Wesley.

Ross, Ronald G. [July 2007]. "What's Wrong with If-Then Syntax For Expressing Business Rules ~ One Size Doesn't Fit All," *Business Rules Journal*, Vol. 8, No. 7.
Available at: http://www.BRCommunity.com/a2007/b353.html

Ross, Ronald G. [March 2008]. "The Emergence of SBVR and the True Meaning of 'Semantics': Why You Should Care (a Lot!) ~ Part 1," *Business Rules Journal*, Vol. 9, No. 3.
Available at: http://www.BRCommunity.com/a2008/b401.html

Rumelt, Richard [2011]. *Good Strategy Bad Strategy: The Difference and Why It Matters*. New York, NY: Crown Publishing, a division of Random House Inc.

SBVR *(Semantics of Business Vocabulary and Business Rules)* (Version 1.0). [January 2008]. Object Management Group. Available at: http://www.omg.org/spec/SBVR/1.0/

Taylor, James and Neil Raden. [2007]. *Smart (Enough) Systems*. Boston, MA: Prentice-Hall.

Zachman, John A. [1987]. "A Framework for Information Systems Architecture," *IBM Systems Journal*, Vol. 26, No. 3. IBM Publication G321-5298.

Current information on the *Zachman® Framework* is available from Zachman International® at http://www.zachman.com/

Index

About...

Business Rule Solutions, LLC

Business Rule Solutions, LLC (BRS): Formed in 1996, BRS is recognized as the world leader in business rules and their use in business analysis. Co-Founders Ronald G. Ross and Gladys S.W. Lam are internationally acclaimed as the foremost experts and practitioners of related techniques. BRS emphasizes building business solutions and creating business requirements based on business models. BRS professional services include mentoring, consulting, and online training. Visit **BRSolutions.com**.

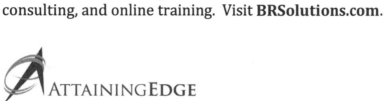

AttainingEdge: AttainingEdge is the world's foremost source of professional training in business rules, business analysis with business rules, and related areas of business innovation. AttainingEdge focuses on the critical juncture where business meets IT. More than simply bridging a gap, its goal is to enable practitioners to eliminate the gap altogether. Participants interact with world-class leaders in the field, who use extensive examples and analogies from real-world experience. Visit **AttainingEdge.com**.

Business Rules Community: BRCommunity.com is a vertical, non-commercial community for business rule professionals. BRCommunity provides articles, commentary, discussion areas, and a variety of other valuable hands-on resources. BRS established BRCommunity.com, and its flagship on-line publication, the *Business Rules Journal*, in 2000. The *Journal* (free) is known for its high-quality, non-commercial editorial focus. BRCommunity.com is the place to be for business rules! Visit **BRCommunity.com**.

Business Rules Forum Conference: Since the first annual conference in 1997, the Forum has been the premier conference worldwide dedicated to business rules and operational decisions. The Forum, chaired by Ronald G. Ross, focuses on real-life success stories and the achievements of experienced professionals. It offers invaluable insights about how organizations can come to grips with rapid change, massive customization, and compliance in a truly scalable, traceable, manageable manner. Along with its product expo, the Forum covers the rule-based technologies and techniques needed to create an agile organization. Visit **BusinessRulesForum.com**.

Building Business Capability (BBC) Conference: The annual Building Business Capability (BBC) Conference encompasses four co-located conferences: Business Rules Forum, Business Analysis Forum (the official conference of the IIBA®), Business Process Forum, and Business Architecture Summit. The BBC offers insight and expertise to help organizations create more effective, complete, and agile business solutions, especially involving automation. Gladys S.W. Lam is BBC Executive Director. Visit **BuildingBusinessCapability.com**.

International Institute of Business Analysts (IIBA®): IIBA® is an independent, non-profit professional association serving the fast-growing worldwide community of Business Analysts. Focal areas include business analysis, requirements management, systems analysis, requirements analysis, project management, and consulting. With local chapters all over the world, IIBA publishes the *Business Analysis Body of Knowledge®* (BABOK®), the standard widely-used in the field. Visit **IIBA.com**.